BLUE ANGEL

DONALD SPOTO

Doubleday

NEW YORK

LONDON

TORONTO

SYDNEY

AUCKLAND

BLUE ANGEL

The Life of
Marlene Dietrich

PUBLISHED BY DOUBLEDAY

a division of Bantam Doubleday Dell Publishing Group, Inc.
666 Fifth Avenue, New York, New York 10103

DOUBLEDAY and the portrayal of an anchor
with a dolphin are trademarks of Doubleday, a
division of Bantam Doubleday Dell Publishing Group, Inc.

Book design by Marysarah Quinn

Insert design by Anne Ling

Library of Congress Cataloging-in-Publication Data
Spoto, Donald, 1941–
Blue angel : the life of Marlene Dietrich / Donald Spoto.
— 1st ed.
p. cm.
Includes bibliographical references and index.
1. Dietrich, Marlene. 2. Entertainers—Germany—
Biography.
I. Title.
PN2658.D5S59 1992
791.43'028'092—dc20
[B] 92-11031
CIP
ISBN 0-385-42553-8

for Kirtley Thiesmeyer,
with gratitude deep and true

"Iron shapes iron, and friend shapes friend."
PROVERBS 27:17

Acknowledgments

In 1984, not long after I completed the final draft of a biography of Tennessee Williams, I decided to prepare a short book on the career of Marlene Dietrich. Published the following year under the title *Falling in Love Again,* it was never intended to be a complete life story but rather a reflective essay with photos on her various film roles. But during the research I was fascinated by the life behind the work, and so I began to dig deeper. Thus *Blue Angel: The Life of Marlene Dietrich* has taken shape over eight years, even as other books were begun and published.

Biographers (perhaps preeminently among practitioners of the writer's craft) owe much to the practical assistance of others. En route to publication, throughout Europe and America, I was the fortunate recipient of kind and generous help from friends and from strangers who quickly became friends.

Crucial interviews relative to the life of Marlene Dietrich were granted by the late Rupert Allan, Robert Anderson, Pierre Barillet, Leonard Blair, Vivien Byerley, Barrie Chase, Alexander H. Cohen,

Robert Colbaugh, Frederick Combs, the late Cheryl Crawford, Laurence Evans, Douglas Fairbanks, Jr., Dean Goodman, Ethel Grand, the late Alfred Hitchcock, Harry Horner, Jean Howard, Hilary Knight, Stanley Kramer, Stefan Lorant, Jean Louis, Col. Barney Oldfield, USAF (Ret.), the late Lotta Palfi-Andor, Eileen Palmer, Hildy Parks, Cesar Romero, Maximilian Schell, Nicholas von Sternberg, Peter White and Billy Wilder.

Librarians and archivists round the world were without exception unfailingly helpful as I pored through documents. Especial gratitude is due Angela Singleton, at the British Broadcasting Service/Data Enquiry Service; the staff at the Billy Rose Theatre Collection of the New York Public Library at Lincoln Center; Alan Braun and Gladys Irvis at the library of the American Film Institute; the staff of the British Film Institute; and the personnel of the Berlinische Galerie (Berlin), the Deutsches Literaturarchiv/Schiller Nationalmuseum, the Süddeutscher Verlag (Munich), the Serkis Filmarchiv, Berlin, and the Akademie der Künste Berlin.

Once again, Marvin Eisenman, one of the world's most knowledgeable film archivists, enabled me to see Dietrich films that were otherwise virtually impossible to locate. His gracious help was invaluable.

Karin Brettauer very generously gave me access to (and permission to quote) important family papers, the unpublished memoirs of her aunt, Grete Mosheim. These lively documents by a noted German actress who knew and worked with Dietrich in the 1920s were, I soon discovered, indispensable for a fuller understanding of my subject's early life and career.

Assistance in translating from the German various particularly formidable papers, letters and documents was cheerfully and patiently provided by Dr. Jon Zimmermann, professor of German at the California State University at Fullerton; by Henriette Fremont; and by Annemarie Moore and Nicholas Vazsonyi.

In Honolulu, Kim Reineman provided warmly supportive hospitality at his home, where I wrote portions of this book; he also read several chapters of the first draft and made incisive suggestions.

Irene Mahoney, who is a highly respected biographer, playwright and historian (and a dear friend for over forty years), urged me to reconsider some vital matters after she read the first several chapters; her counsel was well taken. When she then had to resume her own several projects round the world, another gifted writer gave me generous and tangible proof of his abiding friendship: the playwright, producer and screenwriter Mart Crowley read the completed first draft of my typescript, raised many important issues for my deliberation, corrected several important matters of fact and in more ways than I can detail improved both the content and tone of *Blue Angel.* And Douglas Alexander, my editorial assistant since 1988, again applied his considerable critical skills to every stage of the book's research, and his comments as I was writing it. I salute his keen mind and abiding loyalty.

At Doubleday, I was fortunate indeed to have Shaye Areheart for my editor, for she is a keen-eyed, dexterous and prudent guide through the thickets of a book's final preparation for publication. Shaye also became a good friend, and I am enormously grateful for her wit, her intelligence and her confidence in me and my work. Her associates, Bruce Tracy and Scott Moyers, cheerfully dispatched numerous everyday matters, always facilitating the author's tasks and thus his life.

Likewise in London. From the first day, Mark Barty-King and James Cochrane at Bantam were enthusiastic for this book; they, too, made important editorial emendations and, like their New York colleagues, added leavening friendship to professional contributions. It is difficult for me to imagine, with such a team of international collaborators, that there may somewhere be a writer more fortunate than myself.

But the litany of saints continues: for almost fifteen years I have been represented by my dear friend Elaine Markson, who is ever the most vigilant and attentive agent, a woman of honor as of humor, endlessly indulgent with me, as alert for my contentment as for my career. Elaine's associates—Geri Thoma, Karen Beisch, Sally Wofford, Caomh Kavanagh and Lily Zivkovic—are loyal and spirited colleagues, and I am grateful to them each and all for their many kindnesses.

• • •

ACKNOWLEDGMENTS

THE DEDICATION PAGE OF BLUE ANGEL BEARS THE name of an esteemed and trusted friend who came into my life in 1987, soon after I moved to the West Coast from the East. Kirtley Thiesmeyer is my attorney—and ever so much more. He is a daily counselor in matters of contracts and career, but he is also a cherished comrade whose concern, support and gentleness of spirit enrich my life in more ways than he can ever know. I respect his integrity, just as I learn constantly from his probity and patience, his good humor and his courage. Additionally, he and his wife Dee have countless times extended to me the warmth of their home and included me within the circle of both their family and their friendships. In testimony of my love and appreciation, I offer this book to Kirtley, a small enough return for all he gives me.

D.S.

Los Angeles: January 1992

Contents

CONTENTS

Want to buy some illusions,
   Slightly used, second hand?
They were lovely illusions,
   Reaching high, built on sand.
They had a touch of Paradise,
   A spell you can't explain:
For in this crazy Paradise,
   You are in love with pain.

Want to buy some illusions,
   Slightly used, just like new?
Such romantic illusions—
   And they're all about you.
I sell them all for a penny,
   They make pretty souvenirs.
Take my lovely illusions—
   Some for laughs, some for tears.

—"Illusions," by Frederick Hollander,
sung by Marlene Dietrich in *A Foreign Affair*

CARLOTTA: Time doesn't exist.
PONDELIÈVRE: Perhaps so, but mirrors exist.

—JEAN ANOUILH, *Cher Antoine*

1 : February 1978

FEW PEOPLE IN OR OUT OF THE FILM INDUSTRY
found it easy to believe producer Joshua Sinclair when he announced to the press, late in 1977, that Marlene Dietrich was about
to break her retirement and self-imposed isolation within her Paris
apartment. She had, Sinclair continued, agreed to appear on screen
in her first speaking role in eighteen years, in the German-English
film *Just a Gigolo,* with rock star David Bowie. Lonely for precisely
the human contact she paradoxically but insistently rejected, she also
found irresistible a salary of $250,000 for two half-days of work in a
Paris studio, where the sets for her scene were transported from
Berlin.

On a bitterly cold morning in February 1978, she arrived on
time for work, "her jaw set and her shoulders hunched with deter-
mination," as an eyewitness recalled. Dietrich walked slowly, un-
steadily, because of her failing eyesight, clinging constantly to the
arm of makeup artist Anthony Clavet. She looked, quite simply, like
a wizened old lady.

Two hours later, her makeup painstakingly applied, she emerged from a makeshift dressing room wearing a costume of her own design: a wide-brimmed black hat with a delicate but strategically concealing veil, shiny black boots, white gloves and a black skirt and jacket—everything just right for her brief appearance as the Baroness von Semering, manager of a ring of Berlin gigolos just after World War I. Director David Hemmings, producer Sinclair and a small crew awaited, and in a few moments one of her two brief scenes was easily photographed.

Next morning, Dietrich returned for the more difficult second task—to sing the film's title song, which was to be heard near the end of the picture. "I will sing one chorus of that horrible old German song in two seconds flat," she told Hemmings and Sinclair. Everyone stood by nervously, for it was uncertain she had the strength or the breath to fulfill the promise.

But an astonishing transformation then occurred, attested by all who were present in the studio that wintry day. First she was photographed in close-up, the hat and veil deliberately almost hiding her eyes as she stood to one side of the set, an empty hotel dining room. Then she walked—cautiously but unaided—toward pianist Raymond Bernard, and standing proudly, she began to sing. Far from offering the perfunctory delivery of a song she disliked, Marlene Dietrich sang with heartrending simplicity:

> Paid for every dance, selling each romance,
> Every night some heart betraying.
> There will come a day youth will pass away,
> Then what will they say about me?
> When the end comes, I know,
> They'll say "Just a gigolo,"
> And life goes on without me.

Nothing she had done on stage or screen over a period of sixty years could have prepared witnesses that day (or viewers of *Just a Gigolo* since then) for her astonishing rendition of this simple confessional song. On the words "youth will pass away," there may be heard a tremor of sadness in her voice that was without precedent in any prior recording or theatrical appearance.

And when she came to "life goes on," the voice became plangent, almost a whisper as she managed, to poignant effect, an octave's span. In only one take, the scene and the song were captured forever. There was a moment of reverential silence round her, and then the bystanders broke into applause; many of those who knew her films, recordings and live stage appearances could be seen brushing away tears.

Unable to see them across the bright studio lights, Marlene Dietrich, in her seventy-seventh year, nodded and found her way back to the cramped dressing room. An hour later she was alone again, back at her home on the fashionable Avenue Montaigne, just opposite the grand Plaza–Athénée Hotel. Except for visits to doctors and hospitals, she never left this apartment until her death from kidney and liver failure in her ninety-first year, on May 6, 1992.

2: 1901–1920

WHEN PRUSSIA'S KING WILHELM I WAS PRO-claimed the first Kaiser of Germany in January 1871, his capital in Berlin became the new Empire's government center. For centuries merely a provincial town flanked by smaller villages (Lichtenberg, Friedenau, Wilmersdorf, Charlottenburg, Schöneberg), Berlin grew swiftly and by 1901 had absorbed numerous suburbs, its population of one and a half million spread over 350 square miles. Real estate was in constant development as railways expanded, construction companies thrived and banks and insurance firms prospered. The city was thus a vast cosmopolitan center, alive with every kind of commercial, creative and social expansion.

"He who writes for Berlin writes for the world," trumpeted the newspaper *Berliner Tageblatt* in its first edition. Few would have disagreed, for in a sense the city was a microcosm. Immigrants flowed in from Austria, Italy, Poland, Russia, Hungary and France, all of them attracted by the promise of immediate employment and a superior standard of living. Additionally, the famous Berlin air—cool, fresh and invigorating year-round—offered an appealingly temperate atmosphere for the enjoyment of a sparkling chain of lakes and public parks. Gardens, splendid in their designs, were planted thick with birch, pine, chestnut and lime trees.

The climate may have been moderate, but the city's Teutonic tastes were not. At the century's turn, the classic modesty of old Berlin was replaced by a garish, nationalistic excess. Coveting the paraphernalia of pomp and circumstance, the arch-conservative Wilhelm II became obsessed with military parades and maneuvers, and he encouraged an urban design that virtually defined kitsch. The monument to his grandfather Wilhelm I stood sixty-five feet high on a bronze pedestal, flanked by bronze lions, and the Kaiser personally supervised plans for buildings with classical columns and great staircases leading from the street to the elevated ground floors, as if administrative offices were temples. Inside, the spaces were outlandishly opulent, with a profusion of gold and ebony, parquet floors, still more Corinthian pillars and scenes from mythology painted on fifty-foot-high ceilings.

From this style every designer took his cue. The lavish Adlon Hotel at Number One Unter den Linden, subsidized by the Kaiser himself, featured Italian marble and enormous chandeliers; it was one of the most famous lodging places in the world, frequented by royalty as well as Vanderbilts and Rockefellers. But other hotels—the Central, the National, the Monopol and the Kaiserhof—quickly surpassed the Adlon with even more red velvet, more ivory, more gilt banisters. New residential palaces seemed to spring up each month, along with expensive apartments offering ten, twelve or sixteen rooms. Ambition and pretense were tangible in the Florentine villas of the grand boulevards, their interiors crowded with heavy, expensive furniture: an excess of tables, bureaus and stained glass, elaborate chandeliers, heavy bronze household implements and overstuffed velvet sofas with gold and silver tassels.

Meanwhile, in less fashionable parts of town, modest barrack-like apartments were proliferating to house workers for the locomotive factories, iron foundries and new Daimler-Benz automobile plants. By 1901 the industrial proletariat lived mostly in tenement blocks, with six or eight families sharing a common lavatory.

Life was rigorously stratified. At the summit were Wilhelm II's family and court, fiercely patriotic and ever alert for anything political, literary or aesthetic that threatened established power. ("An art that transgresses the laws and barriers outlined by me ceases to be an art," the Kaiser said flatly in 1901.) Then came the upper middle class, loyal to him insofar as it was in their interest. The majority of Berlin's population was comprised of the working class, those who during the 1890s had won important socialist reforms and strove to keep and extend the benefits deriving therefrom. And finally there was the intellectual bourgeoisie, opposed to everything represented by the court ideology. This last group was largely responsible for the prevalent tone of ironic, sarcastic wit that characterized Berlin's social and intellectual life, and they supported the dozens of newspapers that in turn endorsed the proliferating political parties—among them the Guelphs, Bavarians, Old and New Liberals, Polish dissidents, Catholics and a variety of Conservatives. Since the 1890s, these factions often clashed violently, their confrontations inevitably augmenting the power of the imperial police.

IN 1901, THERE WERE 4,500 ROYAL PRUSSIAN policemen in the upper-middle-class district of Schöneberg, southwest of central Berlin, each man well paid and highly respected by the area's population of 89,143—an astonishing police-civilian ratio by any standard. Groups of more than fifty subordinate patrolmen, detectives and telegraph operators were accountable to their leaders, and one of three supervising lieutenants was Louis Erich Otto Dietrich. An imposing man of thirty, Dietrich was autocratic, humorless and severe, his appearance very nearly a cliché of Prussian military tradition: he wore a monocle subjected to incessant polishing, a perpetually waxed and upturned moustache, closely shaved hair and a slightly ridiculous topknot that betokened his magisterial profession when he was helmetless and at leisure.

Louis Dietrich had married Wilhelmina Elisabeth Josephine Felsing in 1899 and the couple had taken a spacious apartment at 53 Sedanstrasse, Schöneberg. Descended from the wealthy Conrad Felsing family (watchmakers and jewelers for generations at the fashionable shopping address of 20 Unter den Linden), she was at twenty-three a plain but sharp-witted bride whose height (five two) and build (tending to plumpness) belied a quiet sensuality. Wilhelmina had acquired from governesses an enthusiasm for music, poetry and the details of proper housewifery, and when she gave birth to her daughter Elisabeth on February 5, 1900, her household, thanks to her husband's handsome salary and her own small inheritance, included three servants.

Just after nine o'clock on the evening of December 27, 1901, a second daughter was born at home. Although never religious people, the Dietrichs called her Maria Magdalene—a fairly common appellation in Christian Germany, where it was popular to recall saints and disciples. When her mother was playful, however, she sometimes called the girl Paulus or Paul, the name chosen for the boy she never had. At about the age of twenty, Maria Magdalene joined the first and last syllables of her two names and called herself Marlene Dietrich.

Blue-eyed with fine red-blond hair, little Maria was from childhood much admired for her almost translucent complexion and gently serious expression. By the age of two she was remarkably self-confident, curtsying while she repeated the names of guests and utterly lacking the coyness common to a pretty and pampered child. At four, she could read the fairy tales provided by her English nanny, who also taught her to write, add and speak simple French sentences.

Maria's quickness established a polite rivalry with her sister Elisabeth who, perhaps because her appearance and manner were not quite so charming and attractive, claimed less attention; in any case, the older daughter fancied dolls, outdoor games and walks with her father, while Maria preferred her mother's company, sitting contentedly while Wilhelmina played piano, sang madrigals, read aloud from a book of poems and taught her daughter to make apricot jam and buttermilk soup. By school age, the sisters seemed almost to have come from different families, and in fact their mature lives never intersected. Elisabeth Dietrich became a teacher, married and lived quietly in Berlin until her death in 1977. Few of Elisabeth's friends ever knew of her famous sister.

IN 1904, THE DIETRICHS MOVED TO A LARGER apartment not far away, at 48-49 Colonnenstrasse, near a wide thoroughfare. Later, Maria remembered the almost constant sounds of horses' hoofs and men marching, of military pageants, police and cavalry parades and troops of schoolboys in strict formations. Even casual strollers observed exact protocols of formal politeness: uniformed gentlemen saluted ladies; children yielded to their elders in conversation, on sidewalks and in streetcars; and decent women never appeared in public without hats, gloves and a male escort. Everywhere public life appeared regimented, manners prescribed, the forms of dress and address precisely specified.

Just so at home, where life was characterized by duty and discipline. Louis Dietrich's professional commitment to law and order had its counterpart in Wilhelmina's elaborate system of the household chores assigned to Elisabeth and Maria, with concomitant rewards (a Sunday outing) and punishments (a meal forfeited). Maria's father expected his children's clothes to be as presentable as his uniform, their shoes spotless, their High German clearly enunciated and grammatically correct, and their deportment flawless. Social propriety and proper deportment had the sanctions often connected with religious observance.

Wilhelmina's zeal for household virtues was the perfect corollary. Economy was primary: every Friday, for example, the girls accompanied their mother and governess to the hay, straw and wood market for calm but persistent negotiations of wholesale prices. Invariably disappointed with the maid's and cook's performance of their duties, Wilhelmina rescrubbed, waxed and restained the intricate parquet floors of the parlor. Often she hastily remade the sauce for dinner, teaching Maria that the proper execution of such tasks produced the immediate rewards of satisfaction—and of having pleased the girls' father, always a dominant consideration in every matter at home. Making Papa comfortable, gratifying him and deferring to his superior status as a man were in fact official household responsibilities.

Germanic precision and masculine supremacy was thus part of

every detail, and Wilhelmina's rules for honoring these were indisputable. "Sie selbst glich einem guten General," Maria wrote later: "She herself was like a benevolent general," and most of all the commanding officer outlawed idleness. "Tu etwas!" Wilhelmina said if she saw her daughters unoccupied—"Do something!" Performing things correctly was the demand of every day, Wilhelmina reminded, quoting Goethe. One had to approach life conscious of its various requirements, which included a careful concealment of emotion. "My whole upbringing [forced me] to mask my feelings," Marlene Dietrich wrote later.

> The last slap I had from my mother was because of that. I was having dancing lessons and had to dance with everyone in the room, including a young man I did not like. I made a long face. Mother saw it and slapped me as soon as we were alone. "You must not show your feelings, it is bad manners," she said.

But there were compensations. The Dietrichs often took their daughters for promenades, to admire the new brownstones and orderly rows of trees along Unter den Linden, a grand boulevard where the most elegant emporia sold everything from food to toys to clothing. Shopping was now a fashionable pastime, an end in itself: at the richly carpeted boutique Demuth, for example, expensive leather goods, silver inkstands, jade paper knives and silk pencil cases could be admired. Nearby were the Felsing store with its expensive watches, hand-painted music boxes and filigreed picture frames, and elegant tearooms, delicatessens and steamship agencies. Here Maria could see women with fancy parasols and men with straw boaters mingling with career officers in plumed helmets, white trousers and black boots.

It was the twilight of the German aristocracy, and even in the afternoons matrons sparkled with strands of opera-length pearls, cotillions were announced in newspapers, and a rigid social protocol linked money and privilege to heredity. An entire way of life was presented as desirable and even possible for most Berliners, a life of richness in food and furnishings, of large diamonds and powerful colognes, of exciting new forms of transportation. More families could afford servants to care for their children while they took a holiday in St. Moritz; cafés were crowded with housewives who did not work; and while the women chatted and sipped, thoughtful waiters routinely set down pewter bowls with cool water for the ladies' poodles.

On Sundays, the Dietrichs often stopped at the Hovel Confiserie to buy chocolates, marzipan or vanilla creams before proceeding to the Café Bauer on the Friedrichstrasse, where they sat at a marble-topped table and were served steaming cups of coffee or cocoa. Sometimes a few delicacies would be offered from the famous gourmet food store Huster, whose horse-drawn carriages were now all over Berlin, carrying buffets of lobster, salmon, salads and smoked hams to select restaurants and wealthy private patrons in the Bellevuestrasse or the Voss Strasse.

There were special entertainments, too. Maria and her sister were occasionally taken to the vast Scala Theater, home of the most famous variety show in Berlin. Here they saw Rastelli the juggler, Grock the clown, singers, impersonators and sideshow performers who cavorted with noisy abandon. The city was the theatrical center of middle Europe and grand productions filled the State Theater, but actually Berlin itself was a place where every resident and visitor, appropriately garbed, seemed to be a player in a vast social drama. When the Dietrichs left a music hall for Sunday dinner at the Kempinski on Wilhelmina's birthday one year, the restaurant scene resembled nothing so much as an elaborate set piece—lavishly uniformed waiters, choreographed according to an almost religious ritual, served a meticulously presented artwork of roast pheasant.

In early 1907, the family again moved to another rented and furnished apartment, at 45 Potsdamerstrasse. Maria was not yet six years old, and for the third (and not the last) time she had new furnished rooms to become accustomed to, a new governess, a new neighborhood. And then, with shocking suddenness that summer, her father died, apparently of a heart attack after being thrown from a horse. Custom required the dignified masking of family grief, and Wilhelmina affected a stoic calm. Maria could recall no display of emotion as mother and daughters formed a strong, womanly circle, augmented by the protracted visits of two aunts and Grandmother

Felsing. Following an old (and by then increasingly abandoned) Prussian custom, Wilhelmina henceforth wore her late husband's wedding band above her own.

"O lieb, solang du lieben kannst . . ." Maria remembered her mother repeating for weeks after her father's death a lyric by the nineteenth-century German poet Ferdinand Freiligrath:

> *O lieb, solang du lieben magst!*
> *Die Stunde kommt, Die Stunde kommt,*
> *Wo du an Gräbern stehst und klagst!*
>
> *O love, while still it's yours to love!*
> *O love, while love you still may keep!*
> *The hour will come, the hour will come,*
> *When you will stand by graves and weep!*

With money from a small civil service pension, Maria was enrolled that autumn at the Auguste Victoria Academy for girls, 63 Nürnbergerstrasse, where all the teachers were women. (Elisabeth, who suffered a series of childhood illnesses, received tutorials at home for most of that year.)

A hotchpotch of architectural styles—Victorian, Gothic, Florentine, Biedermeier and French Regency—the overappointed school halls were sharply distinct from the severe, chilly classrooms with their hard benches and poor lighting. Although she had enjoyed a prior advantage in her basic educational skills, Maria—a year younger and physically smaller than her classmates—felt lonely. At home she had not been encouraged to look outside the family circle for friends; now, detached from maternal protection and unprepared for quick socializing, she seemed a withdrawn and altogether unremarkable pupil who demonstrated no special aptitudes.

Her mother, however, sensed musical talent in the girl, and soon Maria was receiving piano lessons at home from a plump, jolly lady whose name has not come down to us. But this teacher was discharged after four months, since she seemed to Wilhelmina somewhat too relaxed to instill in Maria the basis for a serious musical career. A violin instructor called Bertha Glass followed—a serious, pale and slender woman more befitting Wilhelmina's intentions; accordingly, the violin was emphasized almost exclusively in Maria's education over the next decade. On her birthdays in 1909 and 1910, encouraged by her mother, she offered recitals at family gatherings. She was also apparently overcoming her shyness, for she argued loudly and often with Bertha, who tried to convert her student from a preference for simple pretty melodies to the graver, more intricate rhythms of Bach and Torelli.

Especially proud of Maria's musical ability was her widowed maternal grandmother, a tall, elegant woman of fifty with dark red hair and damson eyes. Grandmother Felsing took Maria to the family shop on Unter den Linden and taught her details of fashion and fine art—how Fabergé eggs were made, what jewelry should be worn with which dresses, how important were the right accessories and colognes for a lady's wardrobe and boudoir. She gave the child pretty ribbons and small pieces of jewelry and also arranged for her to have lessons in knitting and crocheting. Mrs. Felsing also insisted that the violin was quite proper but that the child also needed skills for common socializing, and so she paid for six months of guitar lessons. Maria's parlor now echoed with jaunty Bavarian folk songs as well as baroque airs.

Jovial and forthright, Mrs. Felsing represented, with her pearls and pomades, a kind of luxuriant sensuality, and she indulged Maria in keeping with her role as a doting grandmother and as a kind of whimsical coach in the arts of womanly appeal. She was, in other words, a welcome and powerful balance to the quiet severities of life with Wilhelmina and Bertha. From her mother and teachers, Maria learned responsibility, self-denial and the necessity of focussed concentration on hard work; her grandmother stressed the equally exacting but more enjoyable niceties of an artfully designed femininity —even if, according to Wilhelmina's judgment, these interests were to be reserved for maturity, and Maria's dress and manner had to remain sober at home. Above all, she was warned never to attract attention.

· · ·

BY THE TIME SHE WAS TEN YEARS OLD, MARIA DIE-
trich had lived almost exclusively in a female environment both at
school and at home. "We lived in a women's world," she wrote
later; "the few men with whom we came in contact were old or ill,
not real [*wirklichen*] men." She had seen the strength of widows in
their resourceful independence from men, despite the prevalent social assumption that they were inferior. Unaided, they were also
forced to make important economic decisions. In 1908, Wilhelmina,
unable to keep servants and a large apartment, moved with her
daughters to a more modest apartment at 48 Akazienallee and then,
in 1909, to even smaller quarters at 13 Tauentzienstrasse. To provide
her growing daughters the luxuries of private music lessons and
reasonably fashionable clothes, and to maintain the appearance of
genteel dignity appropriate to the heirs of a Royal Lieutenant, the
Widow Dietrich (so she was identified in the Berlin telephone di-
rectory for 1908) took a part-time job as a housekeeper for neighbors.

Wilhelmina also seems to have set herself the task of finding a
new husband, for there were several gentleman callers to the Dietrich apartments—most of them military or policemen, always in
full regimental uniform. These various courtings ceased in 1911,
when she accepted a proposal of marriage from Eduard von Losch, a
career colonel in the Royal Grenadiers whom she had met while she
was employed as housekeeper for his parents. Stolid, darkly handsome and ill at ease with his two stepdaughters, von Losch remained
very much in the background for the few years he was in Maria's
life, and of him she remembered little more than his ubiquitous
cigarettes and a collection of sabers. Her stepfather, like the man he
replaced, was simply another somewhat aloof, uniformed authority
figure she had to please.

THE ROUTINES OF SCHOOL, HOUSEWORK AND VIOLIN
lessons continued for Maria from 1912 to 1914, but she entered
adolescence with a sudden rush of new affection. One of her teachers, a slim and cultivated Frenchwoman in her twenties named Mar-

guerite Bréguand, taught French at Auguste Victoria. Maria, who had learned the rudiments of the language at home since the age of three, advanced rapidly in Mlle Bréguand's class, receiving high marks and perfecting her accent in after-class walks with her teacher. With the adulation common to a schoolgirl's crush on an attentive and sympathetic mentor, Maria imitated the woman's hairstyle, tried to duplicate the colors of her wardrobe and earnestly sought to seal the friendship with little gifts of chocolate or lace. As for Marguerite Bréguand, she encouraged Maria's love of things French and took a kindly interest in her general development; any overt display of camaraderie—even if the teacher had been so inclined—was of course strictly disallowed. Whatever were the terms and degree of reciprocity in Maria's attachment to her teacher, the relationship ended abruptly when Mlle Bréguand returned to France immediately after war was declared in 1914.

Of this time, the actress Tilla Durieux remembered soldiers marching proudly out of Berlin to war, showered with blossoms as they went. "Every face looks happy," Durieux wrote. "We've got war! Bands in the cafés and restaurants play [martial tunes] without stopping, and everybody has to listen to them standing up . . . There's a superabundance of everything: people, food and enthusiasm!" But Maria, forlorn over the departure of a teacher she idolized and confused about the attitude of Francophobia everyone was supposed to assume, could not comprehend the prevalent jubilation. Nor would she agree to stop speaking the enemy language, as pupils were asked to pray for the defeat of France; she often peppered her conversations with French phrases, to the indignant stares of classmates and superiors.

The festival atmosphere—as Berliners celebrated a war to establish the Empire's supremacy—was brief. Maria and the other schoolgirls were required to take on extra duties, knitting gloves, scarves and sweaters for soldiers. By 1915, food and fuel were strictly rationed, milk was a rarity, and potatoes were the diet staple. Maria's stepfather, who was on maneuvers during the summer of 1914, proceeded directly to combat without returning home, and before the end of that year her Uncle Max and two cousins were killed in battle. Like many of her friends, she then attached a black band to her left sleeve and wore only a black or grey dress. The rituals of bereavement also required that her long hair (now a luxuriant ash blond) henceforth be tightly wound and pinned up, worn loose only on Sundays at home. (In her adulthood, she was embarrassed by the fact that her uncle had commanded the first Zeppelin raid over London.)

Throughout the war, Maria went regularly to the city hall with her mother or a schoolmate, to scan the lists of wounded, missing and dead. At home there were ominous family meetings, as visiting aunts, cousins or Grandmother Felsing asked news of those fighting relatives from whom no letter had been recently received. By 1916, life became harsher still, for every street had a family in mourning and food was severely limited. At Christmas that year, Eduard von Losch sent a tin of corned beef to his family; it was the first meat they had seen in two years, and they parceled out slices in tiny slivers, heating the empty can several times for the residue of grease in which to fry potatoes. The following year, however, even potatoes were scarce and considerable imagination was brought to the preparations of turnips; there were, for example, turnip jelly, turnip bread and turnip soup, and the top-greens were boiled and reboiled for stocks and teas.

During wartime, Marlene Dietrich later felt, German women

did not seem to suffer in a world without men . . . Our life among women had become such a pleasant habit that the prospect that the men might return at times disturbed us—men who would again take the scepter in their hands and again become lords in their households.

But no master would ever rule the Dietrich-von Losch home again. Early in 1918, Wilhelmina was informed that her husband had been seriously wounded on the Russian border. She was permitted to visit him at a makeshift hospital, and although he seemed to rally, he died of infection not long after her return to Berlin. Since he had entered Maria's life in 1911, Eduard von Losch had lived with the family for a total of about eight months; he was never more than a vague and distant provider. When asked years later if she missed her father or stepfather, she replied flatly, "No. You can't miss what you never had."

For Wilhelmina, however, the second abrupt loss of a husband was shattering. Her ordered life collapsed again, her critical judgments on her daughters' styles and manners became sharp, and her serenity was broken. Never especially demonstrative with her daughters (and never as doting as their grandmother) Wilhelmina became more reserved than ever, as if she feared that any expression of an emotional bond with Elisabeth or Maria might again invite the rupture of death. "She didn't want to know whether I loved her or not," Marlene Dietrich wrote later. "She [simply] considered it more important that I should feel secure with her . . . Perhaps she didn't love, perhaps she was just trustworthy." Wilhelmina assumed a distracted, lost air, moving slowly, sometimes even neglecting the chores with which she had once been so obsessed. More than once, Maria awoke in the night to see her mother, fully dressed, stretched across her daughter's bed. "If only I could sleep," she would whisper wearily. By day, she often read aloud and, while working or walking through the apartment, she repeated verses of the Freiligrath poem: "The hour will come when you will stand by graves and weep . . ."

THERE WAS GOOD REASON FOR GRIEF ALL OVER THE country. Almost 1,800,000 Germans had been killed in the war—more casualties than any other nation—and by autumn 1918 there were few more men to sacrifice. During the conflict, Berlin had endured many strikes in addition to the general political turmoil, but now the crisis was enormous. A general strike on November 9, organized to dissolve the Empire and depose the Kaiser, rallied hundreds of thousands of Berlin workers, soldiers and sailors at the Reich Chancellery. His own generals advised Wilhelm to abdicate, and that day he left for exile in Holland. Within hours, the radical pacifist, anti-imperialist and Social Democrat Karl Liebknecht proclaimed the birth of a free Socialist Republic of Germany from the balcony of the Imperial Palace. At the same time, police headquarters and newspaper offices were occupied by left-wing extremists.

The uprising was immediately opposed. Bloody street battles ensued, and while armed revolutionaries took to the streets—seizing everything from government buildings to breweries to railway stations—private armies loyal to the old regime responded in full force, and in early 1919 Liebknecht was murdered. International peace treaties were being composed as the war ended, but there was nothing like concord in the streets of Berlin.

After elections were held, a new constitution was drafted on February 24, 1919, in the town of Weimar, about 140 miles from central Berlin. The Widow von Losch, eager to provide some kind of safe haven for her daughters, decided to pack them off to school in that city. Elisabeth successfully pleaded to remain behind and begin her teacher training in Berlin, but Maria readily agreed to her mother's suggestion.

The intellectual center of Germany in the late eighteenth and nineteenth centuries, Weimar had been from 1815 to 1918 the capital of the Grand Duchy of Saxe-Weimar-Eisenach. The city of Goethe and Schiller, it housed their archives in major museums and their effigies presided sternly in front of the German National Theater. The Liszt Music College memorialized that composer, and despite the war, the city's permanent political and cultural status was taken for granted throughout Europe. Architect and educator Walter Gropius was in Weimar in 1919, and he became director of the famous Bauhaus school of modern design and architecture; his staff included a remarkable roster of names—among them Josef Albers, Paul Klee, Lyonel Feininger, Wassily Kandinsky and László Moholy-Nagy. Equally renowned for its music conservatories, Weimar was also the residence of Professor Robert Reitz, a noted violinist and teacher. When Maria Dietrich arrived in April, it was to study with him.

At seventeen, she had grown to her full height of five feet, five inches. Like her mother, however, she tended to corpulence, and the short, more fashionable skirt and the short bobbed hairstyle she now adopted made her seem almost Rubenesque. Very much had been restricted in her Berlin life because of family and school obligations, and in Weimar she had no particular polish, nor an entrée to a new circle of friends. She was, therefore, pleased when Reitz, a demanding but kindly instructor, arranged for her to reside at a girls' dormitory near his studio. Her only desire was to please him—that, after all, was virtually the only approach to men she knew—and so she frequently brought him a pastry or offered to do his household chores. Years later, in answer to a question put to her by her lifelong friend Billy Wilder, she claimed that Reitz had been her first male lover.

With her roommates—girls who were studying music or literature at one academy or another—Maria soon began to flourish. They all bought cheap seats for theater and opera productions, and often on Sunday afternoons they took a picnic to the park and read aloud to one another—selections from Goethe's *Faust,* with each of them taking a part; the lyrics of Heinrich Heine's *Romanzero;* a poem just written by one of themselves; or sometimes a letter from a male admirer. During such activities, Maria's friends came to appreciate her witty comments and her brisk, satiric remarks.

For perhaps the first time, she became aware that she could be an asset to a gathering. Eager to be liked and accepted, she dispatched most of the dormitory tasks on their joint behalf and often invited a crowd of students to join them for a hearty goulash; additionally, she readily shared her cigarettes with friends and gave part of her own meager allowance to anyone in need. When her mother visited during the late summer of 1919, armed with supplies of tinned food and soaps, she found Maria far more casual in speech and manner, more gaily independent and perhaps, to Wilhelmina, more alarmingly mature after the experience of living away from home. A photograph of a much older man on her daughter's dressing table evoked her mother's inquiry; Maria smiled, said nothing and that evening introduced her mother to him—Professor Reitz, of course, who seemed very much a surrogate father as well as serious instructor. Of her year in Weimar little else is known, and later Marlene Dietrich rarely spoke of it: it was apparently a time of earnest study and of personality development, but neither written records nor personal witnesses survive to reveal more. In any case, she was back in Berlin before her nineteenth birthday in late 1920, studying with Professor Carl Flesch at the Music Academy and living in a one-room apartment nearby.

Her mother, making an enormous sacrifice, bought her a violin for 2,500 marks—then almost $700, an amount which would have bought a small house in the Berlin suburbs. There seemed to be no doubt, as Professor Reitz had said, that Maria was on her way to a major career as a violinist.

3: 1921–1926

IN 1910, THE CRITIC KARL SCHEFFLER HAD CALLED
Berlin a city doomed to a perpetual state of "becoming," but never
completed. By the end of 1920, a legal ordinance had recently created Greater Berlin, which included four million people, making it
the third largest city in the world. That year, the poet and playwright Bertolt Brecht described it as "a wonderful affair, overflow-
ing with things in the most ghastly taste—but what a display!" The
activity was indeed remarkable, for in progress or recently opened
were dozens of new theaters, cinemas, swimming pools, racetracks,
office buildings, factories, exhibition halls, luxury apartments and
proletarian flats. There was also an abundance of languages: Polish,
Slovak, Hungarian, Dutch, Danish, French and English were spoken
everywhere, for the city was a major European gateway, and citizens
en route to and from their own countries often stayed, attracted by
the cornucopia of a bedazzling life.

That life was, perhaps more than anything, a madcap European
version of the postwar, liberated jazz age; in fact, in a way the

Roaring Twenties began in Berlin. There was first of all, in 1919, a great Russian influence following the mass exodus from that country after the war: their newspapers, restaurants and styles were ubiquitous. Pianist Vladimir Horowitz and writer Vladimir Nabokov were among the first Russian refugees, as was nineteen-year-old Gregor Piatigorsky, who had waded across the Sbruch River holding his cello above his head while border guards shot at him. Dadaism, the anarchic art movement founded at Zurich's Café Voltaire, reached Berlin, too, where an adherent like Kurt Schwitters insisted he was making a political statement by festooning the walls of his home with junkyard trash. More sedately, English tearooms and literary societies opened monthly in Berlin, and soon American influence was everywhere evident—in pop songs, imported Broadway shows, the films of Chaplin and the translated works of Melville, Whitman, Poe, Twain and Sinclair, all of which Berliners were reading in best-selling quantities.

Things were happening quickly, and nowhere was the speed more evident than in the silent "flickers" that became popular as the new German cinema flourished. At the height of the war, General Ludendorf (among others) had seen the potential of film as propaganda, and in 1917 the major production companies were consolidated as the Universum Film Aktien Gesellschaft (known familiarly as UFA)—the Universe Film Company. After the Versailles Treaty, the government's one-third interest was sold, and UFA began to produce commercial and, when censorship was abolished, even unusual entertainments. The titles *Hyenas of Lust* and *A Man's Girlhood* fairly describe their stories.

But there was enduring art in the cinema. Robert Wiene's fantastic silent film *The Cabinet of Dr. Caligari* (1919), a weirdly expressionistic horror tale with a hallucinatory depiction of madness, was perhaps most responsible for the public's interest in movies, and soon Fritz Lang was preparing grave thrillers (*Destiny, Dr. Mabuse* and *Spies*) about society's anarchic impulses. F. W. Murnau, Ernst Lubitsch and Robert Siodmak were also refining skills they later took with them to film work elsewhere, and Billy Wilder, Fred Zinnemann and Alfred Hitchcock came from Vienna and London to make films at UFA's Neubabelsberg studios, which offered the finest technical facilities in the world. Whatever could not be supplied by state funding was provided by wealthy bankers, and by 1922 there were over 275 film companies (up from twenty-eight six years earlier) and a parallel explosion in the number of movie houses.

In the theater there was also unprecedented progress. A twenty-one year-old actor named Max Goldmann had come to Berlin's Deutsches Theater company from his native Vienna in 1894, and under the tutelage of its director Otto Brahm had developed astute performing and managerial skills. By 1905 he had directed plays by Strindberg, Wedekind, Wilde and Gorky as well as operas by Richard Strauss. Now known by the less obviously Jewish name of Max Reinhardt, he succeeded Brahm that year and widened his repertory to include Shaw and Shakespeare, Schiller and Goethe. Committed to the concept of exciting theater for the masses, he introduced revolving stages, spectacular mechanical devices and new approaches to stage lighting in his three-thousand-seat Grosses Schauspielhaus (Great Theater), a conversion of a circus on the Schumannstrasse. This new home of the Deutsches Theater was a steeply ascending amphitheater surrounding the stage on three sides. Here he presented monumental productions of the *Oresteia* and *Danton* with expertly managed, vast crowds of actors and extras. Next door to this vast auditorium, Reinhardt opened the smaller Kammerspiele or Chamber Theater, for staging smaller and sometimes avant-garde pieces, and nearby was Reinhardt's drama school.

German talent often flourished in less formal settings, however, and the cabaret was perhaps the most notorious. Set in a kind of supper-entertainment atmosphere, it had evolved from the circuses and street fairs of the late 1800s to the vaudeville shows of the early twentieth century, and by the 1920s, cabaret shows delighted both the lower and middle classes. Its most famous literary form emerged at the Kabaret der Komiker, where Kurt Tucholsky's satires drew an international audience ("We say no to everything!" was his provocative motto). Also popular were Erich Kästner's casual skits combining classical references, contemporary literary allusions and piquant sociopolitical commentaries often spiced with interludes of topless dancers. In such settings, one was free to perform and discuss any-

thing—and those on- and offstage did just that. Nothing was cen-
sored, everything was fair game for impromptu send-up and every
sort of sexual taboo was challenged—often at the behest of the
conferencier, a witty master of ceremonies who joked with the audience and introduced the acts and playlets.

BUT THERE WAS A DARKER SIDE. THE ARTIST
George Grosz, for one, called the Berlin of that time

> a completely negative world, with gaily colored froth on top that
> many people mistook for the true, the happy Germany before
> the eruption of the new barbarism. Foreigners who visited us at
> the time were easily fooled by the apparently light-hearted,
> whirring fun on the surface, by the nightlife and the so-called
> freedom and flowering of the arts.

Just beneath the surface, Grosz saw (and depicted in his famous
caricatures) "the fratricide and general discord . . . the noise, rumors, shouting, political slogans." He was on target, for all the commercial and cultural activity coexisted with a dizzying postwar infla-
tion. In 1919, a dollar bought eight marks; four years later, it bought
four trillion. Violent crime accompanied massive unemployment
and homelessness, there was a terrible food shortage, and families
routinely dissolved. Often ten or a dozen strangers shared a dingy
room with out-of-work drifters. An influenza epidemic claimed the
lives of seventeen hundred people in a single day in 1919. Not surprisingly, political discontent often became ferocious, and there
were more than five hundred assassinations in street riots between
1920 and 1923; reason seemed as debased as the currency.

Amid such disarray, forms of escape were understandably desired, and casual sex and opium were easily available. When novelist
Stefan Zweig wrote that Berlin had transformed itself into "the
Babel of the world," he was describing a city that seemed to thrive
on contempt for basic decency. Bare-breasted prostitutes chatted
with customers at the Café Nationale, while at the Apollo men and
women danced nude as patrons found rooms and niches for quick

trysts with performers during their offstage moments. At the White Mouse, on the Behrenstrasse, the cocaine addict Anita Berber offered her Dances of Horror, Lust and Ecstasy, usually wearing only chalk-white makeup and a crooked smile. She, like many of the onlookers, died before the age of thirty. Various morbid bars and clubs proliferated, responding to every possible inclination, and on many street corners boys and girls in black leather and shiny boots snapped whips threateningly or used hand fans daintily, to suggest every imaginable caprice.

There was, then, a curious blend of absolute despair and desperate gaiety, as if everyone sensed that catastrophe was imminent. In fact before the end of 1923, Adolf Hitler made an abortive attempt to seize power in Munich. Hermann Göring was wounded in the attendant melee; he withdrew to Austria where he became a morphine addict and, like his Führer, marked time.

INTO THIS WORLD OF 1921 BERLIN RETURNED MAria Magdalene von Losch (as she had been known in school at Weimar). Her violin lessons continued that year, but to support herself she often worked in a small, tacky cabaret orchestra, in a glove factory, a hat shop and even at a newspaper kiosk. Before her twentieth birthday that December she had at least two romantic liaisons —one with a frail young man whose identity is unknown and who subsequently died of dysentery, the second with an older man whose wealth somehow withstood the general economic distress. The sickly lad evoked her pity and tenderness; it was also an opportunity for an unthreatening, undemanding sexual interlude she could effectively control. And from the senior beau she willingly accepted meals and trinkets until she learned he had other romantic attachments as well as a wife and four children, whereupon she booted him out. Very quickly (as often happens when young people come to the swirling freedom of a modern metropolis) her residual shyness was overcome—not, it seems, by conscious effort, but simply by absorbing the *Berliner Luft,* the atmosphere itself.

· · ·

ONE DAY IN THE AUTUMN OF 1921 AT A CROWDED cafeteria she met an aspiring writer named Gerda Huber; that same day, at Gerda's insistence, Maria moved in with her, and for several months—until a job in journalism took Gerda to Hanover—the new friends were inseparable. Dark-haired, intelligent and earnest, she was the first woman with whom the adult Maria fell frankly and fully in love.

The relationship was based not merely on the situation of two compatible young working women sharing expenses in a wretched economy. Gerda—sedate, inclined to be bookish and to spice ordinary conversation with quotations from Goethe or Karl Marx—impressed Maria with her better education and her confident articulation. She discussed politics persuasively and literature from a sophisticated viewpoint, and her concern for the repressed and disenfranchised women in European culture ranked her as an early feminist.

Maria admired Gerda's eloquence and keen mind, while Gerda appreciated Maria's carefree attitude toward life and her comically feigned gravity about a music career whenever Maria was visited by her mother; the two young women were a good balance. Although she had changed violin teachers again, Maria seemed more intent on enjoying life than pursuing a career that seemed wildly unrealistic amid such urban chaos. Maria was also attractive to Gerda for her ability to convert two shabby rooms in Wilmersdorf into a habitable apartment, and to prepare a satisfying dinner from apparently useless scraps or leftovers.

Despite her attendance at girls' academies and the tutelage of her grandmother, Maria at twenty was in fact rather ungraceful, and in this regard she was perhaps seen as unintimidating to the slim and gangly Gerda. When she could, Maria ate heartily, and photographs of her at that time reveal a chubby young woman with a round, fleshy face. She seemed to care little for her figure—indeed, leanness was no social requisite; additionally, she (like very many Berlin women of her time) troubled even less about the image she presented in public. Attracting someone through mere appearance was not a tactic; what she did—or did not do—communicated her inner desires and outward wishes.

"She was anything but a sex bomb," according to the writer and producer Geza von Cziffra, who knew her at that time when she was a denizen of cabarets and late-night bars.

In fact she was quite boyish, with her masculine, buddy-like behavior. She readily joined us at tables where several of the patrons were homosexuals, for in fact [she] was much more interested—although not exclusively—in women. If she wanted a man now and then she simply showered him with sweetness, but any direct offer would have to come from her. So it would happen that she whispered to someone at a luncheon table, "Afterwards we'll go to your place." It would have been wrong for the poor soul to deduce any kind of commitment from such an afternoon, for [she] forgot such a pleasantry almost immediately.

Von Cziffra was not alone in attesting to Maria's participation in postwar Berlin's carefree life. A nonchalant approach to sex was in fact considered absolutely chic and virtually a social requirement for a grownup trying to get through the unpleasantness of every day.

WHILE ATTENDING VIOLIN CLASSES AT THE HOCHschule für Musik, Berlin's finest music academy, Maria met voice students, eager young apprentices hoping for theatrical careers. She managed to enroll in one of the most popular classes, taught by the eccentrically lively Franz Daniel. Many years later, Lotte Andor (then a classmate of Maria's and later an actress in Germany and America) recalled that Daniel had "a very strange system of breathing techniques. He made us run, make faces, jump around, do all sorts of tricks. This was his method of improving voice projection, and Marlene and I obeyed without question. She was remarkably anxious to please"—and, it seems, to broaden her career possibilities, for soon she was asking Lotte Andor (and Gerda, who she thought knew everything) about Max Reinhardt and his drama school. Acceptance there effectively guaranteed the start of a stage career because Reinhardt employed his students in the Deutsche Theater's repertory plays.

But Maria still had to cope with her mother's insistence on the more acceptable life of a concert violinist; Wilhelmina was still supporting her and subsidizing her lessons, and thus felt she had the right to criticize as well as counsel. In early 1922, however, Maria arrived at her mother's home one day with a bandaged left hand. She had an infected wrist, she said, and was forbidden to play the violin for two months. For this predicament we have only her own later vague accounts: she spoke variously of a broken ring finger, a sprained wrist, a diseased muscle, or a growth on a tendon. Of course she did not want to remain idle, Maria cannily told her mother: she was taking voice and acting lessons, just in case. In fact, she had already arranged an audition with Max Reinhardt's staff for entrance to his school.

By spring 1922, Wilhelmina's daughter was no longer Maria Magdalene von Losch. She had fashionably contracted her first two names, reassumed her father's surname and listed herself for the Reinhardt audition as Marlene Dietrich; gone forever were the nominal links to the penitential Mary Magdalene and to von Losch.

Ever after, Wilhelmina remained only coolly resigned to the fact that her daughter (unlike Elisabeth) had settled for a profession still then considered at least inappropriate for a fine lady, and at the worst downright immoral. For quite some time, there was a polite distance between mother and daughter, not bridged when a shocked Wilhelmina saw how Dietrich was supplementing her income: publicizing jewelry or phonograph records in stores and magazines, or advertising shoes or stockings. Legs, Dietrich told her mother: she was well paid to show her legs, which publicists much admired. "And if they want legs, they get legs," as Dietrich bluntly told the actor Wilhelm (later known as the director William) Dieterle later that year. Commercial photos from 1922 show Dietrich with studied coyness, holding a product or standing in a short skirt, her garters indicating the virtues of a brand of durable stockings.

Her legs landed her another job while she was preparing for the audition. From 1922 to 1928, she was among the so-called Thielscher Girls as one of twelve chorines presented by the impresario Guido Thielscher. The troupe performed intermittently with variety acts in Berlin, Hamburg and other cities, kicking and strutting in cabarets and music halls.

By June 1922, Marlene Dietrich was formally listed in the Grosses Schauspielhaus yearbook as a student and actress residing at 54 Kaiserallee in the Wilmersdorf district (just west of Schöneberg), where she shared a small two-room apartment with two or more Thielscher Girls when Gerda Huber was away on a writing assignment. A month earlier Dietrich had finally auditioned for Reinhardt's school—although not before him personally (nor did he ever teach her), for after 1920 he resided mostly in Austria and commuted to Berlin only occasionally. Dietrich recited a speech from Hugo von Hofmannsthal's mystical drama *Der Tor und der Tod* (*Death and the Fool*), in which the spirit of a dead girl speaks to a dying nobleman:

> *Wie dann dein Brief, der letzte, schlimme, kam,*
> *Da wollt ich sterben. Nicht um dich zu quälen,*
> *Sag ich dir das. Ich wollte einen Brief*
> *Zum Abschied an dich schreiben, ohne Klag,*
> *Nicht heftig, ohne wilde Traurigkeit;*
> *Nur so, dass du nach meiner Lieb und mir*
> *Noch einmal solltest Heimweh haben und*
> *Ein wenig weinen, weils dazu zu spät.*

> *Your letter came, the last, the dreadful one;*
> *And then I wished to die. Not to distress you*
> *Do I tell you this. One letter more*
> *I meant to write in parting; no lament,*
> *Not passionate, or fierce, unbridled grief,*
> *But just to make you yearn a bit for me,*
> *And teach you to feel homesick for my love,*
> *And shed a few tears, because 'twas then too late.*

But Dietrich was misguided in her choice. Reinhardt's assistants thought her delivery too grand and without nuance. She simply stood, reciting the lines in a kind of breathless self-pity. She was put off for a month, after which she returned and recited a brief scene from *Faust;* she was then permitted to enroll in small classes beginning that summer, conducted by Berthold Held, a friend and colleague of Reinhardt's. Among her classmates was Grete Mosheim, later an internationally famous actress. Later, Mosheim said,

> One day, Held told me, "Tomorrow I will introduce you to a young woman who really looks like an actress." And next day there was seated there a beautiful young girl who looked really great—blond hair, blue eyes, pretty face—and it was Marlene Dietrich. But he told her the same thing he had told me: "You look very beautiful, but you are no actress, you have no talent." Maybe this shared intimidation made us close friends, but in no time at all Marlene and I confided our problems to each other.

Mosheim and others who knew her at the time remembered a young woman of ebullient and sometimes risqué humor, excited about her prospects of a stage career. Accordingly, Dietrich—no longer the homey girl who shunned the spotlight, was now eager to be noticed, praised and approved. Lotte Andor recalled Dietrich wearing bright red hats with long plumes, or a large bow in her hair, or a feather boa. One day she might arrive at class with exaggerated makeup or an outrageous mix of brightly colored clothes; on another, she would borrow a dog and make a dramatic entrance with a Borzoi or a poodle. "She also loved lacquered shoes," Mosheim added, "silk stockings and a black velvet coat with a chic little hat."

Socially she was just as idiosyncratic and resolutely *sui generis*. As Geza von Cziffra recalled, she in fact had a reputation for rather easy virtue. Affectionate and playful, Dietrich was nothing at all like the sheltered maiden she later claimed to have been at the time; indeed, she was not so much Gretchen in *Faust* as Gloria Swanson in *Her Gilded Cage* (released that year in America and Germany). Like Swanson's Suzanne, Dietrich had gone from sedate music lessons to audacious modelling and cabaret work, falling in and out of love and reinventing herself along the way. And like the Swanson character, too, she would eventually move from Europe to America and become the quintessential star.

Gossip about theater folk was of major interest to the Berlin press. Dietrich was like most struggling actors, living in Spartan lodgings, racing from part-time job to a class in diction, voice or deportment. She was sometimes dependent for her dinner on her ability to crash the wild, bountiful after-parties routinely given at popular restaurants by wealthy playgoers.

But also like the public, Dietrich took her playgoing seriously. Despite the civil unrest and the brutal frugality that afflicted almost everyone's life, the theater was flourishing, and she partook of it all. Dramatist Carl Sternheim was at the height of his popularity in the 1920s, and his antibourgeois satires—like the racy *Die Hosen* (*The Knickers*), about the loss of a lady's stockings and undergarments— combined pointed comedy with trenchant social commentary. Georg Kaiser's trilogy *Gas* indicted the worship of postwar technoc- racy and posited the end of civilization, and the first play of Bertolt Brecht, *Trommeln in der Nacht* (*Drums in the Night*), focused on the predicament of the returning soldier. And with these and other serious dramas, there was always an abundance of musical revues, shows imported from London and New York, experimental cham- ber plays and, in repertory, everything from lavish operettas to starkly ritualistic two-character scenes.

To augment their incomes, actors regularly scoured the call sheets for film studios, where even a bit part offered a day's wages, lunch and the possibility of something more glamor- ous. In April 1922, Dietrich was tested at the Templehof film studios by a cinematographer named Stefan Lorant, who found her uneasy before the camera despite hours of gentle and persuasive reasoning. (Lorant was later highly successful in England and America as both journalist and author of many books, among them an acclaimed biography of Abraham Lincoln.) Quick, lively and ambitious, she was as ever eager to please, but Lorant remembered that Dietrich was unable to appear relaxed and confident, and her expressions and gestures were either extravagant or so muted she seemed catatonic. "She tried to follow instructions as I asked her to look sad, to imagine this, to react in such and such a way—pathetic or trium- phant or so forth—but even before we developed the reel, I felt she

offered nothing to the camera and would have no future in films."
He did not recommend her to Herr Horstman, the studio chief,
even for a crowd scene or a walk-on role.

Indeed, there was nothing particularly polished or impressive
about Dietrich in the early 1920s, and she was not singled out for
special attention onstage or in cabaret. But she was persistent. She
and a friend arranged to meet the director Georg Jacoby, who was
preparing a historical costume comedy—*Der kleine Napoleon* (*The
Little Napoleon*)—about the amorous adventures of Napoleon's
younger brother. Complimenting Jacoby on his earlier work and (as
set designer Fritz Maurischat recalled) openly flirting with him, Dietrich was quickly cast in the single-scene role of a lady's maid; she
worked on the picture for only a few days in late summer 1922.

Rightly, she saw this debut as unremarkable, with no guarantee
that her appearance would bring more film assignments. A woman
of the moment in her work as in her private life, she was merely
seeing to the practical matter of paying her rent and providing a few
luxuries. To this she ardently gave herself, apparently never considering that with some guidance she might be more than merely presentable on film, a medium which could evoke her talent, exploit
her charm and provide a lucrative international career, all better than
the theater could.

She may well have been surprised, then, when soon afterwards
she was chosen from a group of fellow drama students for a small but
effective role in a film called *Tragödie der Liebe* (*Tragedy of Love*), to be
directed by Joe May, a prolific cinematic pioneer. May's assistant, a
handsome, blond and athletic Slovakian-German named Rudolf
Sieber, advertised an open casting call to select dozens of extras for
the picture, whose climax was set in a crowded courtroom. On a
warm September day, Dietrich arrived at the studio, where Sieber
quickly took her from a group of young women and rushed her into
May's office. Asked to stand, then sit, turn this way and that, smile
and nod slowly, she followed the director's instructions with a kind
of diffident bemusement: this seemed much ado about very little
indeed if she were to play an anonymous bit, and she was quickly
bored by May's demands that she repeat a simple gesture or glance.

The following afternoon, Sieber arrived at the Reinhardt rehearsal hall, only to be told that Dietrich had no classes that day. He found her at her mother's home, where she was living temporarily because of a cash crisis; there Rudi made several important announcements. First, *Tragödie der Liebe* was to be a major film certain to attract vast audiences, for the star was none other than the robust, burly Emil Jannings—a leading German stage actor also known for his screen portraits of Louis XV, Henry VIII, Peter the Great and Othello. Second, the film was quite different from the kitschy pseudo-history of *Der kleine Napoleon:* this was a violent story of lust, jealousy and revenge, with Jannings cast as a brutal wrestler standing trial for murder. Third, Joe May had sent Sieber to offer her the role of Lucie, the presiding judge's pert, spoiled mistress who has a brief, pouty scene making a telephone call in bed, and who then whines her way into the crowded courtroom where she causes mild distraction by her giggly insolence—a brief but amusing role injected as a few moments of comic relief. The perfect touch for the wardrobe of this frivolous character, Sieber added, would be a monocle—then a fashionable affectation often worn by young women with perfect eyesight who simply wanted to be noticed. Dietrich accepted the role and offered to prepare Sieber a cup of coffee. Instead, he took Dietrich out to lunch at a nearby café, and very soon they were courting, although the meetings at Wilhelmina's apartment, held under her vigilant eye, were properly chaste.

Born February 20, 1897 in Aussig, Rudolf Emilian Sieber was a dapper twenty-five-year-old who found Marlene Dietrich winsome, pretty and sensual. When Sieber called at her apartment a month later, Wilhelmina flatly said she disapproved of her daughter's busy social life when the duties of work should prevail. "This is too boring for me," Sieber told Dietrich soon afterwards. "I can't come to your home because of your mother. Why? I can have any of the most beautiful Russian girls in Berlin—any of them I please. We need to stop this, it just doesn't please me anymore."

But it was not just her mother's Victorian propriety that Sieber resented. According to Stefan Lorant, who saw them both socially at the time, Rudi was not quite so freewheeling sexually, and he seemed to disapprove of Dietrich's rendezvous with women, which she made no attempt to conceal. If indeed that was his objection, he perhaps harbored the common notion that all she needed was the love of a good man to normalize her preference. Rudi was earnest, conventional and obviously taken with this spirited, energetic woman who was most affectionate and responsive when he was tired or worried. At such times she hovered with concern, nurtured and encouraged him, acted as she had been trained—to gratify a man— and then more than ever willingly applied the soothing unguent of sex. But he was impatient with Wilhelmina and her snobbism.

THE FILMING OF *TRAGÖDIE DER LIEBE* PROCEEDED smoothly, and Dietrich's brief appearance as Lucie delighted the other players and then audiences. Although the film is silent, no dialogue intertitles are needed to appreciate Lucie's coy manipulation. Dietrich's eyelids flutter, her shoulders seem almost to project her request, her lips to promise a rewarding kiss. But in the courtroom finale she steals the scene from a hundred other players, exchanging her monocle for opera glasses—her idea, and it must have exhilarated Joe May, for he intercut close-ups of her comic reactions to the tense legal proceedings as she fluttered, laughed and yawned, everything in counterpoint to the solemnity of the situation. This remains the earliest documented evidence of a sly theatrical wit and a sense of how best to direct a director's attention to herself.

September 1922 was triply busy, as Dietrich travelled to the studio in early morning, rehearsed in her drama classes in the late afternoons and was onstage several evenings each week in her first roles. Beginning September 7, she had a small, four-line role in Wedekind's *Die Büchse der Pandora* (*Pandora's Box*) at the Kammerspiele, which she played nine times until March 3, 1923; her friend Grete Mosheim was also in the cast. The director was an amusing man named Friedrich Holländer, who was also a musician and composer; he occasionally coached Dietrich in singing, for her voice lay uncertainly between soprano and (perhaps because she had been smoking heavily for five years) a rather gauzy baritone.

She also appeared forty-two times, from October 2 to April 22, in a German translation of *The Taming of the Shrew* at the Grosses Schauspielhaus. The popular star Elisabeth Bergner played Kate, and

Dietrich the Widow, a small part made smaller by the director's generous cuts of the text. She was, however, so frankly awestruck by Bergner's beauty and poise that she diluted what little character the Widow had and made no impression on colleagues or audiences. Not much more promotion was given to her career by her appearance (again with Mosheim) in two small roles in a forgettable play by Hennequin and Veber called *Timotheus in flagranti* (which was permanently removed from the repertory after only twelve days). This she immediately followed by twenty-three performances (from January 24 to March 5, 1923) at the Kammerspiele in yet another small, colorless role, Anna Shenstone in a translation of Maugham's *The Circle*—again with Elisabeth Bergner in the lead. Looking like a refugee from a road tour of *Die Walküre,* she also appeared nine times as an almost comically overdressed Amazon warrior in Kleist's epic tragedy *Penthesilea.*

Her relationship with Sieber, which proceeded thornily, was also very nearly as tragic as the play. "The realization that he might marry another girl just about drove her to suicide," according to Grete Mosheim. "Finally she stole some coal and food from her mother and one winter night she went through the snow to his house. She gained access to his quarters, laid on a hot meal and waited for him to return." From that night the affair flourished, and next day Rudi gave her the money to take a small flat on her own—Wilhelmina to the contrary notwithstanding.

But by April 1923, Dietrich was professionally bored. Her several stage roles were minuscule and unrewarding, and she had just spent four days dressed as a peasant girl in a pious trifle called *Der Mensch am Wege (Man by the Roadside)*, a film starring, written and directed by Wilhelm Dieterle. "One had the impression that she came from a milieu where one had to go through the kitchen to get to the living room," Dieterle said years later, describing her directness and simplicity. "Despite this, she could seem very much the *grande dame."*

The affectation of sophistication may have been assumed for the sake of Dietrich's escort, for by this time Rudi was virtually her constant companion and accompanied her to the suburban studio where the film was made. To make herself more attractive, she also joined Grete Mosheim in an exercise regimen under the direction of a powerful Swedish gymnast named Ingrid Menzendick, who had a studio in the Lützowplatz.

Then, on Thursday, May 17, 1923, at the town hall of Berlin-Friedenau—as if on a whim—Marlene Dietrich (then twenty-one) married Rudolf Sieber (twenty-six). The newlyweds moved into her apartment on the Kaiserallee.

The marriage, according to friends like Stefan Lorant, Grete Mosheim and Lotte Andor, had its own capricious logic. For Rudi's part, he was beguiled by her sensuality and wished to settle into a conventional marriage and raise a family. At the time of the wedding, Dietrich did not object to this plan; besides, she appreciated his influence at the film studios and his professional recommendations on her behalf. He was also handsome, polite and articulate—and a man to care for and attend, which was very much part of her training. In this regard, she eagerly assumed the role of *Hausfrau,* cooking and housekeeping for her husband.

But two weeks after the wedding, it was clear that Marlene Dietrich was not to be confined by matrimony. She made no secret of her infatuation with a girl she had met at an audition for a Bjornstern Bjornson play about budding romance (aptly titled *Wenn der junge Wein blutt/When the Young Vine Blooms*), and Rudi, as she might have predicted, was suitably concerned. Once the play began regular performances (as Dietrich's fellow cast member Lotte Andor recalled), Sieber delivered his wife to the theater each evening and waited backstage to escort her home. The object of his wife's attention was quickly discouraged.

Dietrich's career was not much advanced by the Bjornson play —nor by either her two-minute bit part in the movie *Der Sprung ins Leben* (*The Leap into Life*), filmed in July, or her stage appearance as Hippolyta in *A Midsummer Night's Dream* at the Theater in der Königgrätzer Strasse in February 1924. For the remainder of 1923 and 1924 she was essentially unoccupied, and so it was not surprising to friends when she told them she was pregnant. On December 12, 1924, after a difficult delivery, Dietrich gave birth to Maria Sieber.

There must have been complications and perhaps even some danger attending the event, for Dietrich was confined to a long recuperation; as she wrote in a card of thanks to her former violin teacher, Julius Levin, in May, she was still resting at home and unable to look for work. But she was in no hurry, for the role of doting mother eminently suited her. She would not accept a servant to help care for the baby, she nursed her lovingly for eight months, and when friends invited the Siebers to a vacation in Westerland on the North Sea during the summer of 1925, she accepted on condition that Heidede was welcome too.

This holiday immediately preceded Dietrich's return to the UFA studios in Neubabelsberg, where she was hired to play the coquette Micheline in Arthur Robison's sumptuous production of *Manon Lescaut.* In a half-dozen scenes with the stars Lya de Putti and Fritz Greiner, Dietrich had the most screen time of her career thus far.* Flirting at a sidewalk café by merely lowering her head and affecting weary insouciance that would soon become a virtual trademark, she impressed at least two critics with a provocative kind of repose—as if she might seduce by merely waiting in a kind of languid indifference. While many other performances of the silent screen era (and later) were almost theatrically overripe, Dietrich knew how to do nothing brilliantly. And this quickly became a way to attract attention by a sort of inversion: while everyone round her seemed almost hysterically fussy, she claimed a scene by appearing detached, liberated from the action.

But the image of cool independence was not entirely simulated. By early 1926, Rudi was again (as often) unemployed: he kept house and cared for Maria while Dietrich went to auditions and casting calls and effectively supported the family. As he might have anticipated, this arrangement had serious risks, for marriage and motherhood were no hindrances to his wife's autonomy.

---

* Some recent chroniclers of Marlene Dietrich's career (among them Cadden, Higham and Kobal) have insisted she appears as an unbilled extra in a crowd scene of G. W. Pabst's classic *Die freudlose Gasse* (*The Joyless Street*). But no archival materials or subsequent cast list support this, and she is nowhere recognizable. Because no complete version of the original film exists, it is remotely possible she fell to the cutting room floor; even this explanation, however (advanced by Dickens), seems unlikely, for the crowd scenes were shot in February 1925, when Dietrich was still resting at home after her daughter's birth.

4: 1926–1929

In February 1926, Marlene Dietrich as-
sumed the role of Lou Carrère in Hans Rehfisch's social satire *Duell
am Lido*. Cast as an amoral girl tottering on the brink of the demi-
monde, she arrived at the first rehearsal and was told by director
Leopold Jessner that she looked just right in her own outfit—silk
trousers, a dark jacket and a startling monocle—and that she should
wear all these in the performances. He may not have known that she
had come directly from an all-night frolic at a transvestite bar called
Always Faithful, whose patrons were certainly not. Dietrich may
have taken her performance cue from that place, too, for she played
Lou as frantically decadent. "The role should have been acted by
Marlene Dietrich not in a demonic revelry but icy-cold," remarked
critic Fritz Engel.

From that season on, she was a well-known public presence, and
not at all because of her professional accomplishments. Known in
seedy Kurfürstendamm bars as well as at elegant dances sponsored by
producers and musicians, Dietrich was typical of many Berlin ac-

tresses—freewheeling and unconventional in her conduct and eager to meet those who could advance her career; they were often more approachable at night, after they'd had several whiskeys and some cocaine. At such times, however, she always kept a clear head.

Often, as actress Elisabeth Lennartz recalled, Dietrich got attention at restaurants and cafés by "wearing neither bra nor panties, which was very modern and daring." Dancer and actress Tilly Losch, a leading doyenne of the Berlin lesbian bar scene, recalled that Dietrich was no stranger to such places. "It was chic for girls not to be feminine. I knew Dietrich in those days and she was a tough little nut. But unlike the others, she somehow looked glamorous." A photograph of the time shows Dietrich as glamorous indeed in a gentleman's smoking jacket at a ladies' supper club, flanked by Leni Riefenstahl (soon to be Hitler's documentarian with her films *Triumph of the Will* and *Olympiad*) and the Chinese-American actress Anna May Wong.

In lounges, cabarets and jazz clubs, however (as Gerda Huber and Grete Mosheim, among others, confirmed), Dietrich had a reputation for combining the most outrageous dances, jokes and sexual capers with unbending opposition to drugs and excessive drinking. She was, in other words, a curious combination of her mother's Prussian upright moralism and her own sturdy, antic individualism. Käte Haack recalled a formal ball in the mansion of Eugen Robert, director of the Tribune Theater, attended by Reinhardt, playwright Ferenc Molnár, the actors Peter Lorre and Conrad Veidt, and Carola Neher (soon to star in the original production of *The Threepenny Opera*).

> Only one woman stood out: Dietrich, who appeared and took the hand of Carola Neher, who was also a great beauty. And then the two of them danced a tango. It was an unforgettable sight, and the entire crowd, astonished, made room and watched.

The tango was of course a dance of considerable style, and it drew attention by its controlled, almost stoic eroticism. Dietrich and Neher glided, swooped and dipped without ever unlocking a breathless embrace. The bystanders cheered.

But there were other ways of attracting attention. Elli Marcus, known for her celebrity photographs, was approached by Dietrich with the blunt request, "Take some pictures of me that will make me a star." Warily, Marcus complied and Dietrich sat obediently for three days of photography; despite the pleasing results, fame still eluded her.

At home, Sieber at first took his wife's eccentric liberties calmly, as if they were an actress's transient fancies or a phase from which she might emerge. Indeed, Dietrich openly discussed her casual amours, which included men from film studios with whom she spent an occasional night, actors from the theater who she thought required a little attention, and those like Anna May Wong and Tilly Losch, who were clever, amusing and exotic companions. She did not proffer sex as barter, to win a role or a favor; it was simply an acceptable form of flattery and a way of being appreciated. From men she was perhaps winning the approval she had been denied by her father and stepfather, while intimacy with women was always natural and easy for her.

IN LATE SPRING 1926, DIRECTOR ALEXANDER KORDA cast Dietrich in the role of a pretty, sophisticated society girl in a film showcasing his wife Maria. In *Eine Du Barry von Heute* (*A Modern Du Barry*), billed oddly as Marlaine Dietrich, she had only three brief scenes as a nameless coquette—but she nevertheless revealed a real flair for comedy. After ordering a new dress that requires time for alterations, she sees the shopgirl wearing it at an elegant restaurant that very evening. Furious, she demands that her escort take her away at once, and her quick shift from surprise to annoyance to prissy outrage is comically acute. Next morning, languishing in bed, she telephones the dress shop to demand the clerk's discharge, only to be told the girl has already resigned (and become an overnight social sensation). Her understated fury—conveyed by simply narrowing her gaze and slowly pursing her lips—is a model of discerning adult acting in silent film.

Despite the small role and modest income—Dietrich was paid only three hundred marks, which was one percent of the star's salary—she agreed that August to appear for Korda as a mere dress extra for the party scenes of a comedy called *Madame wünscht keine Kinder* (*Madame Wants No Children*). This she accepted on condition that Rudi be hired as a production assistant, a courtesy won through the intercession of cinematographer Karl Freund, who years later in America was the cameraman for the television series *I Love Lucy*.

But there was no time—nor did she have the inclination—to be despondent over a negligible film career. In late August, Dietrich was busy rehearsing daily at the Grosses Schauspielhaus when an ailing actress (Erika Glässner) withdrew from Eric Charell's eighteen-scene musical revue *Von Mund zu Mund* (*From Mouth to Mouth*). This show, which opened September 1, was important for several reasons.

First, this was Marlene Dietrich's initial appearance in a singing role—an assignment for which she did not believe herself well suited and a skill she had hardly refined. Nevertheless, on short notice she worked with Charell (a noted choreographer and director of operettas, revues and folk musicals) and with composer Hermann Darewski. By opening night, Dietrich had learned three songs that were inserted into her spoken material as the show's mistress of ceremonies. Wearing a bright yellow dress with a long train and rose-colored ruffles at the neck and wrists, she stood—quite still, as she insisted to Charell at dress rehearsal—and sang the undistinguished melodies, barely acknowledging the grandeur of her surroundings or the vast audience. Her apparent detachment created, as she must have suspected, an atmosphere of intrigue about herself and what experience might have been behind the lyrics of the song; she barely regarded her audience, half-closing her eyes and never smiling until she walked, slowly and with a kind of muted eroticism, along the extended ramp over the orchestra pit. With one glance and a hushed word, as actor Hubert von Meyerinck recalled, she communicated more than any performer who cavorted wildly in the show.

It was with the delivery of her second song in *Von Mund zu Mund* that Dietrich brought the audience to a standing ovation. Altering her stance and tone to present a slightly tense, perky sexiness, she revealed a voice not of great beauty or warmth, but one with unusual spirit, range and subtlety. A recording released the following year was a minor sensation among private collectors in Berlin, along with her renditions of "Wenn ich mir was wünsche" (patently modeled on American blues singers) and "Leben ohne Liebe," sung in a disarmingly innocent style, rather like a sad, distracted nightclub performer offering a weary conviction that "You can't live without love," and that an abandoned woman knows this better than anyone.

WITH THESE FIRST RECORDS, MARLENE DIETRICH was about to join an array of German actresses who tried to sing (and singers who tried to act). Many, like her, had distinctive styles, but many were facile mimics of other Europeans or Americans who vocalized with more or less a personal manner. Among the most famous was Lilian Harvey, the British actress raised in Germany (where she became a star), who was perhaps closest to an accomplished operetta artist when she sang onstage or in film (as in her 1926 film *Prinzessin Tralala*). Renate Müller, on the other hand, had a slightly nervous vibrato when she sang "Ich bin so glücklich heute —I'm so happy today," rather as if she were protesting too much (in fact she committed suicide at thirty). They avoided the blunt attack of those like Fita Benkhoff (who liked to flavor her songs with Americanisms like "Oh, baby!"). On the other hand, Trude Hesterberg was certainly one of the most trained voices—almost operatic—and Evelyn Künneke was one of those most influenced by American popular song.

But Zarah Leander and Claire Waldoff were perhaps the most famous, controversial and prominent singers at the time and later— and the most influential on the development of Dietrich's singing style. Leander had an astonishingly smoky, androgynous baritone, but her delivery was in a strange way strongly, almost severely feminine. When she sang about a pursuit of casual amours ("every night brings me a new stroke of luck") there was a strain of knowing defeat, of loneliness; just so in a lyric of fatigued waiting ("each night, by the telephone . . .") or Gallic compromise as she thanked

a lover as he (or she) departed ("Merci, mon ami . . ."). Enormously popular, Zarah Leander—with her adult, apparently unemotional but acutely felt trademark of knowing distance—was certainly
a model for Marlene Dietrich in the late 1920s. She prepared the
way for Dietrich's delicate balance between eternal romantic optimism and tiresome self-pity.

Much less womanly but equally influential was Dietrich's co-star
in *Von Mund zu Mund,* the redoubtable Claire Waldoff, a barrel-
chested little Valkyrie who—seen in photos and heard on recordings
decades later—resembled no one so much as Mickey Rooney in
drag. Waldoff's theatrical songs and recordings, crudely refined in
cabaret, were not so much sung as rasped or bleated with an almost
painful, choking coarseness that many Berliners loved precisely for
its unconventionality. Spitting and punching her way through the
measures of "Hannelore" (a paean to a rudely educated peasant girl)
or "Willi" (in which she poked fun at the deposed Emperor), Claire
Waldoff raged along like a boozy stevedore. An intelligent performer
unafraid to offend with her openly gay songs, she also enveloped
everything with a self-mocking humor.

In fact—unlikely a pair though they might have seemed—the
now occasionally blond Marlene Dietrich and the red-headed Claire
Waldoff became lovers (or at least sexual partners) in the autumn of
1926. Geza von Cziffra, Elisabeth Lennartz and Stefan Lorant knew
that Dietrich was quite besotted with her new friend, with whom
she often dined after midnight, sometimes singing along the
Kurfürstendamm or (to the delight of theater patrons) in the alley
near the theater. This brand of professional-personal intimacy, however briefly it lasted, was typical throughout Dietrich's life; it seemed
to have its own truth and reward, and when the affair ended Waldoff
remained a genial buddy to her. Fritzi Massary, the reigning queen
of musicals and operettas at Berlin's Metropol from 1904 to 1932,
later wrote that Dietrich learned from Waldoff to laugh at herself as
well as at the pretensions of hypersophisticated audiences.

Dietrich was also (according to Mia May, the leading lady in
Tragödie der Liebe) "constantly pursued by people who found her
fascinating, [and] she went around with a group of young actresses
who adored her. Usually she wore a monocle or a feather boa,

sometimes as many as five red foxes on a stole." Perhaps inevitably, an increasing number of adoring colleagues and theater fans were therefore responsible for Dietrich's growing self-confidence in Berlin from 1926 to 1930. At a party she gave for friends at home at Christmastime 1926, word circulated that she was going to change her outfit. Käte Haack recalled that Dietrich had ordered an ensemble with seven silver foxes that had just arrived, and she made a second grand entrance, forcing (as she doubtless intended) everyone's attention on herself. Such tactics often assured that she would be noticed in public, too—at the Cabaret Nelson, for example, a notorious nightspot where high art could be found one moment and low humor the next. On the other hand, she discouraged others from calling attention to themselves. When the actress Lili Darvas admired Dietrich's fur coat but compared it unfavorably to her own, she was told, "Oh, don't worry, Lili, dear—no one is ever going to bother to look at *you.*"

AFTER THE BRIEF BUT MEMORABLE PRESENTATION OF *Von Mund zu Mund,* Dietrich supplemented her income from late 1926 through early 1927 by rushing through three films. In *Kopf Hoch, Charly!* (*Heads Up, Charly!*), she again assumed the small role of a French coquette; in *Der Juxbaron* (*The Imaginary Baron*), she had a major comic role as a young woman whose parents hope to marry her off to a nobleman; and in *Sein Grösster Bluff* (*His Greatest Bluff*) she was a high-priced prostitute involved in a jewelry theft. In each of these productions were actors (Michael Bohnen, Trude Hesterberg, Albert Pauling) who recalled Dietrich's thoroughly professional attitude; indeed, she had a lifetime reputation for punctuality and preparedness. She was also remembered for honoring colleagues' birthdays with cakes or strudels or trinkets—gestures that were certainly sincere but also perhaps reflected her wish to gratify and to be considered generous and thoughtful.

Dietrich was herself pleased when she won a small role in the European premiere of George Abbott and Philip Dunning's American play *Broadway,* a tense romantic melodrama still selling out in New York after a year's run. The premiere was given at the Vienna

Kammerspiele on September 20, 1927, where she made a brief appearance as Ruby, a chorus girl in a spicy jazz-age story about speakeasy gangsters, bootleggers, corrupt police and a vaudevillian's climb to stardom.

The role was almost negligible, but once again Dietrich managed to attract attention by raising her hemline just a trifle higher than the other chorines' (although there was no dancing). In the first-night audience was Karl Hartl, then in Vienna as executive producer for a movie with characters similar to those in *Broadway;* two days later, he invited Dietrich to his office and offered her a part in the film *Café Electric.* "She showed only a mild enthusiasm," Hartl said years later,

> and I had the feeling her heart wasn't in film. But she accepted, and she showed up the first day with a red suit and a hat like a pot. Marlene knew how to wear clothes of mediocre quality in a way that seemed elegant; her taste and her choice of colors made up for the cheapness of the material.

She accepted the role not only for the salary but also because it was an opportunity to work with the dynamic and popular Viennese actor Willi Forst. As Erni, Dietrich was to be seduced by a young gigolo named Ferdl (Forst), a denizen of the notorious Café Electric, gathering place of pimps and hookers. In a swift blurring of the distinction between art and life, Dietrich and Forst became the talk of Vienna's café society within a week. "We had to repeat several love scenes between her and Willi Forst," said Hartl. "Considering their romance, this was no hardship for them, and finally she was outstanding."

The production had another social advantage for her. Igo Sym, also in *Café Electric,* was a handsome Bavarian actor and musician who taught Dietrich to play the musical saw, a long strip of thin metal like a toothless saw, played with a thickly waxed bow. With her knees grasping the handle of the saw, she bent the metal—more for higher tones, less for lower—and slowly applied the bow to its edge; the sound could be politely described as a kind of mournful vibrato. For decades, Dietrich had a kind of vaguely comic renown in Germany and America as the first lady of this "singing saw," although she always regarded this talent with absolute solemnity, as if it authenticated her earlier hopes for a career as a concert violinist.

Not long after the Dietrich-Forst romance became an open secret, Rudi arrived in Vienna and demanded that Dietrich end the affair. This was never the judicious approach to take, for it had the predictable effect of confirming her on the independent route she always marked for herself; his wife apparently barely reacted to this entreaty. Rudi had hoped that the responsibilities of motherhood would alter her conduct, but this was a hopeless fantasy. When he then countered that he had the chance for his own extramarital romance—with a darkly attractive young woman named Tamara Matul—Dietrich was delighted and encouraged him.★

"I haven't a strong sense of possession towards a man," she said somewhat airily not long after her confrontation with Rudi, "perhaps because I am not particularly feminine in my reactions. I never have been." This was the closest Dietrich ever came to justifying her continuing marriage to Rudolf Sieber, a relationship that was henceforth always cordial. From 1927 to 1930, the Siebers lived together only part of the time in Berlin (and rarely thereafter anywhere). Dietrich never seriously considered divorce, perhaps because even a nominal marriage forestalled another offer and acted as a kind of protection. But that same year, Tamara Matul became Rudi's constant companion and an attentive surrogate parent to Maria when her mother was absent.

Before returning to Berlin, Dietrich—acceding to Willi Forst's fervent request to prolong her Austrian sojourn—took a small role in the satiric play *Die Schule von Uznach* by Carl Sternheim, Germany's reigning comic dramatist. After the November 28 premiere at Reinhardt's Theater in der Josefstadt, critic Felix Salten (author of *Bambi*) wrote, "Among the girls, Marlene Dietrich was the most refreshing as a beautiful, sensual young woman who rambles on without thinking."

★ During all this, Dietrich was rumored to be romantically linked with Igo Sym and with the actor-playwright Hans Jaray. Although there is no evidence to support the talk of these affairs, her complicated (and well-documented) love life at the height of her international fame suggests that the delicate management of simultaneous liaisons was well within her competence.

. . .

DIETRICH RETURNED TO BERLIN IN EARLY 1928, arms full of belated Christmas gifts and toys for Maria; she then devoted two weeks to the child's amusement, taking her to the zoo, parks and children's pageants. Then she was back in rehearsals for the Berlin opening of *Broadway* on March 9, and for a celebration in honor of her old boss Guido Thielscher, whose fifty years in show business were marked by a midnight cabaret at the Lustspielhaus on March 27. These two events, following the Berlin premiere of *Café Electric* (retitled for Germany as *Wenn ein Weib den Weg verliert/When a Woman Loses Her Way*) and linked to her increasing prominence as a colorful doyenne of theatrical social life, gave Dietrich the widest press exposure she had so far enjoyed.

She still tended to a portliness all too evident on her short frame, and she worried that her nose (which turned up slightly at the tip) made her less photogenic than she would have liked. But her legs were ideal—perhaps because she was now exercising daily with a prizefighter's trainer who forced her to lie on the floor for hours, pedalling an imaginary bicycle. Casting directors, not to mention most men and many women, were quick to notice the elegant, sensual line of her legs; she could, therefore, risk an even higher hemline than that dictated by mere fashion.

In addition, Dietrich's partiality for an onstage pose of profound unconcern continued to work wonders for her image. To receive an almost rapt attention Dietrich had only to lean against the scenery, lower her eyes and light a cigarette with utter indifference to everyone round her. In a comic role, this gave her a deadpan appearance and seemed somehow all the funnier; in a serious part, she seemed more than ever a mysterious, eternally ineffable presence. By such tactics, she effectively stole scenes and was immune to criticism from other players. She was, in other words, refining the theatrical counterpoint of creative indolence to a highly successful technique.

IT WAS PRECISELY DIETRICH'S IMPRESSION OF VARIous inner moods and mysteries that inspired writer Marcellus Schiffer and composer Mischa Spoliansky to cast her in their fantastic musical revue *Es Liegt in der Luft* (*It's in the Air*) at the Komödie Theater that spring of 1928. Set in a department store, the show was a series of twenty-four episodes about those who visit and work among an array of luxurious, useless items; most notably, it offered a series of short sketches about those who became lost in the crazy array of goods, died and remained there as wandering spirits.

Dietrich appeared in seven of the twenty-four scenes, and one of them caused a sensation. Schiffer's wife, the tall, boyish French actress Margo Lion, was already known to be openly bisexual, and a number was prepared for her and Dietrich called "Sisters." Ostensibly a parody of the sort of friendly girls' duet offered by the Dolly Sisters, the song deliberately pointed to the bond between two women, happily buying underwear for one another while temporarily released from the company of their boyfriends.

Audiences and critics loved the frank but elegant sexual inferences of the number. Then, after the first week, Dietrich—protesting that their dark outfits needed a touch of color—naughtily capitalized on one of the most notorious sexual symbols of the day and pinned bunches of violets on herself and Lion. These flowers were a widely understood token, since the popular German poet Stefan Georg (and those he inspired, called the Georgists) had taken the color lavender as an emblem of homosexual love and violets as markers of its erotic expression. The play *La Prisonnière* by Edouard Bourdet, a compassionate assessment of modern lesbianism, had recently been successful in Paris and Berlin and one of its most daring visual motifs was violets shared by women in love. That edible flower, prized by French gourmets, also had a long Gallic association with sexual pleasure.

Each night there were several curtain calls after Dietrich and Lion strolled back and forth across the stage in an expressionless daze of mutual obsession, clasping hands and singing—Lion in a high falsetto, Dietrich in a smoky, low register that Spoliansky had found to be just right for her. "Marlene Dietrich," reported that dean of critics, Herbert Jhering, "sings with delicacy and tired elegance. The number ["Sisters"] goes beyond anything so cultivatedly daring we've ever seen."

The success of *It's in the Air* led film writer and director Robert Land to Dietrich's dressing room, where he offered her a handsome salary to appear in a romantic comedy as a Parisian courtesan famous for her lessons in lovemaking. The film was quickly produced that summer with Dietrich in the title role of *Prinzessin Olala*—an obvious satire of Lilian Harvey's chaster story of *Princess Tralala,* who won hearts by song rather than sex. When the picture was released in September, critics took notice of Dietrich's resemblance to another European star: "When Dietrich mimes her coquette role," gushed the critic of *Film-Kurier,* "here's another Garbo! It seems the director had all he could do to tone down her deliberate Garbo imitation."

The reviewer was on the mark, for by this time Marlene Dietrich was well on the way to modelling herself on the mysterious and alluring Swedish actress. She had the same coloring as Garbo, and she mimicked the expression of cool diffidence that was meant to imply fires within. Dietrich had seen Garbo in several films, *The Saga of Gösta Berling, The Torrent* and *The Temptress,* which was already released in Berlin. She spoke with Mosheim and Andor (among others) of her passionate admiration. Garbo, then working in Hollywood at MGM, had quickly become one of the world's biggest stars, and Dietrich was much taken with her remote, sphinx-like beauty.

By late summer, Dietrich was rehearsing back at the Kömodie for her role in Shaw's *Misalliance* (presented as *Eltern und Kinder/ Parents and Children*). Windy and meandering, this is not usually rated a Shaw masterpiece: "It never stops—talk, talk, talk," whined Dietrich (as Hypatia Tarleton), describing the Tarleton family; she might have been reviewing the play. The author's stage directions describe Hypatia as living in "a waiting stillness, [with] boundless energy and audacity held in leash," and from this stillness Dietrich, Garbo-like, took her cue. As a woman eager to marry only for adventure ("Who should risk marrying a man for love? I shouldn't . . . it would make a perfect slave of you"), she played Hypatia with an almost stoic self-confidence—but the character's sentiments were not, after all, so different from her own. Her co-star, Lili

*W*ilhelmina Felsing after her marriage to Police Lieutenant Louis Erich Otto Dietrich.

*M*aria Magdalene Dietrich at the age of five (1906).

*E*lisabeth (left) with Maria, about 1909.

*M*aria Dietrich (front row, second from right, with black hair bow) at the Auguste Victoria Academy: Charlottenburg, 1914.

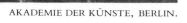

*A*s a gypsy violinist in a school production, 1916.

*P*ortrait of Maria from a family album, 1918.

*M*odelling in Berlin, 1922.

*F*lanked by two drama classmates in front of the
Kammerspiele: Berlin, 1922.

*D*ietrich (left) as a chorus girl,
dancing with the Thielscher Girls:
Berlin, 1922.

*O*n the day of her marriage to Rudolf
Sieber: Berlin, May 17, 1923.

*M*argo Lion and Claire Waldoff.

*B*eginning a lifetime of entertaining on the musical saw: Vienna, 1927.

*W*ith Igo Sym (left) and Willi Forst during the filming of *Café Electric*: Vienna, 1927.

*W*ith Margo Lion, singing "Sisters" in *Es Liegt in der Luft*: Kömodie Theater, Berlin, 1928.

*P*ublicity photo, 1928.

*T*he last of Dietrich's sixteen silent films: *Gefahren der Brautzeit*, with Willi Forst, 1929.

As an American millionairess, with Hans Albers in *Zwei Krawatten*: Berlin, 1929.

With director Josef von Sternberg, on the set of *The Blue Angel*: Berlin, December 1929.

As Lola Lola in *The Blue Angel*.

*D*eparting from Berlin for Hollywood:
April 1930.

*O*n the set of *Morocco*, 1930.

*V*on Sternberg at home in California,
about 1930.

Darvas, later recalled how Dietrich made Hypatia's independence even more arresting by speaking in a low, sultry voice, scarcely moving. "She simply sat down on the stage and smoked—very slowly and sexily—and everyone forgot the other actors were present!" Dietrich's pose seemed so natural, her gestures so economical, that she already seemed to have the tranquil energy of a Modigliani female.

The critics, however, were not entertained. Alfred Kerr, Ludwig Sternaux and Franz Leppmann complained that she did too little, that she was simply showing off her lovely legs instead of any real dramatic ability—an objection again levelled at her in her next job, another Robert Land comedy—*Ich Küsse ihre Hand, Madame (I Kiss Your Hand, Madame)*—filmed in late 1928. In this romantic comedy she played a rich Parisian divorcée named Laurence Gérard, in love with a headwaiter who turns out to be a Russian count down on his luck. When Laurence's overly attentive and obese lawyer (played by an actor aptly named Karl Huszar-Puffy) offers to do "anything in the world" for her, she replies, "All right, you can take my dogs for a walk." The moment—as Dietrich scarcely glances at the hapless fellow through half-closed eyes—is both cruel and comic.

The beginning of 1929 found her still in film studios, this time in *Die Frau, nach der man sich sehnt (The Woman One Longs For,* released in America as *Three Loves)*, cast as a sophisticate who is the mistress of her husband's murderer and then falls in love with a third man, eventually getting herself killed in the bargain. Director Kurt Bernhardt (later successful in America as Curtis Bernhardt) had seen her in *Misalliance* and fought, against the producers, to have her play the leading role. This he later regretted, finding her difficult on two counts. First, "Marlene waged intrigues—one man against another" in life as in the story, he recalled. Exploiting the infatuation of her co-star, Fritz Kortner, she fueled petty disagreements between him and Bernhardt, the better to advance her own favor in the eyes of both. "She is an *intrigante,*" according to the director, who added in plain language that Dietrich "was a real bitch."

This angry assessment was due to the second difficulty she caused Bernhardt:

She was so aware of her face that she would not let herself be photographed in profile because her nose turned up somewhat. She drove Kortner crazy (although he would have loved to go to bed with her). She never moved her head from the spotlight over the camera, facing forward and refusing to move her head to speak with other actors—she simply looked at them out of the corner of her eye. I wanted her to turn to Kortner, to be natural with him, but she wouldn't do it. She was completely aware of the lighting and how it hit her nose. Marlene looked fantastic, but as an actress she was the punishment of God.*

Her insistence had an odd payoff, for with her austere languor and apparently affectless gaze there were more comparisons than ever to Greta Garbo. "Directors have to get her out of this Garbo mimicking!" the critic of the *Berliner Tageblatt* had cried on January 20, 1929 (after the first screening of her preceding film); now, the *Deutsche Allgemeine Zeitung* (on May 4) said of her latest performance that she was merely "a Garbo double in her somnambulist attitude and heavy-lidded gazes—as if she were exhausted in her playful laziness." On May 22, *Variety*'s Berlin correspondent concurred in virtually identical words, and at once the Berlin representatives of at least two Hollywood studios—Paramount and Universal—cabled home to report a new international star. MGM had the real Garbo; would a reasonable facsimile be acceptable? To find and engage such a copy these men were paid handsome salaries. (When the picture was finally released in America that autumn, the *New York Times* hailed her "rare Garboesque beauty.")

Two more films followed in rapid succession that spring and summer. In *Das Schiff der verlorenen Menschen* (*The Ship of Lost Men*), she was an American aviatrix who is rescued by a shipful of lusty thugs when her plane goes down in the Atlantic. Guided by the French director Maurice Tourneur, Dietrich (plumply attractive even though made up to be windblown and grimy in unflattering male garb) had little to do but rouse fever among the beasts. After

---

* One young flame, the architect Max Perl, later recalled that during the summer of 1929 she finally decided to correct the shape of her nose and submitted to the discomfort of cosmetic surgery; in this she was something of a hardy trailblazer, for such procedures were not the commonplace they later became.

this—perhaps because she was still occasionally spending an evening with her old flame Willi Forst—she joined him in *Gefahren der Brautzeit* (*Dangers of the Engagement Period*), playing a sweet girl seduced by a friend of her fiancé.

In the sixteen silent films she had made in six years, Marlene Dietrich's leading roles had been few, and these were in films that caused no great sensation. The same was true of her eleven Berlin stage appearances (and two in Vienna), so that if her name was dropped in acting circles in mid-1929, no great echo resounded.

On the other hand, despite her appearances as a calmly detached supporting player, she had a reputation among actors who knew her as a woman of untamed energies who led a tempestuous love life unfettered by her married state. Friends could not quite keep up with her romantic escapades, for she quite openly had serial (and sometimes simultaneous) liaisons with colleagues like Willi Forst and Claire Waldoff.

FROM HER NEXT ROLE, HOWEVER, WOULD COME AN association that would forever change her life and destiny as well as the history of twentieth-century film.

On September 5, 1929, a nine-scene music and dance revue called *Zwei Krawatten* (*Two Neckties*) opened at the Berliner Theater, with text by Georg Kaiser and music by Mischa Spoliansky. In this comic satire about a waiter (Hans Albers) who changes his black tie for white tie and tails (and becomes a gentleman) Dietrich was cast in the minor role of an American millionairess named Mabel who had but one line of dialogue: "May I invite you all to dine with me this evening?" Otherwise she stood with a composed but sensual allure ("plump but agile, with a smoky voice and droopy eyelids," reported one critic).

During the first week of performances that September, there was an especially observant spectator in the audience. He was scouring Berlin's theaters looking for a singing actress for a film he was preparing. *Zwei Krawatten* was a logical stop, for it featured two players he had already signed for smaller roles. On hearing Dietrich's one line and watching her lean against the scenery "with a cold disdain for the buffoonery," he stood up and left the auditorium—but not until he had found her name on the program. "Here was the face I had sought," he later wrote, "and, so far as I could tell, a figure that did justice to it. Moreover, there was something else I had not sought, something that told me that my search was over."

The director was Josef von Sternberg. Marlene Dietrich never worked again as a stage actress.

5: 1929–1930

"I FEEL AS IF I DIED IN HOLLYWOOD AND HAVE now awakened in heaven," said director Josef von Sternberg without obvious irony. It was August 16, 1929, and he had just arrived in Berlin to work on the preparations for his new motion picture, a German-American co-production and one of Europe's first sound films. Greeting the assembled press amid the opulence of the Hotel Esplanade's grand foyer, von Sternberg—then a thirty-five-year-old of lively intelligence and multiple talents—was looking forward to working in Germany for the first time. He was surrounded that afternoon by producer Erich Pommer; the star of the film, Emil Jannings; writer Carl Zuckmayer; cameramen Günther Rittau and Hans Schneeberger; and composer Friedrich Holländer.

Born in Vienna as Josef Sternberg, he had had a gruellingly destitute life, even after arriving in America in 1901 at the age of seven. Years of severe malnutrition had stunted his growth (his full adult height was only five feet four inches) but not his agile mind. Denied formal education by the need to work, he read widely and in adolescence began to amass an impressive library of books on anthropology, comparative culture studies, psychology, art history, mythology and erotica. By the age of twenty-five he had held a variety of factory jobs and had served in the United States Signal Corps during the World War. He then decided to go to Los Angeles, where an earlier experience in an East Coast film laboratory prepared him for work as an editor, writer and assistant director. Among the pictures he worked on in 1923 was a trifle called *By Divine Right,* whose producers—impressed by the names of other Europeans in Hollywood (Erich von Stroheim, for example)— added an aristocratic-sounding *von* to his name—"without my knowledge and without consulting me," as he later insisted in his autobiography. Unlike von Stroheim, however, he spoke English without any trace of a foreigner's accent.

His account may be accurate, but over the next several years von Sternberg certainly became the kind of egoist who could have changed his own name. An autocratic and secretive man, he was fond of sporting Oriental dressing gowns, riding boots and even a turban, but he was not simply a flamboyant eccentric. An accomplished painter and photographer, von Sternberg was also an inspired designer of visual effects for motion pictures. By 1929, he had directed seven remarkably original and successful features, one of which (*The Last Command*) had helped earn Emil Jannings the first Academy Award ever given for best performance by an actor.★

Von Sternberg's idiosyncratic, often iconoclastic pictures— among them *The Salvation Hunters, Underworld, The Docks of New York* and *The Case of Lena Smith*—were characterized by intense rhythms, structural perfectionism and a pitilessly realistic view of human perversity—all combined with a deeply felt and highly personal romanticism. Von Sternberg, the painter, patiently composed each frame so that his films are astonishing in the way they tell stories by the play of light and shadow on the landscape of the

★ Jannings received the Oscar for his combined work in that film and in *The Way of All Flesh*.

human face. In these black and white movies he fully exploited the techniques and props of the trade—diffused light, scrims, gauze, smoke, trees and shrubbery; von Sternberg expertly evoked psychological effects by the uncommon arrangement of common elements.

He was also, like many directors, more concerned with the craft of filmmaking than with the special treatment of actors; much less could he be bothered with turning them into stars. Considering indifference to actors essential for the right final visual effect, he once said, "I regard actors as marionettes, as pieces of color [on] my canvas." Some puppets can be manipulated more easily than others, however. Jannings refused to be one of von Sternberg's puppets (they fought constantly during the making of *The Last Command*), but he acknowledged his director's genius and insisted that UFA and Paramount engage him for Janning's first German talkie.

The project finally selected for this was Heinrich Mann's 1905 novel *Professor Unrat,* about a bourgeois teacher who marries a woman of easy virtue, thereby losing his standing in polite society. He then becomes a gambler and crooked politician, exploiting his wife until their mutual downfall. After some preliminary contributions by writers Carl Zuckmayer and Karl Vollmöller (and by Robert Liebmann, who also wrote the English lyrics for songs by Fredrich Holländer), von Sternberg himself was responsible for the final screenplay and the cinematic form it was to take. He omitted Mann's social-political diatribe and concentrated entirely on one theme: a man's self-abasement and ultimate degradation by his fatal obsession for a bawdy cabaret singer. This emphasis was at least partly inspired by Jannings, who had cornered the market on his portraits of pathetically humiliated men—in G. W. Pabst's *The Last Laugh,* for example, as well as in von Sternberg's *The Last Command.*

THAT AUTUMN, WHILE THE SCRIPT WAS POLISHED, the sets designed at UFA's Neubabelsberg studios and a cast gradually assembled, von Sternberg had one persistent difficulty: finding the right actress to play the tawdry Lola Lola (a name he derived from Wedekind's deadly Lulu). Jannings and Pommer advocated Lucie Mannheim or Trude Hesterberg for the role, but von Sternberg insisted audiences would find the former too attractive and the latter too familiar. Von Sternberg then decided to see two players he had already contracted for his film (Hans Albers and Rosa Valetti), who were appearing in *Zwei Krawatten*. From that evening, as he said, the film director's search for Lola Lola was over; he would have no one else but Dietrich in the role. Looking at her, he saw an image of natural eroticism and bewitching indifference, a woman entirely (if unwittingly) capable of effecting a man's complete ruin.

The following afternoon, von Sternberg brought Dietrich to meet Jannings and Pommer. The star and the producer asked her to remove her hat and pace the room, the usual procedure to determine that an actor at least had hair and no limp. Dietrich casually complied, strolling, as von Sternberg put it, with "bovine listlessness, a study in apathy, her eyes completely veiled." Jannings and Pommer promptly rejected her for being both too plump and too casual; with equal alacrity, von Sternberg threatened to renounce the project and return to America unless he was accorded the right to give her a screen test. (In his autobiography, Jannings conveniently claimed to have championed Dietrich from the night he took von Sternberg to see *Zwei Krawatten*—a fiction denied by everyone else present at the time.)

Presuming that she was being considered for yet another minor role, Dietrich returned so they could hear her singing voice, but she appeared even more bored and unprepared than before, and was without the sheet music they had requested. She admitted that she had doubts as to how well von Sternberg could handle women onstage. And, in addition to all this, she had worn a characterless dress that hung formlessly from her body, but covered about twenty excess pounds. Von Sternberg, undeterred by her indifference, pinned the dress seductively and poured the right lights on her; by such technical wizardry, Dietrich seemed suddenly alive and casually carnal. She then sang, not beautifully but with a kind of defiant allure, a song about the end of an affair. "She came to life and responded to my instructions," von Sternberg recalled. "Her remarkable vitality had been channeled." Dietrich's critics capitulated —Jannings presciently muttering that her sex appeal might threaten his dominance in the film—and at once Lucie Mannheim and the other aspirants were dismissed. From that moment, according to Dietrich, "von Sternberg had only one idea in his head: to take me away from the stage and to make a movie actress out of me, to 'Pygmalionize' me." This was true, but theirs was a complex collaboration, which could not be so easily categorized.

Once she learned she was to play the leading role of a tarty *femme fatale,* Dietrich was both exhilarated and nervous, afraid she would look and sound inadequate alongside seasoned professionals like Jannings, Albers and Valetti. But she and her director worked brilliantly together, and he quickly allayed her anxiety—while she, eager to please, offered herself to him as Galatea, pupil and lover. "Even while rehearsals were in progress, they seemed to live for each other only," according to Willi Frischauer, who was present during the making of what was soon called *Der blaue Engel* (*The Blue Angel*), after the cabaret where Lola Lola sings. Indeed the director and star did live for each other; everyone on the film knew von Sternberg and Dietrich met privately in his hotel suite, sometimes in the morning, often after the day's work. Rudi knew of this at once, for his wife blithely introduced them, telling Jo she hoped one day the Siebers could meet Mrs. von Sternberg, who was in California. As Marlene hoped, the two men became quite friendly; thenceforth— because the Sieber marriage was now only a legality—there was in fact no rivalry between them. "At first," according to Stefan Lorant, "Rudi was naturally let down: I think he always hoped for some kind of romantic reconciliation between them. But when it became clear she was on her own he settled for a good friendship. After all, he had Tamara, and probably some other partners, too."

FILMING OF *THE BLUE ANGEL* LASTED FROM NOVEM- ber 4, 1929, to January 30, 1930, a span necessitated by the filming and recording of each scene in German and English (because post- dubbing was not yet possible). From the first scenes, the picture stresses the teacher's harsh and humorless moralism with his stu- dents, boys who trade postcards of the naughty Lola Lola in top hat, short skirt, bare thighs and a provocative gash of black garters. Professor Rath sets out to scold the theatricals and the shameless woman for her bad influence, but after only one visit to her dressing room his long-repressed libido is hopelessly demolished by her sensuality. Amused and touched by the attentions of a scholar, Lola Lola spends the night with him. He subsequently proposes marriage, she accepts, and he abandons his profession to become a member of her tacky, peripatetic little repertory company.

Eventually, Rath is so degraded by his passion for Lola Lola that he becomes a clown in cheap vaudeville routines; she, true to her bawdy nature, blithely turns to other lovers for excitement. At the conclusion, the professor returns to the town where he taught and they met, only to find that he's become a laughingstock. Mad with jealousy and rage, he nearly strangles Lola Lola after seeing her once again in the arms of another man. Finally he wanders distractedly back to his old classroom, where he dies clutching the desk that once represented dignity. Lola Lola, however, calmly survives, and at the end we see her provocatively straddling a chair at the Blue Angel, defying her cabaret audience to risk the fate of Professor Rath.

BOTH DIETRICH'S FEARS AND AMBITIONS PARALLELED her desire to please von Sternberg, whom she idolized. "Her behavior," he recalled,

> was a marvel to behold. Her attention was riveted on me . . . She behaved as if she were there as my servant, first to notice that I was looking about for a pencil, first to rush for a chair when I wanted to sit down. Not the slightest resistance to my domination of her performance. Rarely did I have to take a scene with her more than once.

As for Dietrich, she admitted forever after, "I didn't know what I was doing. I just tried to do what he told me." Her obedience guaranteed him complete control over every facet of her appearance, from which he drew the character of Lola Lola just as he designed the cabaret and the smallest prop. Everything was subject to his command and approval—her voice, walk, gestures and clothes.

Still embarrassed by what she considered her broad Slavic nose (despite surgery), Dietrich approached von Sternberg. "He pulled out a small vial of silver paint and drew a line right down the middle of my nose. Then he climbed up onto a catwalk and adjusted a tiny spotlight to shine directly on the silver line from above my head. It was like a miracle: he had reduced the width of my nose by nearly a third." By such simple techniques can an actress's lifelong gratitude be secured. Over the next six years, his authority and her docility would assure Dietrich's complete education in the craft of film.

On the other hand, her acquiescence and subservience on the set of *The Blue Angel* (and her lifelong admission that she owed her entire career to him) was in clear contrast to her loud offstage complaints about the horrific torture to which she was daily subjected on the set. She complained to all who would listen that von Sternberg controlled her every gesture, every word—in German as well as in English—and predicted that the film would be an utter failure. She also broadcast Jannings's almost pathological jealousy (which in fact led him to perform the attempted strangulation of Lola Lola somewhat too realistically).

But what really caused the actress such profound anxiety was an unforeseen conflict derived from her awareness that von Sternberg was making not so much a film about Lola Lola as about Marlene Dietrich herself. "I did not endow her with a personality that was not her own," he always insisted. "I gave her nothing that she did not already have. What I did was to dramatize her attributes and make them visible for all to see." And what he portrayed represents his sly, almost clinical amusement over Dietrich's backstage life—not only as he knew it from his own affair with her, but also from her dedication to free love, something widely known because she made no secret of it. "The truth of the matter," according to her good friend Stefan Lorant, "was that she was quite a free agent, although in this regard she was not exceptional. Berlin in the 1920s was a very free and open society, and theater people more than any others were committed to an unpuritanical pursuit of such love affairs as seemed mutually agreeable."

In *The Blue Angel,* Dietrich/Lola Lola is like a force of nature, as the film's most famous song says—"from head to toe primed, geared for love . . . and that is my world." She is indeed a saucy little strudel, but her impact is not so much calculated as inevitable, like the doom of certain men at her mercy. She simply *is,* without premeditation and certainly without malice, although not without tragic effects on the unwary.

In the melding of von Sternberg's Lola Lola with Dietrich, her life fused with his romantic-realist fantasies, creating a coalition of motifs that came to dominate each of the succeeding Dietrich-von Sternberg films. Thus the director's frequent statement—"I am Miss Dietrich, Miss Dietrich is me"—has great significance. His personal supervision of every detail in his films made von Sternberg's work remarkably confessional and accounts for his reluctance to discuss any aspect of his pictures except matters technical. This dominion over a product (justifying the designation of what the French critics call a movie *auteur*) depended on a kind of creative freedom and control rarely found in the business of filmmaking then or later. This unusual prerogative, independent of pressure from studio executives, was exerted only by von Sternberg and a few other great filmmakers —perhaps most notably Alfred Hitchcock, whose work is everywhere as emotionally and spiritually self-revealing as von Sternberg's. Hitchcock, too, resolutely refused to discuss anything except technical matters, lest he make explicit the self-disclosure he had already presented onscreen. This unusual degree of control was permitted by studio executives only because their films, completed on time and within budget, were financially successful.

THE OVERARCHING MOOD OF *THE BLUE ANGEL* IS one of careless cruelty in a Berlin of dangerously loosened instincts. The film opens as a woman throws a bucketful of water against a window, behind which stands a defiantly risqué poster advertising the appearance of Lola Lola in cabaret. Moments later, Professor Rath discovers his canary dead in its cage: "No more singing," his housekeeper sighs, calmly tossing the bird in the stove. This seemingly negligible opening actually announces the major linking device of the picture, for Lola Lola is soon singing to the staid professor—thus becoming his little birdie, as he becomes her strutting, crowing and ultimately dead mate.

Dietrich sings four numbers in the picture, the lyrics for each composed according to strict instructions from von Sternberg: "Ich bin die fesche Lola—I'm naughty little Lola"; "Ich bin von Kopf bis Fuss auf Liebe eingestellt," rendered in somewhat diluted English as "Falling in Love Again"; and "Nimm dich in Acht vor blonden Frauen—Watch out for blondes, for they have a certain flair for stripping you bare and then leaving you." But most provocative was her delivery of "Kinder, heut' abend—A Regular Man." The song (in a recording taken from the soundtrack) became almost an anthem for the Berlin woman of the 1920s hoping to meet a regular (*richtige*) guy:

> *Spring has come, the birdies sing,*
> *All is bright and cheerful—*
> *Hear the cuckoos in the trees*
> *Givin' us an earful.*
> *Funny how this time of year*
> *Always gets you feelin' queer—*
> *There's nothing to it,*
> *I gotta get a man that's a man—*
> *That's a regular man!*
> *If I can't find one*
> *there's not a girl who can—*
> *that's a man—that's a regular man!*
> *Say, if I find one I'll sure teach him a few—*
> *That's a man, that's a regular man!*
> *Men there are both thin and fat,*
> *Large and small and stocky—*
> *Rich and poor and nice at that,*
> *Bashful and quite shocking.*
> *How he looks I care a lot,*
> *I can pick him like a shot.*
> *There's nothing to it—I gotta get a man—*
> *that's a man, that's a regular man.*

And so, contrary to the housekeeper's remark, there is indeed more singing, most notably at the wedding of Lola Lola and Rath, where he crows for joy—an overgrown rooster animated by passion for his little chickadee. "Me? *Marry?*" she had cried when he proposed, almost hysterical with laughter. Does he not *know* better? From the discovery of the dead canary we had moved earlier to his disgust over his breakfast eggs, then to his imitation of a lovebird at his wedding meal. Finally, he is plastered with rotten eggs as a stage clown, and then, in the throes of madness, the crowing becomes an uncontrollable, manic shriek.

The Blue Angel is suffused with images of willing enslavement: cufflinks become handcuffs, a professor's gown becomes a straitjacket; and Rath assumes the role of the company clown, with a wide collar resembling a slave's neckband. (In our first view of Rath, he is teaching from his desk, tyrannically taking his students through Hamlet's "To be or not to be." The tragic resolution of the soliloquy is realized at the film's conclusion, when he dies clutching that same desk.)

In concrete terms, then, *The Blue Angel* and its tale of a man destroyed by his own illusions is drenched in decadence, saturated with images of voyeurism (by the schoolboys, by Rath himself, by the slavering cabaret audiences), fetishism (the cherished relics of Lola Lola's underwear, her stockings, her hat) and sadomasochism; everything is dark and perilous in this twilight world of semifurtive eroticism. No wonder that the officials at UFA (now led by the tycoon Alfred Hugenberg, later a member of Hitler's cabinet) did not take up Dietrich's option. They felt *The Blue Angel* was un-German; it was, after all, directed by an Austro-American, it offended the strict ideals of the German academic system, and it outraged traditional morals in the bargain. In 1933, the film was banned in Germany by Nazi decree.

As von Sternberg recalled, Dietrich had a kind of brilliant tactical reaction to UFA's lack of enthusiasm. She claimed the film would ruin her (she would be typecast as a whore) whether it became successful or not. She also resented the publicity released prior to the premiere, complaining that Jannings and the director were being emphasized while she was being ignored—and this, she stoutly maintained, at least partially explained why UFA was not offering her additional work. As von Sternberg noted, "Regardless of her conviction that the film just being assembled [edited] would ruin her forever, she wanted that ruin to be properly publicized." Dietrich also realized that what von Sternberg had promised would soon be true: her name would be known everywhere.

Clearly, then, Dietrich's lifelong assertion that she "simply wasn't ambitious, nor have I ever been" cannot be taken seriously. She wanted success most desperately, hence her earnest cooperation with a man whose abilities and intelligence she greatly respected. She was not, in other words, a woman who since 1923 had masochistically sustained deprivations, rejections and uncertainties without any hope, conviction or desire that perseverance would ultimately show a profit. If she had not been ambitious all this time, if she had really preferred being a simple *Hausfrau,* then (one might ask) why had she been dashing from rehearsal hall to studio, auditioning for roles she says she did not want?

Quite the contrary. That February she wrote to critic Herman Weinberg, who had sent her reviews of her film performances prior to *The Blue Angel,* asking him to send her three copies of each original newspaper that mentioned her. When he complied, she sent an autographed studio photograph—hardly the style of a woman indifferent to her career and her future. Dietrich's indifference had always been a wily affectation; by 1930, the pretense was refined to a social art that she could turn to her professional advantage. Soon the insolent pose of indifference would make her one of the most rapturously photographed women in history with a career three times as long as Garbo's.

If UFA did not want her, she then asked von Sternberg, what about Paramount Studios in Hollywood, his home base? His reply came in the person of B. P. Schulberg (the studio's chief production executive), who in late January visited Berlin, where von Sternberg showed him Dietrich's test and some excerpts from the film still being edited. Schulberg made Dietrich an offer she thought absurdly low and forthwith rejected. Von Sternberg then departed for America in early February 1930, after completing the final cut of *The Blue Angel*. Apparently Dietrich's mood altered in his absence, because before the month was out, she went to the office of Ike Blumenthal, Paramount's Berlin representative. He offered her a new one-picture deal at $1,250 per week, for a film to be made in Hollywood that spring—with Josef von Sternberg as her director.

This contract she signed, informing Rudi that she would be leaving him and Maria for only a few months, and that she would return with handsome savings for them all (Tamara included). The prospect of American employment was enormously attractive, especially because life in Germany was growing more perilous daily. She would embark on a kind of reconnaissance mission, she told her husband, to determine how her life and career might be eventually pursued in the United States.

Eager to depart, she did so within hours of the premiere of *The Blue Angel* at the Gloria Palace on the evening of March 31. But first she made her obligatory appearance at the gala, dressed in a full-length white fur coat and carrying a spray of red roses. Cameras clicked and people applauded, but when she put the coat and flowers aside, there was a ripple of knowing laughter from the press and public: "She had pinned a bunch of violets in a place where no woman ever wears flowers—just where the legs part," as an eyewitness recalled. Afterwards, according to the *Berliner Zeitung*, "Young people rushed her and begged for autographs. She had to be rescued by police so she could get to her car." Rudi was working in Munich as a production assistant on a film, so it was Willi Forst who escorted Dietrich to the boat train from Berlin to Bremerhaven.

Leaving so quickly, she missed the superb reviews. "Marlene Dietrich is the event," reported Berlin's respected critic Herbert Jhering, in the *Börsen-Courier* on April 2. "She sings and performs almost phlegmatically, but this she does in an exciting way. She is common without being common, and altogether extraordinary." The *Licht Bild Bühne,* in but one of dozens of typical raves, called her "fascinating, like no other woman before on film, [with] the silent, narcotic play of her face and limbs and her dark, exciting voice."

Among the other passengers bound for New York on the *Bremen* were James Stroock—owner of Brooks, the New York theatrical costume company—and his wife, Bianca. Common professional interests created a friendly rapport with Dietrich, and at first Bianca (unaware of the connotation) was simply flattered when a bunch of fresh violets was delivered to her each morning. The meaning of these little posies became clear, however, when Dietrich invited the pretty, stylish Bianca to her cabin, offered her a glass of champagne and showed her a book on the techniques of lesbian lovemaking. Surprised at what was by now an obvious proposition, Bianca declined; Dietrich, amazed by the rebuff, simply said, "In Europe it doesn't matter if you're a man or a woman. We make love with anyone we find attractive." And not only in Europe, as it turned out: her remark to Bianca Stroock would neatly summarize her conduct even in Hollywood, becoming a kind of lifetime motto in the coming decades.*

But in New York there was no opportunity for Dietrich to devise such provocative scenes. Arriving April 9, she was met by Paramount's East Coast publicity team and a squad of reporters they had dragooned, and over four days she was put on intensive display. Because the studio hoped to present her as their version of Greta Garbo, Dietrich was instructed to imitate her reticence and to deflect all questions about her private life; hence Paramount's executives were not at all pleased when she told the press that yes, she was married and had a child. In Hollywood's so-called golden age, such an admission quickly threatened the studio's carefully placed veil of mystery. (Dietrich was also shrewd enough to know that this forthrightness about her family could lower any raised American eyebrows about her freewheeling sexual life.)

The interviews peaked on the evening of April 12, when Marlene Dietrich was introduced to the American public on the ABC radio network's "Paramount-Publix Hour," broadcast to the entire nation. Her English, tolerable in Germany, now sounded unsteady and heavily accented, and she spoke slowly, translating everything before she spoke. But the press (and thousands of listeners, judging by the subsequent enthusiastic mail) found her intriguing.†

* Geraldine Brooks (as she called herself professionally), daughter of James and Bianca Stroock, later married Budd Schulberg, who was the son of Paramount's B. P. Schulberg.
† Among many other Continental imports over the years: Greta Garbo and Ingrid Bergman (from Sweden); Simone Simon and Leslie Caron (from France); Vilma Banky (from Hungary); Pola Negri

Typically, the Hollywood welcome was more elaborate. When Dietrich arrived by train in Los Angeles, she was met not only by von Sternberg and photographers from the city's eight newspapers but also by a five-piece German band in full regimental regalia playing Viennese waltzes and Silesian polkas; her reaction to these inept selections was not documented.

Within days, Paramount arranged for a formal reception at the Ambassador Hotel to introduce Dietrich to the press. According to photographer John Engstead, who later created some of her most alluring images, she arrived in a blue chiffon dress that was unflattering to her rather opulent figure. Next day, on mandate from von Sternberg, she began a strict regimen and after three weeks of diet and exercise had lost fifteen pounds. When she began her first American movie that spring, she weighed 130, but von Sternberg considered even that too much for a woman who, at five feet five, was an inch taller than he.

(from Poland); Alla Nazimova and Anna Sten (from Russia); Luise Rainer and Hedy Lamarr (from Austria); Alida Valli, Sophia Loren and Gina Lollobrigida (from Italy); Melina Mercouri (from Greece).

6: 1930

IN 1930, MARLENE DIETRICH JOINED AN IMPRES-
sive list of stars at the Paramount studio on Marathon Street in
Hollywood: under contract were personalities as diverse as Claudette
Colbert, Miriam Hopkins, Jeanette MacDonald, Carole Lombard,
the Marx Brothers, William Powell, Harold Lloyd, Clara Bow,
W. C. Fields—and Maurice Chevalier, who was filming *Playboy of
Paris* and whose dressing room was adjacent to Dietrich's. Glad for
the opportunity to be with another immigrant and to speak French
—the forbidden language during the great war—she was soon having tea with Chevalier and then dining frequently with him.

In addition to von Sternberg, still her mentor and a regular
visitor to her rented apartment, there were other notable directors
under contract at Paramount—among them William Wellman, who
directed *Wings,* which had won the very first Oscar for best picture;
Victor Fleming, who had directed Jannings in *The Way of All Flesh;*
and Ernst Lubitsch, much admired for a series of elegantly crafted
pictures (among them *Forbidden Paradise, The Patriot* and *The Love*

Parade). These and other Paramount films were remarkable among Hollywood's products for a unity of visual style, an achievement deriving as much from budgetary considerations as from artistic intent. To save time and money, directors, writers, designers and cinematographers routinely worked in close collaboration from the earliest stages of a film's preparation.

This was precisely the method employed in the development of Dietrich's first American film, a project for which *she* had provided the inspiration. When von Sternberg left Berlin in February, she had given him for shipboard reading Benno Vigny's minor novel *Amy Jolly*. Paramount, delaying the American release of *The Blue Angel* so that Dietrich's debut would be in a role more glamorous than Lola Lola, had given von Sternberg free choice of a project for her. After reading *Amy Jolly,* he conceived a film about another cabaret entertainer—this time in exotic Morocco—who meets a wealthy artist but eventually declines the stability of his love for the uncertainty of life with a wandering legionnaire. The picture would, therefore, be a variation on *The Blue Angel,* but without quite so much decadence —and with the romance required by Hollywood. Typically, the film would also explore the ambiguity of von Sternberg's own attachment to his leading lady. The film, he decided at once, would be called *Morocco*.

Sets were constructed and casting completed in April and May, while Dietrich quickly accustomed herself to life in California according to the regulations of those responsible to the studio for star-creation. Although the Depression had affected the vast majority of Americans, film actors seemed to live in an ideal world. To secure an image of almost inviolable glamour, studios often provided the stars with expensive cars and lavish wardrobes; von Sternberg insisted that Dietrich be no exception. Paramount issued her a Rolls-Royce convertible and chauffeur, and her one-bedroom apartment on Horn Avenue (just above Sunset Boulevard not far from Beverly Hills) was decorated and furnished with the movie-fan magazines in mind—a leopard skin rug, overstuffed chintz-covered sofas, a wall of mirrors and crystal whiskey decanters. In matters relative to Dietrich, said photographer John Engstead, "von Sternberg controlled everything." As for the car (which appears in the final scene of *Morocco*) and driver, Dietrich always had the impression that von Sternberg's aim was to limit her independence by preventing her from going off on her own.

Although she posed languorously at home for photographers, there was, in fact, little leisure time. In June Dietrich, Gary Cooper and Adolphe Menjou began work on *Morocco*. Von Sternberg did not provide his cast with the script he had virtually dictated to Jules Furthman, a writer who had borrowed so much money from Paramount to support his gambling habit that they kept him working at the studio simply to collect the debt. Instead, the actors received pages of dialogue as they proceeded; in any case, as von Sternberg cavalierly insisted, the images told the story. So they did, in a picture astonishing for its narrative simplicity and a psychological complexity that makes it an album of the increasingly poignant von Sternberg-Dietrich symbiosis.

Paramount, as the director was repeatedly told, wanted Dietrich to be what the press had for years recognized—a more glamorous, more mysterious and alluring version of Greta Garbo, an image Dietrich had actively sought to imitate long before coming to Hollywood. So von Sternberg and cinematographer Lee Garmes presented Dietrich as a Garbo double for her first scene in *Morocco*. She moves toward the camera, veiled, swathed in black, enveloped in nighttime fog aboard ship. The final scene of the film perfectly reverses all that, as Dietrich moves away from us, without veil or hat, dressed all in white, bathed only by the bright sunlight in the arid desert. Between these two images occurs an almost mythic transformation.

TAKEN MERELY AS A STORY, *MOROCCO* IS ELEMENtary indeed, but it advances the director's peculiar vision of Dietrich as a fateful and fated woman, bound to a code of love that may be exotic but is certainly admirable in its integrity. Whereas in *The Blue Angel* she had played an unfaithful floozy, in *Morocco* she is a faithful follower, exactly as he hoped she might be offscreen.

Amy Jolly, a cabaret performer (Dietrich), comes to work in Morocco and, although pursued by the wealthy, idle artist La Bessière (Menjou), she is drawn to the younger, handsome woman-izer Tom Brown (Cooper), a soldier with the foreign legion. She slips him the key to her quarters, but when Brown visits her that night (after he is also propositioned by the wife of the local adjutant) their meeting is tense with mutual wariness. Soon Tom announces that he will give up the Legion for Amy's sake—a promise he in-stantly regrets, abandoning her and resuming his wandering life. Amy accepts La Bessière's offer of marriage, but at their engagement party she learns that Tom may have been wounded on maneuvers, and she leaves her fiancé to find him.

As it happens, Tom is quite well (and as usual in the arms of a passing fancy), and is soon to depart again on his endless desert trek. At the end Amy, grateful for the devotion and generosity of La Bessière, leaves him forever and follows Tom into the desert: certain to be hurt, she is still bound to the honor of her love. Our last glimpse of her (one of the most famous images in American film) is a long shot as she slowly disappears over the horizon of a windswept desert, the only sound the receding Legion drumbeats and the eter-nal wind. Her scarf and white chiffon dress blowing wildly, the sirocco against her face, she doffs her high-heeled shoes, hurrying to join the line of wanderering men and their women camp followers.

THE FIRST DAY'S FILMING THAT SUMMER DID NOT augur well. Recording her first scene, von Sternberg was forced to devote numerous takes to a simple shot with only a single line; on the words "I won't need any help," Dietrich had difficulty with the word "help," as she repeatedly inserted a vowel between the final consonants. There had been considerable difficulty recording the English version of *The Blue Angel* because of the actors' thick ac-cents, and Paramount was insistent that Dietrich's diction be clear. (In fact when *The Blue Angel* was released the virtually inaudible English version was everywhere supplanted by the more popular German print, with the addition of English subtitles.)

Once the problem of "help" was solved, however (after more

than forty takes), others arose. Not yet fluent in English, she was meticulously prepared for each shot by von Sternberg, who (much to the annoyance of Gary Cooper) spoke with her in German, a practice star and director continued long after she learned English, and one that enabled them to maintain a certain intimacy among their colleagues. Not as maniacally jealous or fearful of Dietrich's star power as Jannings had been, Cooper (exactly her age) was almost preternaturally handsome, yet wary of Dietrich's emerging primacy in the picture. This led to several unpleasant exchanges between him and von Sternberg. "Cooper was neither intelligent nor cultured," Dietrich said rather ungallantly in 1991. "Just like the other actors, he was chosen for his physique, which, after all, was more important than an active brain."

But her inclination that season was quite different, for Dietrich smoothly engineered an evening *à deux* at Horn Avenue, and soon there flourished an affair that was (at least for Cooper) as hot as Morocco itself. This was no real challenge for Dietrich, since Cooper, although married, readily succumbed to the offer; he had also been involved with Clara Bow (as who was not) and, even more seriously, with Lupe Velez. Of course, von Sternberg was not at all pleased with this new development, but he knew better than to complain.

Some people can evoke from their lovers an attention that is frankly deferential. This ability Dietrich seems to have raised to the level of a fine art, for remarkably often in her life her lovers were not only grateful admirers but somehow felt bound to her. Men were especially vulnerable to this, Cooper among them: for the remainder of *Morocco,* he was her devoted ally, far more ardent to please and attend her in life than in the story they were filming. Von Sternberg, though firmly out of this romantic running of the bulls, quietly raged with jealousy and resentment, according to both Dietrich ("They didn't like each other . . . [it was] jealousy") and actor Joel McCrea, a friend of Cooper's ("Jo was jealous . . . and [Cooper] hated him").★

But to make things more complicated still, Cooper soon had his

★ Ironically, McCrea had rejected the role of Tom Brown before it was assumed by Cooper.

own reasons for jealousy when he learned that Maurice Chevalier had briefly become a rival. Chevalier's autobiography claims the friendship was "simply camaraderie," but his wife used it as the basis for a successful divorce petition. This affair coincided with the Cooper romance. Several evenings each week there was a game of musical automobiles for the limited parking spaces near Dietrich's apartment, where the situation was one of first come, first served.

It would be easy to regard Marlene Dietrich's vigorous sexual life as irresponsible, frankly hedonistic or even symptomatic of an almost obsessive carnality. But her affairs, no matter how brief or nonexclusive, were always focussed and intense, never merely casual, anonymous trysts. Lavish in bestowing amatory favors, Dietrich in fact equated sex more with the offering of comfort than with the pursuit of her own pleasure—or perhaps more accurately, the complex, benevolent control she exerted in romances *was* her gratification. Sex was something nurturing she offered those she respected (like von Sternberg), those she thought were lonely (like Chevalier) or those she thought to be in need (like Cooper, who complained, poor man, that he was being nagged by both his wife and by Lupe Velez). None of these affairs seems to have been characterized by any aim of permanence.

Hence, Marlene Dietrich entered on them according to her usual lights: to please others, to win confidence and to secure a place in someone's life. She was also a healthy and beautiful twenty-nine-year-old woman, alone in a new country and responsive to ardent attention. In this case, the pair she romanced aligned her with the new Hollywood glamour (Cooper) and the old European charm (Chevalier). They represented, in other words, the two realms she wished to combine in herself. At the same time, the quiet intrigues made her the focus of considerable attention. Since she comported herself with dignity and discretion, however, and because she was so thoroughly cooperative in her work, she easily deflected Hollywood's usual high-toned and hypocritical accusations of moral turpitude.

· · ·

WHATEVER HIS FEELINGS OF ROMANTIC ABNEGATION (and they were clear to everyone working on the project, including Cooper and Lee Garmes), Josef von Sternberg was a calm and creative center for Marlene Dietrich, and she knew it.

In 1924, he had written "The Waxen Galatea," published in *The Director* the following year. This short story tells of a shy man who becomes obsessed with a plaster mannequin in a dress shop. He gazes each day on the lovely image until he sees a real woman breathtakingly like the figure in the window. He follows her, but she meets a man who, at the woman's request, then humiliates the silent pursuer, now an annoying intruder on her rendezvous. Shattered, he vows never to love anything other than a wax figure.

"The Waxen Galatea" is an important clue to the character of its author, a secretive and obsessive romantic known to very few. Von Sternberg was enormously successful in keeping his private life from scrutiny, although as with many men with intensely creative instincts there seems not to have been much exterior drama. Reticent and often alone, he indulged a preference for painting and study instead of a Hollywood social life. (His first two marriages ended in divorce, but his third wife—also a painter, whom he wed after World War II —gave him a rewarding stability and his only child.)

Von Sternberg was a dispassionate man whose emotional detachment from women enabled him to look at them analytically in his art. In this regard, he resembled other important filmmakers who hankered for waxen Galateas and who transferred their images and fantasies about women to the screen. For D. W. Griffith, the favored actress was Lillian Gish; for Erich von Stroheim, Mary Philbin; for Charles Chaplin, Edna Purviance; for producer David O. Selznick, Jennifer Jones. Alfred Hitchcock's inner life was revealed in a series of romantic films starring actresses he fell in love with, among them Madeleine Carroll, Ingrid Bergman, Grace Kelly and Tippi Hedren. For Josef von Sternberg, it was Marlene Dietrich. He found, she wrote in her memoirs, that she corresponded perfectly to his own complicated dream-life.

. . .

In *The Blue Angel*, he had presented the triumph of decadence over dignity, establishing her as the unwitting cause of an impassioned man's destruction by simply being true to her nature; in *Morocco,* however, the wandering cabaret performer Lola Lola becomes the faithful follower Amy Jolly, still singing of the perils of romantic attachment—but now offering faithful love to a man who seems unsure of his attraction to her and may lack any real passion at all. The first time we see her after the shipboard introduction she wears white tie, tails and, like Lola Lola, a black top hat. Full of confidence, puffing a cigarette, indifferent to the café audience's initial laughter at her cross-dressing, she strides through the crowd, surveying them through a haze of smoke. She sees an attractive woman, stops, removes a flower from the woman's hair then kisses her full on the lips—and seconds later tosses the flower to Cooper.

The sequence is freighted with significance. "I planned to have her dress like a man," von Sternberg later claimed, "sing in French and, circulating among the audience, favor another woman with a kiss, [because] I wanted to touch on a lesbian accent"—a motif inspired, as he wrote in his autobiography, by seeing Dietrich wearing full male evening dress at Berlin social events. This outfit had already been part of the hallowed image of "La Garçonne," the boy-girl androgyne that Paris and Berlin found so alluring in the 1920s and that gay culture sometimes glorified. Females dressed in men's formal wear were as hallowed a music hall tradition as men in drag. At the turn of the century, entertainer Vesta Tilley (later Lady de Frece) wore men's clothes and delighted English audiences as she sang, "I'm Burlington Bertie, I rise at ten-thirty, and toddle along to the Strand." Hetty King and Ella Shields were other women popular when they performed in tuxedos and gentlemen's suits.

But the cross-dressing—a recurrent motif in the von Sternberg-Dietrich films—was not merely designed to shock American audiences. "Woman is no different from man," the director said often and with various emphases during his life, "and man does not differ from woman other than [that] the female conceives . . . All my characters are modelled on myself as I would behave under [the same] conditions and circumstances." In this regard, momentarily suppressing Dietrich's femininity not only capitalizes on an aspect of the actress's own bisexual nature: it also enables women in the audience to love her and simultaneously establishes (however vaguely) an identification with men.

The matter goes deeper still, and beyond any mere postulation of homosexuality, bisexuality or even a kind of hip unisexuality. The von Sternberg-Dietrich films—inspired by his observation and knowledge of Dietrich's variegated erotic life, do not satirize gender roles, they fuse them ("Woman is no different from man") by presenting passive men and aggressive women; in this regard, von Sternberg may have been decades ahead of the liberationists. According to Henry Hathaway (who was on the crew of *Morocco* and later became a director), von Sternberg "always felt that a woman, deep down, dominated the man . . . [She] was the one pulling the strings, [and] that reflected in a man's behavior."

In *The Blue Angel,* Jannings was the archetypally passive "female" character, undone by Lola Lola, the top-hatted "male" character. Thenceforward, the six Dietrich films offered a ruthless, dreamlike critique of traditional gender roles by making their reversal acceptable. In *Morocco,* Dietrich arrives (as she had in real life) by ship; she respects but does not love a painter (Menjou as surrogate for the painter von Sternberg, complete with mustache), and she captivates Cooper, who is astonishingly passive, almost delicate. When Dietrich tosses him the flower taken from the woman she has just kissed, he places it behind his ear, wearing it even in public—he becomes, in effect, the new "girlfriend" of the "man" Dietrich. This suited Marlene Dietrich perfectly, and she relished the scene: "I would much prefer to be a man" was a constant refrain in her public and private utterances. "I can think of no advantage in being a woman that compensates for the mental superiority of men." And she was certainly, as her lovers attested, the most aggressive partner any of them had ever known.

Von Sternberg could perhaps execute such a conceit only with players like this pair. Aware of Dietrich's affairs with men and women (and her sexual life, as she had said, "with anyone we find attractive") the director did not give her any qualities she did not have; rather he took what she *did* have—her frank conjunction of male-female roles and her capacity for the oxymorons of aggressive nurturing and passive service. In *Morocco,* men use fancy hand fans, wear earrings, flutter, wear flowers, while Moslem, Spanish and American women energetically proposition men and openly cuckold their husbands.

Much of this is integrated in Dietrich's second song—"What Am I Bid for My Apple?"—sung in an aptly provocative short outfit and a feather boa; the other (womanly) nature has at last emerged from the evening suit. But now she is like the temptress Eve, freely selling the forbidden fruit to both men and women with lyrics especially written for (and apparently about) Dietrich:

> *What am I bid for my apple,*
> *The fruit that made Adam so wise?*
> *On the historic night when he took a bite,*
> *They discovered a new paradise.*
> *An apple, they say, keeps the doctor away,*
> *While his pretty young wife*
> *Has the time of her life,*
> *With the butcher, the baker, the candlestick maker!*
> *Oh, what am I bid for my apple?*

"There's a foreign legion of women, too," she tells Cooper privately, moments later. "But we have no uniforms, no flags, and no medals when we are brave. No wound stripes when we are hurt." Later, seeing the women camp followers, she asks Menjou just who they are. "I would call them the rear guard," he replies.

"How can they keep pace with their men?"

"Sometimes they catch up with them and sometimes they don't —and very often when they do they find their men dead."

"Those women must be mad."

"I don't know—you see, they love their men," he concludes.

Menjou was clearly the director's deputy, the protective mentor and artist, externally calm but deeply in love and doomed to rejection. "You see," Menjou says again to his guests, when Dietrich leaves him to find Cooper, "I love her. I'll do anything to make her happy." Just so von Sternberg, who gladly responded to Dietrich's every wish and whim during production and after hours, squiring her (to his wife's dismay) to Hollywood restaurants, offering her luxuries at work and at home and contenting himself with being a devoted Pygmalion whose Galatea fancied other men.

He also presented her to Paramount and to the world as a sublime but recognizably human creature—a new Garbo, but warmer, somehow more complex. Completely faithful to her own emotional logic, Dietrich/Amy has a tenderly radiant resignation throughout the film. And so carefully did von Sternberg set up every shot of her, so meticulously were the lights arranged that he could not often allow the more diffuse illumination of travelling shots. "The light source," Dietrich commented later, "created my mysterious-looking face with hollow cheeks, effected by putting the key light near the face and very high over it." This technique seemed to isolate her in the film, to detach her from the surroundings—until the great final retreat into the desert, where she is absorbed by the geography. She seems, until then, to inhabit her own continuum of time and space.

FROM HER APRIL ARRIVAL THROUGH THE SUMMER'S shooting, Dietrich had maintained constant contact with Rudi and Maria, sending gifts every few weeks, with brief notes describing her life at home and at the studio (with discretionary exclusions). Her time with gentleman escorts had to be carefully scheduled to allow for press interviews, publicity and photo sessions, and enough rest to face von Sternberg's camera six mornings each week. By the time production concluded in late August, she had seen none of California outside Los Angeles County. Her life, however rapidly her fame was spreading, was restricted to the precincts determined by work.

The premiere of *Morocco* was held at Grauman's Chinese Theater on November 24, 1930; just as Paramount's executives had predicted during preview screenings, it was an instant and enormous success, and soon there were four Oscar nominations (none of them final winners): for von Sternberg, Dietrich, cinematographer Lee Garmes and art director Hans Dreier. This was the closest Dietrich ever came to an Academy Award.

With a rapidity only a high-powered promoter could appreciate, things began to happen quickly. Paramount bought advertising and billboard space across the country heralding the arrival of a new Garbo, and as rave reviews poured in from critics and platoons of new fans, the studio was forced to send Dietrich two secretaries to cope with the avalanche of letters and requests for signed photos. Garbo, asked her opinion of this apparent counterpart, is supposed to have replied airily, "And who is this Miss Dietrich?" But actors, producers and directors jockeyed for a position near this Miss Dietrich's table at the Coconut Grove, the Hollywood Roosevelt or the Club New Yorker. She was also mobbed at places like the Frisky Pom Pom Club, where she frequently went to see the lineup of female dancers in its revue called "Glorifying Hollywood's Most Beautiful Girls." At these venues the studio cannily arranged for her to be photographed—usually with von Sternberg or another escort, for the faint implication of scandal was very much part of the glamour. At the same time, Dietrich received letters proposing marriage or concubinage with unknown men, and offers of a lifetime of devotion from smitten women.

All this adulation was in the starkest contrast to daily life at Paramount, where Dietrich worked hard to please her director—not only because she greatly respected him but also because she and Paramount needed him for the maintenance of her career. During *Morocco* as during the film they undertook immediately thereafter, she was tirelessly pursuing the demands of a difficult and exhausting craft. At work, instead of being rushed for autographs she was hurried from makeup to wardrobe at Marathon Street; in place of adulation from strangers at restaurants, she heard brusque orders from her director on the set: "Turn your shoulders away from me and straighten out . . . Drop your voice an octave and don't lisp . . . Count to six and look at that lamp as if you could no longer live without it . . . Stand where you are and don't move—the lights are being adjusted." She was neither the first nor the last movie actor to sense a profound divergence in what life presented, a confusion of realms effected by brilliant celebrity and public adoration on one side, and on the other a fragile but arduous employment she knew could be terminated at the public's or producers' whims.

To these separate signals Dietrich responded shrewdly, adding a touch of the heroic. She told the press she was Greta Garbo's greatest fan and that no *arriviste* like herself could compete with so accomplished an actress. She then took the approach of the humble servant, repeatedly acknowledging her total reliance on von Sternberg's genius with the subtle implication that she was a dutiful girl at the mercy of a ruthless sadist. For the final scene of *Morocco* (she told the press), he had forced her to walk barefoot in the desert, and when she fainted from the heat von Sternberg was so relentless that he corrected her pronunciation of the dialogue as soon as she was revived, and then asked for another take. By such methods she stressed her valorous, abject nature. Surely Hollywood had never seen her equal in this kind of self-promotion; even Garbo had limitations.

BEFORE *MOROCCO*'S GREAT SUCCESS AND IN ADvance of the American release of *The Blue Angel,* Paramount renewed Dietrich's contract that autumn, doubling her salary to $2,500 a week. Boldly imitating Garbo, who had her choice of director, Dietrich first insisted that her next film would also be under von Sternberg. The studio acceded to their respective terms, offering him complete freedom. "I made seven films with Marlene Dietrich," von Sternberg said later; "in reality I wanted to make only two: *The Blue Angel* and *Morocco*. But she was bound by contract to a studio and she refused to work with anyone else. I did it reluctantly." Bound she may have been—but only after she signed. She could have returned home, or requested another director; the collaboration, in other words, was due entirely to her insistence. And it endured because, for a time at least, the public wanted to see her.

Aware of the Dietrich-Cooper affair and eager to exploit it to professional advantage, Paramount executives presumed he would agree to co-star in her next picture. They had not, however, sufficiently assessed the tension between the actor and director. Cooper

announced his refusal to collaborate on Dietrich's next film while
von Sternberg was dictating the story and dialogue to Daniel N.
Rubin, who had written *The Texan* the previous year for Cooper.
Victor McLaglen was the unlikely substitute. *Dishonored,* as it was
eventually called (against von Sternberg's preference for *X-27,* the
spy code name assigned to Dietrich's character), went into production that fall, and at once the director's initial vacillation was overcome in the story's realization and the emotional pursuit of his
presentation of Marlene Dietrich. According to the director's son,
the antiwar sentiments extolled in *Dishonored* were exactly those of
von Sternberg, who had lost his brother in World War I combat.

Morocco ended with Dietrich in white, in the blinding daylight of
desert heat; *Dishonored* begins with the reverse image—she is
wrapped in black on a city street corner at night, in a cold rainstorm.
The narrative is basic *Mata Hari,* concerning a Viennese streetwalker
(Dietrich) first seen adjusting her stockings and garters while pursuing her profession. She calmly tells a policeman, "I'm not afraid of
life, but I'm not afraid of death, either." Her remark is overheard by
an intelligence chief who, after testing her loyalty, engages her to spy
for Austria against Russia. She accepts, reflecting prophetically, "I've
had an inglorious life; it may become my good fortune to have a
glorious death." At first she succeeds brilliantly, uncovering the
traitorous activities of an Austrian general (Warner Oland). But then
she falls in love with his contact, a Russian enemy agent (McLaglen),
and after first collaborating in his capture, she arranges his escape.

For this, she is convicted of treason and condemned to death. In
her cell, she insists on wearing her prostitute's clothes to the execution ("a uniform of my own choosing—any dress that I wore when I
served my countrymen instead of my country"). Preparing to meet
the firing squad, she asks a young officer for a mirror so she may
adjust her veil; he draws his sword and she gazes at herself in its
reflecting blade. He then escorts her to the execution site, offering a
blindfold she uses instead to dry his tears. As the drumbeat begins,
she marks herself with the sign of the cross and then we see, gradually, a luminous, triumphant smile on her face.

The young officer then interrupts the execution: "I will not kill
a woman! I will not kill any more men, either! You call this war? I

call it butchery! You call this serving your country? You call this patriotism? I call it murder!" She takes advantage of this interruption to adjust her stockings (the exact gesture at the film's opening) and, one last time, to apply lipstick. The young officer is replaced and the execution proceeds; the drumbeat accompanying the faithful Dietrich at the conclusion of *Morocco* is reprised here, but now the drums and rifleshots resonate like a carillon of honor. X-27 falls dead.

In *Dishonored,* Lola Lola's easy charm has been refined, subjoined to Amy Jolly's sober melancholy. X-27, an accomplished pianist, wears a medley of outfits, from a pilot's rough leather suit to a padded disguise as a plump and giggling peasant girl. Tough but vulnerable, cynical but devoted, Dietrich and the character completely fuse; unpredictable, dangerous and irresistible to both countryman and enemy, she is ever intelligent and beguiling—exactly the adjectives a few perceptive critics often used to describe her when *Dishonored* was released. Her name led the billing for the first time, and deservedly so, for there was a new confidence, not merely an occasional, affected swagger.

Languorously paced though it is, *Dishonored* advanced von Sternberg's obsession with the complexities of a woman's personality as he saw it refracted in Marlene Dietrich. *The Blue Angel* had disclosed something of his own feelings about her during and after their meeting, for he both saw and knew her as the unwittingly callous cabaret singer Lola Lola, with her artless ribaldry and unfeigned earthiness causing emotional chaos.

But this had not described every possibility: in *Morocco,* Amy Jolly's equally cynical and nomadic life as a performer finally revealed her own intrinsic yearning for a new nobility in love. *Dishonored* continued the logical development: the tarnished, wise and wandering Amy has become the jaded streetwalker, living within the code of her own honor and, at last, constant in love unto death —thus she can face the end with an almost blithe faith, blessing herself with the absolving sign of the cross.

With *Dishonored* completed, *Morocco* widely released and *The Blue Angel* about to be, Dietrich took advantage of a hiatus in her contract to revisit Germany; when she departed, von Sternberg announced that in her absence he would make a film of Theodore Dreiser's novel *An American Tragedy.*

Dietrich longed for Berlin society and was eager to return at Christmastime bearing the financial fruits of her labor for her daughter and for Rudi, to whom she felt she owed much. By this time her views on Hollywood were widely reported: she thrived only on her work with von Sternberg and she admired the efficiencies of the modern film industry, but there her fondness for the business ended. *The New Yorker,* on December 20, further reported that she stopped in New York to visit with James and Bianca Stroock, whom she surprised with a cache of lavish holiday gifts, in memory of their shipboard meeting.

She stopped in London for the British premiere of *Morocco,* and by Christmas she was in Berlin where, in less than nine months, dramatic changes had occurred: the Nazis were now Germany's second largest political party. Just as she was arriving home, many of her old friends and colleagues were preparing to depart. Soon she understood why.

7: 1931–1932

FROM CHRISTMAS 1930 TO MID-APRIL 1931, Marlene Dietrich was on holiday. Her family reunion by all accounts was happy, lively and uncomplicated, as Dietrich gave time and gifts to her daughter and shared her Hollywood income with Rudi and Tamara. According to Dietrich's friend and colleague Stefan Lorant, one of the binding elements in the lifelong Dietrich-Sieber friendship was precisely the amicable financial arrangement between them. Sieber was working as an associate producer and assistant director for Paramount, usually at the UFA studios. Six-year-old Maria, meanwhile, although tended mostly by Tamara, seemed to lack the neuroses one might have expected in a child to whom her mother was a virtual stranger.

Unaware of budgets and indifferent to the concept of saving for the future, Dietrich had learned in Hollywood to be a free spender; much, after all, had been provided by the doting von Sternberg or the indulgent studio. By early 1931 she had accumulated the handsome after-tax sum of ten thousand dollars, much of which she began to spend prodigally.

Away from the demands of moviemaking, Dietrich enjoyed the usual social whirl, and in the first weeks of 1931 she resumed a romantic liaison with the composer Peter Kreuder, for whom she had commissioned a song called "Peter," which she recorded. Kreuder was intelligent and attractive, but sometimes there seemed something vaguely disconsolate about him that no one could quite decipher. The combination of wit, sex appeal and wistful ennui was a federation of charms she found irresistible. Together they frequented the theater, concerts and opera.

Ever mindful of maintaining her controversial new eminence, however, she attended some events without escort. Learning that Charles Chaplin was visiting Berlin but was constantly protected from adoring hosts by ranks of police and bodyguards, she used the sheer force of her personality and a striking, mannish ensemble (grey serge suit, matching hat and shoes and a dark red tie) and forced her way past a security convoy into the Hotel Adlon. There she corralled a strolling photographer to take pictures of her strategically seated beside Chaplin, who stood by smiling but somewhat uncertain of her purpose. The photo makes it appear as though Chaplin is offering her a huge bouquet. She sent copies of the snapshot by the score to friends near and far, but mostly to her Hollywood secretary for distribution to the American press. In the film world she had quickly learned much more than technical matters.

That April, Dietrich attracted her own mob of admirers. At half past midnight, she and Maria boarded the boat train at the Lehrter Bahnhof, with Paramount's Berlin staff and representatives of the Lloyd steamship line assembled. The press had been duly alerted for the ceremony of her return to California with her daughter. Kreuder, weeping unashamedly, led a brass band, and a medley of sentimental farewell songs filled the night air. Wearing a leopard coat and a green felt hat, Dietrich waved, smiling one moment and solemn the next, perhaps to synthesize her mixed emotions. Rudi would not be leaving Berlin, she explained, because of professional commitments, but the correspondent for the *New York Times* added the widely known accessory fact—that Sieber did not want to go to Hollywood merely "to be Mr. Dietrich."

Mother and daughter had two other attendants: Gerda Huber had turned up again in Marlene's life, and she was coming to America as private secretary and companion; and there was a nanny for Maria who also served as Dietrich's maid. Whether the relationship between her and Gerda was still passionate cannot be determined; but with a few exceptions, Dietrich's affairs with both men and women usually ran a swift, exhilarating carnal course before settling on the surer terrain of undemanding friendship.

AFTER A SERENE TRANSATLANTIC CROSSING, THE foursome could not have been prepared for the crush of reporters and photographers in New York—nor for the unexpected greeting by a lawyer who leapt forward, nervously asked Dietrich's identity and then pressed a thick envelope into her hand. Not until she reached the hotel did she read the enclosed documents, and then at once she cabled von Sternberg in Hollywood. His former wife, Riza Marks (known in her few minor screen appearances as Riza Royce, and by then living in New York State), was about to file suit retroactively against Marlene Dietrich for alienation of her ex-husband's earlier affection, a charge newly made in light of an interview Dietrich had supposedly given to an Austrian journalist. Thus a libel charge was added to the so-called heart balm suit. The damages sought for these offenses would be a total of $600,000.

The situation was somewhat bizarre from every viewpoint. For one thing, the von Sternbergs had been divorced since June 1930 and so he was evidently free to pursue his own life, with Dietrich or anyone else. But Mrs. von Sternberg's attorneys claimed that she had a major case in light of the article in the *Neues Wiener Journal,* in which Dietrich had, a year earlier, slandered her: "Mr. von Sternberg would have obtained a divorce even if he had never met me," Dietrich was quoted as saying. "Between him and his wife serious differences have arisen. I may tell you that I value in him not only the artist but the man." Dietrich stoutly denied ever uttering such indelicate and inflammatory remarks.

Von Sternberg was outraged at Riza, and this led to an imprudent step taken in retribution: he ceased sending her regular alimony payments. This of course further complicated the problem, and as spring warmed to a torrid 1931 summer across America, so did Mrs. von Sternberg's wrath blaze hotly. She cited him for contempt, he countered by paying only some of the moneys owed, and dates were set for court appearances in Los Angeles and New York. At the request of the cited parties, these were postponed until later that summer, and perhaps because no one involved was eager for the publicity, the case remained unknown to the press until then.

AS WITH EVERYTHING RELATIVE TO HER PUBLIC LIFE, Dietrich depended on von Sternberg to manage the matter. In California, he had already rented an elegant, ten-year-old Mediterranean home for her at 822 North Roxbury Drive, on the northwest corner of Sunset Boulevard in Beverly Hills. The house had a large rear yard with swimming pool, ample space for Gerda and the maid, and a large kitchen. For the first weeks, however, Dietrich religiously avoided that room: von Sternberg had greeted her with mild but firm criticism of the ten to fifteen pounds she had gained in Berlin, and until mid-May she subsisted on a diet of tomato juice and soda biscuits.

Josef von Sternberg was, that spring of 1931, still more than mentor, manager and trainer to Marlene Dietrich. As a nod to the prevalent mores, he maintained a separate address, but soon it was widely known that he was living at Roxbury Drive and sharing the master suite with his star; their matching Rolls-Royce automobiles (hers bullet grey, his midnight blue) could be found parked each night in the crescent-shaped driveway. "Mr. von Sternberg loved good food," Dietrich said with a wink years later. "So I went to the studio every day and did what he told me, and then I came home and cooked." Dashiell Hammett, for one, kept his friends informed of industry gossip: von Sternberg and Dietrich, he reported to his mistress Lillian Hellman with typical irony, were "living in sin."

· · ·

THE SPORADIC CHARACTER OF THE DIETRICH-VON Sternberg relationship can only perhaps be understood as part of the entire complex they maintained between themselves. He performed the cinematic legerdemain securing her advancement from minor performer to international movie star, and this evoked her admiration and affectionate gratitude, of which sex was often Dietrich's natural expression. She was especially inclined thus to comfort men like von Sternberg who seemed emotionally deprived and somewhat morbid in their aesthetic isolation. His self-imposed mission, she later said, was "to photograph me, make me laugh, dress me up, comfort me, advise me, guide me, coddle me, explain things to me" —and there has perhaps never been a more cooperative apprentice.

Although confident of his talents as director and cameraman, von Sternberg nevertheless bore a deeply rooted inferiority complex, and he sometimes alienated colleagues and friends with the kind of high-toned or egoistic posture that tries to masquerade such feelings. In the anteroom to his office at Paramount, for example, was an enormous diorama with commentary and still photos comprising the history of his films for all to see, as if they were approaching a museum or a great cathedral: "Opus One: *The Salvation Hunters.*" . . . "Opus Two: *The Exquisite Sinner*—Sabotaged by Thalberg," and so forth.

His relations with men were usually characterized by some degree of jealous rivalry, and directing men was often a trial: "Cooper was very tall and Jo was not, and he couldn't stand it if I looked up to any man in a movie . . . I didn't understand that kind of jealousy," Dietrich recalled. Additionally, women found his intellect formidable but his manner cool and tyrannical, and so he failed to attract precisely the sort of female attention he longed for (especially since his divorce). Von Sternberg also had the logical doubts often felt by the gifted autodidact: he had read widely and could discuss many fields with impressive knowledge, but he was uncomfortable doing so, fearing that his lack of formal education would unavoidably reveal vast gaps. Consequently, he occasionally allowed himself to be overwhelmed by those who spoke more but knew less. This led some who experienced his sergeant-major tactics at the studio to mistake his silence for smug superiority.

Divorced from a beautiful, dark-haired, doe-eyed actress, von Sternberg had eccentricities of dress, manner and speech that did not put him in great demand socially. Despising polite small talk, he preferred silence, or withdrawal to his studio for painting. Artist and dreamer, Josef von Sternberg was a touching combination of both the intellectual analyst and the aching romantic.

Because she was emotionally sympathetic to him, Dietrich was quick to fill his loneliness. "Marlene worshipped my father with a tremendous respect," Nicholas von Sternberg said years later. "She loved his intelligence and abilities. He saw her as paint on his canvas —and she agreed wholeheartedly with this."

Essentially a woman of clear preferences and antipathies, Dietrich concealed none of them. She disliked most modern art (von Sternberg's occasional tutorials notwithstanding), noodles, horse races, evangelism, fish, after-dinner speeches, politics, American sandwiches, opera and slang; she favored Punch and Judy shows, apple strudel, circus performers, speeding in an open roadster, pickles, perfumes, romantic novels by Sudermann and doleful poetry by Heine.

There was, however, nothing about her of the Byronic heroine, and her attitude toward intimacy (as toward most things in life) was a great deal simpler than von Sternberg's, and without much reflection. "I had nothing to do with my birth," she said around this time, "and I most likely will have nothing to do with my future. My philosophy of life is simply one of resignation." Entirely a woman of the moment, she readily admitted that year, "I never think about the future. I am not religious. I never think about anything there is no good in thinking about." And von Sternberg knew this: "She attached no value to anything so far as I could ascertain, with the exception of her baby daughter, a musical saw and some recordings by a singer called Whispering Jack Smith."

Her convictions, accordingly, were based simply on experience, and this had unequivocally taught her that Josef von Sternberg was certainly good for her. While he saw her as a beautiful woman who could wreak emotional havoc by simply being, he was at the same time one of the moths drawn ineluctably to her flame. Dietrich was an exciting woman whose eroticism was, to those she liked, neither cheaply accessible nor teasingly withheld. For von Sternberg, she also seemed to promise more than she at any one time delivered— not only more sensual satisfaction but also more artistic possibilities for her exploitation as an actress. Thus he continued to work with her and to present new facets of the jewel. She listened, learned, complimented, frankly depended on him; in other words, she nourished his need to be important and necessary to a woman. She did not tire of him, as she could of Cooper or Chevalier, who were charming and handsome but, she implied, intellectually limited.

However, intimacy revealed to von Sternberg another part of her nature: that there was perhaps nothing in her emotional life reserved for only one or even a dozen people she liked. And this realization prompted von Sternberg to withdraw. The coolly detached seducer of the self-destructive man, she was an earthy woman who simply cavorted according to her nature (thus *The Blue Angel).* But the tarnished performer could also be a faithful follower *(Morocco),* a hooker with a curious higher morality *(Dishonored),* a weary traveler living by wit and charm *(Shanghai Express),* a mother devoted to her child *(Blonde Venus).* Although she always insisted her roles had nothing to do with her true character, the truth was just the opposite: they were in fact coded chapters in a kind of tribute-biography von Sternberg made of her, a series of essays that could have been called "All the Things You Are." It was, then, precisely when he filmed her that this director attempted to justify her.

But he also saw her, in everyday life, as capricious, even sometimes shallow; his fantasy about her was therefore being chastened and his goddess revealed as thoroughly human, frail and fallible. Therefore, when he needed to draw on the reserves of dream and imagination for a new picture, he began to withdraw from intimacy. The Dietrich he was to offer to the camera could not be the one he had just known privately. There had to be veils left in place, shadows and mists still separating the seeker from the object of desire: von Sternberg needed always to imagine her as the leading character of one of her own silent films, *die Frau nach der man sich sehnt*—the woman one ever longs for.

But they were not Svengali and Trilby—a designation attached to them from their earliest days in Hollywood. "People have said he

casts a spell over me," Dietrich said. "That is ridiculous. I am devoted, but I made the devotion myself because my brain told me to.
It is only common sense to me. Can you think of anyone casting a
spell over me?" In an odd way, the situation was effectively reversed:
Marlene Dietrich cast the spell, Josef von Sternberg was enthralled.

FOR THE PRESENT, MARIA WAS UNAFFECTED BY HER
mother's fame and the occasional controversies. Enrolled at a private
school with other celebrity children, she had an amiable personality,
although she was necessarily somewhat reserved until she became
proficient in English. Dietrich, perhaps with more blithe imagination than prudence, ordered Maria's wardrobe—dresses, pajamas,
robes, shoes—in exact replicas of her own fashions and styles (but
without the gentlemen's suits Dietrich came to favor more and more
in Hollywood). This might have initially pleased the girl, but she
was left with the distinct impression that she was little more than an
awkward adjunct in her mother's life. Dietrich shuttled her to stores,
purchased expensive gifts for her (even miniature rings and bracelets)
and frequently took her to the beach and to riding lessons. But an
easy rapport never seems to have been established. "I felt that she
wanted to be with other people," Maria said later of her Hollywood
childhood.

> I remember how I used to cry at night. I remember a whiff of
> perfume, and my mother in furs standing there in my room,
> looking so beautiful. I was so jealous when she went out—I
> knew she wanted to see someone else rather than me . . . She
> would tuck me in, kiss me, and *hurry, hurry* . . . I wasn't left
> alone. But I knew the servants and bodyguards were simply
> hired to take care of me, and I disliked them. I never told
> mother that I was unhappy.

With a curious irony, the pleasantest time of Maria's first year in
America paralleled the intensification of the Riza Marks–von Sternberg debacle. Rudi's presence was required in California as a sign
that the Sieber marriage was stable, and this, at least for a month that

summer of 1931, created the facsimile of a traditional family unit. Riza's deposition had been taken in a Los Angeles court, where she had told Judge Lester W. Roth that her husband (before their June 1930 divorce) had "furnished an apartment for [Dietrich], and she charged clothing to his accounts." She then added a comment that caused some amusement: "He never let *me* charge clothing to his accounts." With such remarks the case was beginning not to be taken seriously.

As attorneys for the injured party continued to complain more publicly, the press naturally swung into action at the Pasadena railway station when Rudi arrived on July 19. From then on, at restaurants and at sporting events the Siebers frequented during the following four weeks, photographers leaped from behind trees, bushes and taxis to document father, mother and daughter—a happy trio, embracing, smiling, unconcerned for the mills of rumor. The better to confirm their innocence, Marlene and Rudi widened the family circle to include von Sternberg, who moved temporarily into quarters at the Beverly Hills Hotel. "I am here," Rudi told a reporter about his wife that summer,

> to testify by my presence and any other way that I can testify, that I know that these charges against her are utterly unfounded. I have known and agreed with her attitude that rather than avoid the publicity of these suits she should welcome and face these charges . . . Both of us, as good and moral friends of Mr. von Sternberg, sympathize with him in the attack that is being made against him by his former wife.

Sieber had constructed a brilliant riposte, one possible only because the complex logic of his marriage defied American comprehension. Several months later, after the editor of the *Neues Wiener Journal* admitted that the interviewer had fabricated Dietrich's remarks concerning the von Sternbergs, Riza dropped all charges.

But there was one sour note. Rudi Sieber resented not so much his wife's flagrant adulteries (such, after all, virtually defined her private life) as he did the potential effect of her conduct on Maria; he considered her, in this regard, something of a bad influence. Only when von Sternberg agreed not to return to live quite so openly with his wife and daughter did Sieber drop his threat to take Maria back with him to Germany—an ultimatum that caused Dietrich real panic (and a situation that directly inspired the plot development of the Dietrich-von Sternberg film *Blonde Venus).* Finally, Rudi departed Los Angeles in August to work at Paramount's Joinville studio near Paris, a job facilitated through the intercession of none other than von Sternberg himself.

THEIR NEW PROJECT, WHICH BEGAN FILMING IN AUtumn 1931, was set in the most exotic of the four locales so far chosen for the von Sternberg-Dietrich pictures; Berlin, Morocco and Eastern Europe now seemed overshadowed by the ersatz China of *Shanghai Express.* As Madeleine (a slight variation on her own uncontracted name, after all), Dietrich was—to quote the script— "the notorious woman who lives by her wits along the Chinese coast," and for whom "it took more than one man to change my name to Shanghai Lily." Aboard the eponymous train she meets a former lover (Clive Brook, as a British medical officer), whose life she saves when Chinese revolutionaries waylay the train.

Von Sternberg (taking his inspiration from parts of a story by Harry Hervey) dictated his outline and script to Jules Furthman and finally had something reminiscent of *Tosca.* Dietrich was never more alluringly rendered, photographed through an endless series of veils, scrims and smoky filters—all of it apposite for the latest version of von Sternberg's tarnished woman. As before, she is a character capable of a deeper fidelity and a higher morality than what anyone might expect—higher even than that of the minister who advises her to pray and is himself converted by her subsequent genuine piety. This happens in a single moment that transcends the film's simplistic story, when von Sternberg illuminates only Dietrich's cool white hands, as she slowly joins them in prayer for the safety of her former lover against a bloodthirsty Oriental brigand. (Her hands are constantly emphasized in this picture; her legs are never exposed.) Shanghai Lily, who has abandoned her name (as Marlene abandoned Maria Magdalene, the original form of hers), now risks her life precisely because she can only be true to her onetime love: thus *Shanghai Express* carries forward motifs from *Morocco* and *Dishonored*. The train takes these principals on a kind of journey toward integration—thus the final scenes, in which the former lovers tentatively rediscover the love that once bound them. And once again, the roles are reversed: Dietrich wears the officer's cap, brandishes his whip, takes control. She is, in fact, more active, more passionate here than in any prior film.

Von Sternberg, alternately delighted and (he felt) abandoned by Dietrich, spun a tale in which she is faithful in her infidelity while the hero remains loveless in his disjointed memories. According to cinematographer Lee Garmes (who won an Oscar for the film), "Clive Brook wanted to be Clive Brook [but] von Sternberg wanted him to be von Sternberg." The character Jannings/von Sternberg (in *The Blue Angel)* was ruined by this woman; Menjou/von Sternberg (in *Morocco)* was abandoned; Oland/von Sternberg (in *Dishonored)* was betrayed; but Brook/von Sternberg (perhaps because of the recent history of Dietrich and von Sternberg) has another chance.

In this regard, the laces and veils through which we glimpse Dietrich in *Shanghai Express* are more than just sexy peekaboo: on the contrary, the shot of her folded hands is central to von Sternberg's point, for it italicizes the fundamental mystery of the woman he perceived in Marlene Dietrich. "When I needed your faith, you withheld it," she says to Brook. "Now when I don't need it and don't deserve it, you give it to me." In the romantically complicated world of von Sternberg, love is of course never a matter of balance sheets, and needs and compensations rarely equalize.

After the filming was complete, Paramount arranged almost daily sessions for still photographs with cameramen like Eugene Robert Richee and John Engstead. Over these von Sternberg exerted his usual control, insisting that a high spotlight be used to bring out the shadows under her cheekbones. Often, according to Engstead, von Sternberg asked Dietrich to assume the most uncomfortable positions—to lean over a chair, for example, in an awkward contortion without support. Such a pose she held without complaint while he studied the situation and spoke to her only in German. When the stance was suitable, he began to work on her face, and at his command her head rose and fell, her lids lowered, her mouth opened slightly and his dream took shape. If Dietrich's expression did not suit von Sternberg, he lapsed into angry English: "Think of something—think of anything! Count the bricks on the wall!" Only when he was satisfied did he then nudge Richee or Engstead, and at last the shutter clicked.

Because of this meticulous attention to her image and the enormous publicity machine operated by Paramount, Marlene Dietrich was, by the end of 1931, simply the most famous actress working in America, and the most chronicled worldwide. *Vanity Fair* gushed its wonder over the "genuine and tremendous hold she has on the public today," and the London *Times* hailed her "careful elimination of all emphasis; the more seemingly careless and inconsequent her gestures, the more surely do they reveal the particular shades and movements of her mind."

Gary Cooper and Maurice Chevalier were still in Dietrich's life, escorting her (sometimes together, by her arrangement) to nightclubs and restaurants. Paramount's press department tried to finesse the openness of these rendezvous by claiming their meetings were really about business—that she might appear in a new film with Cooper or Chevalier, but not even the fan magazines took this subterfuge very seriously. Von Sternberg, ever accommodating, sometimes agreed to further confound the press by being the third diner at a restaurant table.

The bewilderment multiplied when Dietrich donned a man's tweed suit, knotted a four-in-hand and danced the tango at a dimly lit Hollywood club frequented by gay women in cross-dress but not, ordinarily, by image-conscious stars. Her partner on at least two such occasions was Imperio Argentina, the popular female dancer, singer and star of Spanish films, whom Dietrich courted with the usual bouquets of violets. Their evenings together were soon quieter and more intimate—at least until Argentina's husband, director Florian Rey, revived the ancient marital rights of an Iberian male. He appeared at Roxbury Drive late one evening with a pair of steamship tickets and ordered his wife to pack for an imminent departure—thus Imperio had danced her last tango in Hollywood.

BY SPRING 1932, DIETRICH'S GAZE WAS ALSO DI-
rected toward Europe, and she startled the press and the public (not
to say the studio) by announcing her intention to return to Germany. "I have enjoyed myself in Hollywood," she told journalist
Whitney Williams, "but the urge to be among my own people is
stronger than the desire to remain here. Germany is not satisfied
with me. It wants to hear me in German-speaking roles."

This was a typical Dietrich ploy; in fact she was quite aware that
in 1932 few Germans abroad were going home and hundreds of
thousands were emigrating. The reason for her announcement
(which Paramount took as a threat if she did not like her next
assignment) was to force an issue relating to von Sternberg. Before
the release of *Shanghai Express* he had decided that his career (and
possibly hers) would be best served if he no longer directed Dietrich.
But he had not foreseen her reaction. First she accused him of simple sexual jealousy; additionally, von Sternberg said,

> She accused me of being determined to demonstrate that she
> was worthless [and] to aggrandize myself by letting her stand on
> her own feet; she was nothing and could do nothing without me
> [she insisted], and all I had done with her was to show how great
> I was.

Dietrich then went further, informing the studio that she simply
would not work under another director—a threat she reinforced by
her public statements about returning home. As she doubtless expected, there was panic on Marathon Street before economic considerations, as so often, resolved the dilemma: Paramount offered
von Sternberg—then inundated with alimony obligations and attorneys' fees—a substantial increase in salary for his new contract if he
would prepare one last picture with Miss Dietrich. He capitulated,
and she spoke no more about Germany.

And so, by April 1932, von Sternberg had drafted *Blonde Venus*
(with the usual assistance on some dialogue from Jules Furthman)—
yet another story of an entertainer, this time a wife and mother

named Helen Faraday who returns to the stage to earn money for her mortally ill husband, Ned (Herbert Marshall). While he is abroad undergoing an expensive cure, she adds to her professional success a glamorous life as mistress of Nick Townsend, a wealthy politician (Cary Grant). Her husband, returning cured, learns about her life and claims that her immoral conduct denies her the right to keep their little boy, Johnnie (Dickie Moore). She flees with the child, is reduced to prostitution to support him, and is forced to give the boy up to her husband. Her sacrifices are duly rewarded, however, when she is later restored triumphantly to international fame and (against von Sternberg's wishes but on the insistence of Hollywood's moral watchdogs) to her family.

The screenplay was not completed without considerable friction between von Sternberg and Dietrich on one side and B. P. Schulberg, Paramount's production chief, on the other. Director and star were told that her character was unsympathetic to the point of depravity, and that von Sternberg would have to tone down the episodes of the woman's descent into prostitution. (Particular objection was made to a scene in which the child is hidden under a table while his mother flirts with a prospective customer.) Von Sternberg refused to submit to the required changes, blithely departing for a New York holiday after Schulberg brought in another writer (S. K. Lauren).

To no one's surprise, Paramount then suspended von Sternberg, discontinuing his weekly salary when he failed to report for the first day's shooting on Monday, April 25, 1932. But Schulberg and company did not adequately assess Dietrich's devotion to her mentor, for she was also absent that day, announcing through her attorney Ralph Blum that she would certainly not appear in *Blonde Venus* with the newly assigned director, Richard Wallace. They had no choice but to suspend her as well, and a threat of lawsuits was announced on April 28. Some script compromises were hastily drafted, and on May 26 shooting began with scenes requiring Dietrich to act the doting mama, bathing and fussing over her little boy. By an odd coincidence, Dietrich felt her real-life motherhood threatened at the same time.

That March, the infant son of aviator Charles Lindbergh had

been kidnapped, but the baby was found murdered before the abductors specified how the $50,000 ransom was to be delivered. Throughout America, wealthy and famous parents panicked, and locksmiths, bodyguards and providers of security gates were kept busy round the clock in Hollywood. The children of movie stars (those of Harold Lloyd, Ann Harding and Bebe Daniels among them) were constantly attended, and Dietrich supervised the installation of iron bars over the windows of Maria's room. Dietrich's chauffeur, an austere ex-prizefighter named Briggs, escorted the child to school, and she was not permitted to wander undefended even in the enclosed yard at Roxbury Drive.

Perhaps predictably, the widespread promulgation of these security tactics provoked the very threats they were meant to forestall. In mid-May, extortion letters were received by Dietrich and by one Mrs. Egon Muller, wife of a German linen importer: if money was not delivered according to specific instructions, their children's lives would be in danger. After Dietrich obeyed police advice to ignore the threat while they tried to trace the letter, a second was received, doubling the extorted sum to $10,000. This was to be left in a package on the rear bumper of an automobile at a particular location. Meantime, Mrs. Muller (also acting under police counsel), placed $17—instead of the $500 demanded—under a designated downtown palm tree.

At this point, frightening though the situation seemed, an atmosphere of comic unreality prevailed, for the swindlers were stupid and incompetent—straight from an episode of *The Gang That Couldn't Shoot Straight*. On May 30, Dietrich was puzzled when she opened her morning mail demanding "the $483 you forgott to leave!" That same day, Mrs. Muller received a letter:

You Marlene Dietrich, if you want to save Maria to be a screen star, pay, and if you don't she'll be but a loving memory to you. Don't dare to call detectives again. Keep this to yourself. Say, what's the big idea! Attention! Is the future of your girl worth it? Wait for new information. $10,000 or pay heavily later on. You'll be sorry. Don't call for police or detectives again.

District Attorney Buron Fitts and Chief of Detectives Blaney Matthews revealed nothing when they ceremoniously called a press conference: "The people clipping and sending these letters are just a bunch of cheap chiselers. They are probably inexperienced, too, and the threats are more or less idle." And so they were. The Sieber and Muller children were never threatened again, the clumsy extortionists were not apprehended, and by midsummer (although Dietrich kept her bodyguards on full-time alert for several months) the matter was no longer a prime concern to anyone.

THROUGHOUT THE ORDEAL, VON STERNBERG WAS the most anxious and vigilant protector, and in fact the danger of losing Maria that spring directly inspired the revised plot of *Blonde Venus*—wherein, despite her maternal devotion, Dietrich must forfeit her child. Perhaps because of his own childhood poverty and the enormous sacrifices lovingly made by his mother, *Blonde Venus* began as a paean to motherhood, as von Sternberg's son later recalled: "When I was young, my father showed the film to me as an example of what he thought about motherhood, which he regarded with an almost maudlin sentimentality. *Blonde Venus* shows his great attachment and gratitude to his own mother for holding the family together in hard times."

But the picture also contains the usual network of references to Josef von Sternberg's relationship with Marlene Dietrich, and the plot synthesizes every love triangle in their previous quartet of films. Like von Sternberg, both the husband Ned and the lover Nick fall in love with the cabaret performer Dietrich when they see her onstage (shades of *Zwei Krawatten);* like von Sternberg, Nick then becomes her lover while the husband (Sieber) is in Germany, and the latter returns with threats to take her child away. There follows Helen's half-willed descent to the life of the demimondaine—von Sternberg's continual fascination for Dietrich's prodigal erotic life (as also in *The Blue Angel, Morocco, Dishonored* and *Shanghai Express)*—and her final victory as a performer, dressed triumphantly in white top hat, tie and tails, a manly woman boasting she neither loves nor is loved.

By the finale Dietrich has, then, revealed the significance of her justly famous first song in *Blonde Venus;* whereas she had not sung at all in *Dishonored* or *Shanghai Express,* she is here given three important numbers. The first, "Hot Voodoo," she sexily croons after emerging from a gorilla costume—her beauty latent even within the beast; the sequence directly recalls Dietrich in a woman's sexy outfit after changing from a man's evening suit in *Morocco.* This is followed by "You Little So-and-So," in which the crooning Dietrich (smiling, winking, pointing a gentle accusatory finger at men in the audience) is teasingly photographed through potted palms and past rows of spectators. Finally, she sings—in her victorious male garb— "I Couldn't Be Annoyed"; any crazy inversion of the so-called natural order is acceptable to her ("if bulls gave milk . . . if everyone stood on his head and on his hands he wore shoes . . . if we ate soup with a fork, and if babies brought the stork").

BECAUSE OF THE DANGER TO MARIA, THE ATMOsphere during filming was tense, but throughout the summer Dietrich worked bravely and without evident anxiety. According to lyricist Sam Coslow she was "a joy to be with . . . a good trouper and nothing at all like the secretive, Garbo-like woman of mystery the Paramount press agents and fan magazine writers were selling to the public." She was also affectionate and reassuring toward child actor Dickie Moore, whose parents also feared kidnappers, and who recalled that she was "obviously on close terms with [von Sternberg]. They yelled at one another constantly in German, but always ended up laughing and embracing."

Blonde Venus was a surprise hit for Paramount when it opened that autumn, earning three million dollars in its first release. But most critics were as unenthusiastic as they had been about the previous von Sternberg films: by this time there was a consensus that her director rendered Dietrich enchanting to behold, but that as an actress she had little range. As for her own estimation of her talents, she was remarkably self-aware and candid: "I do not care," she said at the time. "I am not an actress, no . . . I don't like making pictures, and I haven't got to act to be happy. Perhaps that is the secret."

The criticism of her talents was in a way justified; no one ever accused Marlene Dietrich of being one of the great actresses of the century, convincing in a variety of roles. Subsequently, as if by sheer repetition and increasing confidence, she would display an occasional flair for comedy. But in a sense analysis of her movie acting fails to acknowledge that the primary requirement of the job is a mysterious connection between face and camera—and, as well, the careful presentation of a presence by studios and directors able to exploit appearances.

Marlene Dietrich brought to the roles, after all, precisely what was required by von Sternberg's variations on a theme. The deeply muted passion, the affectless gaze, the slow and moody reactions, the grey envelope of suspicion that ever surrounded her character—everything had been calculated by him and realized by her for a specific effect. The public seemed to realize what reviewers and essayists in Depression America did not: that Lola Lola, Amy Jolly, X-27, Shanghai Lily and Helen Faraday were not women who begged for admiration or endorsement. Much less did they, according to the tradition of movie romance, plead for the counterfeit salvation of romantic love. Wounded and cautious, tainted by experience, wise, sometimes diffident but always accessible to the astonishment of living, they were at once all women von Sternberg imagined and the one woman Marlene Dietrich was.

NONE OF THIS HELD ANY INTEREST FOR HER. "IT IS behind the cameras I should like to be," she admitted that year, "as Mr. von Sternberg's assistant director. But he will not let me." He did, however, offer her the kind of complete education in filmmaking technique directors rarely offer actors. D. W. Griffith was virtually a professor to his actresses, and Alfred Hitchcock often gave leading ladies extensive training in everything from story development to the final cut, but such tutelage is the exception in the swift, ordinarily impersonal business of moviemaking.

Von Sternberg taught Dietrich the fine points of cinema magic, especially as it pertained to the exhibition of herself. In addition to the positioning of lights and props there was of course a meticulous approach to makeup, and by 1933 (the fourth year under his guidance) she knew more about transforming the face, as John Engstead recalled, than makeup artists Elizabeth Arden, Max Factor and the Westmores combined. She knew that if she held a saucer over a candle a black carbon smudge would form on the underside, and that if a few drops of lanolin or mineral oil were warmed and mixed with the soot, this could be effectively applied to the eyelids. Painstakingly, she learned to use this concoction throughout the 1930s, heavier at the lash line, then fading up toward the eyebrow. (The entire procedure is detailed as Dietrich/Helen prepares backstage for her first cabaret number in *Blonde Venus.)*

But it was the camera's potential for artifice that Dietrich learned most about from her mentor. The photographer George Hurrell recalled Dietrich pausing on a staircase between setups of a von Sternberg film, casually surveying the technicians and knowing, by this time, what each man was doing and why. For a session of still photos afterward, she assumed a pose, checked herself in a mirror and called, "All right, George—shoot!" The full-length mirror positioned near her, just to the side of the camera, was in fact Dietrich's invariable requirement and she could be (as Hurrell recalled) quite angry if it had been forgotten.

But as 1932 drew to a close, there were other reasons for her to be annoyed. Von Sternberg's conflict with Paramount over the development of Dietrich's role in *Blonde Venus* had precipitated a number of private meetings with Schulberg and with vice-president Emanuel Cohen, and they agreed with von Sternberg that star and mentor might be well served if her next film—her last under her current Paramount contract—could be created with another filmmaker. The project chosen was *Song of Songs,* based on Edward Sheldon's dramatization of the famous Hermann Sudermann novel; for it von Sternberg suggested Rouben Mamoulian, who had successfully directed *Applause* and *Dr. Jekyll and Mr. Hyde*—and who, as everyone in Hollywood knew, had already been selected by Greta Garbo for *Queen Christina* later in 1933.

Song of Songs, tightly scheduled for an eight-week shoot that winter, required Dietrich to be on the set the morning of December 20, 1932; her attorney announced a few hours later that she would, in fact, not appear at all. Ignoring the possible legal and financial consequences of her actions, she would not submit to direction from Mamoulian (or any director other than von Sternberg) and renewed her threat that when her contract expired in February she would simply embark for Germany.

8: 1933–1935

ON JANUARY 2, 1933, EXECUTIVES AT PAR-
amount filed a breach of contract suit against Marlene Dietrich,
asking the courts for $182,850.06—the precise amount the studio
insisted they had lost since her failure to report for work on *Song of
Songs*. Fearing her departure from the country, they also appealed to
Judge Harry Holzer for an arrest warrant. This he denied, but he did
issue a temporary restraining order against her employment by another studio, and he demanded her appearance in court the following week. Relaxing over the weekend with Maurice Chevalier at
her Santa Monica beach house on Ocean Front Boulevard (later
Pacific Coast Highway), Dietrich affected an airy unconcern worthy
of Lola Lola or Shanghai Lily. Ralph Blum, her attorney, repeatedly
telephoned her about the obvious professional (not to say monetary)
ramifications of her recalcitrance, but she was inflexible. She would
not work until von Sternberg promised to return to her for one
more picture before the year was over.

And so on January 5 her secretary, Eleanor McGeary, telephoned the studio to say Dietrich would be at Marathon Street prepared to work the following week. Paramount immediately cancelled all legal action and simultaneously offered her a new five-year contract, starting with (and ultimately advancing beyond) $4,500 per week—almost four times her original starting pay and a royal emolument in that worst year of the Great Depression. (The studio was not simply acting magnanimously. On his return from a European trip, director Ernst Lubitsch reported to Paramount that abroad the most popular movie stars were Dietrich, Garbo and Jeanette Mac-Donald.) This deal she wisely signed, and on January 9, wearing a man's tweed suit, tie and beret, she joined Mamoulian for lunch in the studio commissary to discuss the first scenes of *Song of Songs*. "Like every German girl, I regard this as one of the great works of fiction," she told the press. Her outfit, however (which she claimed was simply for the sake of comfort, economy and simplicity) accentuated the difference between the actress and the pious, shy peasant girl she was about to portray, and this the press gleefully noticed.

That year, Marlene Dietrich was rarely seen in public wearing women's clothes; in fact some said she was the best-dressed man in Hollywood. Chevalier—who objected more to her unconventional wardrobe than to the press prying around her rented beach house—demanded that she wear more traditional clothes, at least when they dined out or went dancing.

"Her adoption of trousers and wearing of tuxedos," commented the *Los Angeles Times* on January 24, "[was] extreme showmanship, but on the other hand it may also prove a hit." Her apparel was indeed widely remarked—and this greatly displeased Chevalier, who perhaps thought journalists would look for even more scabrous details if he were regularly seen with a mistress wearing only high-fashion drag. In this matter she was implacable, and the affair (but not the friendship) ceased.

The reason for the end of the Dietrich-Chevalier liaison was not simply her wardrobe, but the woman for whom she was now wearing it almost exclusively. Early in 1933, she became deeply involved in an affair with the stylish Spanish immigrant Mercedes de Acosta, a playwright, screenwriter and feminist who was also a charter member of America's creative lesbian community.* A dominating personality in any situation, de Acosta was, as actress and writer-photographer Jean Howard described her, "a little blackbird of a woman, strange and mysterious, and to many irresistible."

De Acosta (who was forty in 1933) moved easily in the aesthetic worlds of Eleanora Duse, Pablo Picasso and Igor Stravinsky, and among her friends she counted at various times Mrs. Patrick Campbell, Sarah Bernhardt, Jeanne Eagels, Laurette Taylor and Helen Hayes. During and after World War I she knew well the dancer Isadora Duncan, and her own career as poet and screenwriter was firm after 1930. Although she was married to the artist Abram Poole from 1920 to 1935, the relationship was never anything but a warm friendship.

In her published memoirs, *Here Lies the Heart* (1960), de Acosta acknowledged that the most ardent relationships of her life were with Le Gallienne (who starred in her plays *Sandro Botticelli* and *Jeanne d'Arc),* Garbo and Dietrich, although she was indeed as busy as the notorious Natalie Barney, the doyenne of Parisian gay women. De Acosta's accounts of her intimacies are fragrant with details not only of flower deliveries but also of candlelit evenings, long, late bedroom conversations and lovers' quarrels. Friends who resented her frankness tried to deny the most torrid romantic revelations, often referring to her book as "Here the Heart Lies." But there is the concomitant witness of many third parties, among them the men in Dietrich's life; the basic truth of de Acosta's book (if not the accuracy of every detail) is indeed unassailable.

According to the custom of that time and the requirements of law, Mercedes de Acosta employed meaningful circumlocutions: Marbury (nicknamed Granny Pop) "seemed such a man to me"; Nazimova acted "like a naughty little boy"; John Barrymore's wife Michael Strange (an apt monicker if ever there was one) looked "like a healthy young Arab boy"; Garbo ("more beautiful than I ever dreamed she could be") overwhelmed her so much that on first

---

* Among a legion, this group included Edna St. Vincent Millay, Willa Cather and Anita Loos (writers); Cheryl Crawford, Elizabeth Marbury, Eva Le Gallienne, Alla Nazimova, Katharine Cornell, Blanche Yurka, Natasha Rambova and Mary Martin (in the theater); Janet Gaynor, Jean Arthur, Kay Francis and Dorothy Arzner (in Hollywood).

meeting her, de Acosta removed a bracelet and slipped it on her wrist. Two days later she managed to accelerate their mutual attraction.

Their common friend Salka Viertel (wife of writer-director Berthold Viertel and screenwriter of several Garbo pictures) arranged for them to meet privately in an unoccupied house near her own on Mabery Road in Santa Monica Canyon, where Garbo and de Acosta "put records on the phonograph, pushed back the rug and danced 'Daisy, You're Driving Me Crazy' over and over again." The scene ends on a closed door, behind which the relationship became more intimate ("I was moving in a dream within a dream," de Acosta wrote tremulously).

When Garbo returned to Sweden for a holiday in 1933, Dietrich, now her rival offscreen as well as on, was quick to replace her, delivering roses and violets to de Acosta's home—"sometimes twice a day," the recipient recalled, "ten dozen roses or twelve dozen carnations [and] many Lalique vases." Dietrich, grandly overstating, told de Acosta, "You are the first person here to whom I have felt drawn. I want to ask if you will let me cook for you." She then suggested they go swimming together at the beach, and next evening the affair began. "You have exceptional skin texture that makes me think of moonlight," de Acosta whispered as if reciting from her current screenplay assignment *(Rasputin).* "You should not ruin your face by putting color on it." Thenceforth Dietrich never again wore rouge in her friend's presence.

Mercedes de Acosta and Marlene Dietrich, almost unique among women in Hollywood, carried on their affair quite openly throughout the 1930s—despite the fact that, then as later, homosexuals were subjected to the fearful suppressions of a hypocritical movie industry. But Dietrich was not to be restricted by the norms of polite expectations any more than by the annual shifts in female fashions. With de Acosta, as with other women and men, it was often important for her to gratify someone she respected. Cooking for them, offering gifts, cleaning their homes, even doing their laundry—no gesture was too humble to demonstrate her desire to ingratiate herself and thus be included in their society. Trained by her grandmother in the arts of feminine attraction and by her mother in the crafts of domesticity, she effectively linked the Victorian model of the loyal and dutiful woman with the Prussian ideal of the tireless, attentive companion and the Berlin prototype of an unfettered, worldly maverick.

It would be tempting, in this regard, to postulate that the men in her life represented a continuing search for a father-figure, and that the women were surrogate mothers she wished to please. But human affects do not conform so tidily to the rudiments of textbook psychology. It is perhaps more accurate to argue that Marlene Dietrich was attracted to those whose styles she admired, whose intellects she respected and whose social influence she wished to share. Sex could be a useful component in a relationship—a bevel with which she could achieve emotional balance—but none of her affairs had even the temporary exclusivity that betokens a desire for loving attachment, much less permanence. Not one of her paramours, men or women, ever reported that she gave herself up to a truly grand passion; always she was remarkably self-aware and in control of the directions her relationships took.

THE FILMING OF *SONG OF SONGS* LASTED FROM MID-January to early April, a protraction required by the almost daily arrival of new writers to tackle the script's problems. Dietrich was cast as Lily, a devout provincial girl with an impossible ideal of romantic love, sent to Berlin after her father's death. There she takes refuge from a boozy aunt (Alison Skipworth) in the studio of a sculptor (Brian Aherne) who convinces her to pose nude for a statue based on the faithful lover of the biblical Song of Solomon. (With more alacrity than Lily, Dietrich did model nude especially for the movie—for sculptor S. C. Scarpitta, whose statue was provocatively exploited throughout *Song of Songs.*) Fearing that marriage will compromise his career, the artist abandons her; and Lily's aunt marries her off to a lecherous old baron (Lionel Atwill). Marital misery leads to accidental infidelity and the predictable descent to the demi-monde before a happy reunion with the fickle sculptor.

Mamoulian remembered her as a disciplined worker but one whose performance was entirely calculated and lacking the spontaneity that derives from intuition. This may have been partly because she was working for another director for the first time and was fearful of her appearance in the picture.

Paramount makeup artist Wally Westmore recalled that Dietrich at the time was fully aware of her own special requirements—especially a key light about eight feet above her and a little to the right. "This created the hollows under the eyebrows and cheekbones which gave her that sculptured look. She never worked without that key light hitting her from above." Dietrich continued to refer to a large mirror just off-camera to assure that this light was properly positioned for the best presentation of her face—a moment that occurred when she saw a small butterfly-shaped shadow under her nose. "If you look carefully," Westmore pointed out, "you can see that little butterfly shadow in every movie and still picture she made."

Cinematographer Lucien Ballard recalled that Dietrich became so skillful that she could simply lick her finger and hold it toward the key light, determining from the heat if it was exactly the proper distance from her face. As for the mirror, it was becoming a kind of totem: the reflection she saw, harbinger of the image on the screen, became her only permanent partner. Just as she was ever confident and controlling in her intimacies, so was Marlene Dietrich the epitome of the Hollywood Narcissus. Gazing at her own reflection, she became transfixed with what she saw and dedicated herself inexhaustibly to its refinement and perfection. But like the figure in the Greek myth, her self-involvement, indeed self-obsession, would lead at last to an isolating and loveless solitude. Perhaps no star was ever more trapped by her own image.

Predictably, Dietrich's directorial tactics on the set annoyed Mamoulian, who was certainly not placated by her impolitic action each day before the first shot. "I had the sound man lower the boom mike," she admitted years later, "and I said into it, 'Oh, Jo—why hast thou forsaken me?' " Rightly, von Sternberg ignored her pleas to be present as photographic counselor—until Dietrich, on March 28, carefully but deliberately fell from her horse during a scene and, in a performance better than any she had ever given onscreen, wept for his assistance. He sped to her side and took her home, where she rested for three days. Perhaps the only memorable moment in the finished film was Dietrich's singing of Frederick Hollander's "Johnny," which gave her the opportunity to convey elegant raciness even as she wandered about trying to find the right key ("We'll disconnect the phone, and when we're all alone, we'll have a lot to do-o-o-o . . . I need a kiss or two—or maybe more").*

PARAMOUNT ALLOWED HER A EUROPEAN HOLIDAY before her next assignment. Although she had spoken for almost a year of returning to Germany, she was now receiving bad press there. "One would like to see so famous a German artist show some German spirit and work in German productions," proclaimed the Berlin trade journal *Lichtbildbühne* in May 1933.

> It is inconsistent with our national revolution that our most famous movie star should be playing foreign roles in a foreign country under foreign directors, speaking English instead of her mother tongue. As long as she opts for the dollar and has shaken the dust of her fatherland from her feet, can the new Germany place any value on the importance of her movies?

Nazi Germany's resentment of her was sealed when *Song of Songs* was submitted for German release soon after. It was, of course, banned, for it was based on a novel by a Jew, was financed by "Jewish Hollywood money" and, added the codifiers of the *Lichtspielgesetz* (which specified the requirements for a play or film to conform to Nazi ideology), it used a German actress to impugn the moral purity of the German people by claiming that adultery could go unpunished in their own country, where the story was set.

Still, Dietrich longed for a summer in Europe, and so with Maria—and luggage containing twenty-five suits of male clothes, dozens of men's shirts, neckties and socks—she boarded the *Europa* in New York and arrived in Paris on May 19. Within hours the Pari-

---

* In America, Friedrich Holländer became Frederick Hollander. He had written "Johnny" as a birthday present for Johnny Soyka, Dietrich's agent at the time of *The Blue Angel*. Soyka's wife Mady later had a fateful encounter with her in London.

sian newspapers were detailing her shocking outfit: a chocolate-colored polo coat, a pearl grey suit, white shirt and tie—and aviator's goggles perched saucily atop a felt hat. One Paris magistrate suggested next day that she be threatened with arrest for impersonating a man, and in fact the police seriously considered a warrant. This idea collapsed when (of all people) Maurice Chevalier told a journalist that Dietrich was a friend to all Frenchmen who loved freedom.

That week she recorded German melodies in a Paris studio and began a week's work dubbing the French version of *Song of Songs;* then she, Maria, Rudi and Tamara toured France, Switzerland, Austria, Italy and the Riviera. But it was Paris most of all that she thenceforth regarded as a refuge. "I am very happy here," she told the press. "My daughter can play in the gardens of the hotel or in the park without fear [of publicity or abduction]."

On September 26, she and Maria left Paris for New York, her garb and makeup as controversial as ever—a black and silver suit over a Chinese red blouse, matching red and black gloves and snakeskin bag, red heels on black patent pumps and her lips and fingernails painted a blazing scarlet. Hours before her departure, she was visited by German film distributors authorized to solicit her to return home to make films. But Dietrich condemned to their faces the recent dismissal from Germany of prominent intellectuals (most of them Jewish) and expressed her outrage at the May book-burnings on the Opernplatz, in which the works of Heine, Marx, Freud, Mann, Brecht and Remarque were especially targeted. Contemptuous not only of her own recent press but also of everything that the Nazis stood for, she coldly rejected their offer—as she did at least two later invitations before she sealed her loyalties by swearing American citizenship.*

WHEN MARLENE DIETRICH RETURNED TO THE States in the autumn of 1933, she was (although not a refugee) one

---

* In March 1934, Carl Ousen, president of the Nazi National Film Chamber, claimed that Dietrich sent a $500 check to their welfare fund. This was a neat tactic to discredit Dietrich in America, but it failed: her contribution, it was soon determined, was sent to a nonpolitical winter relief fund for poor children in her home district.

of almost two hundred thousand Germans who settled in the United States in that decade.* Quite apart from their fierce rejection of Nazi ideology there was a subtle but well-documented self-loathing among many of these immigrants. Once champions of German culture—as Dietrich often referred to herself from 1930 to 1933—they now almost denounced their roots. Bertolt Brecht, who also settled in California, proclaimed that "everything bad in me" was of German origin, and Thomas Mann, speaking for many, lamented, "We poor Germans! We are fundamentally lonely, even when we are famous! No one really likes us."

Marlene Dietrich could not say with any truth that she was disliked. By the same token, she seemed to exhibit the common schizoid pattern of the German émigré, rejecting her Teutonic past and refusing to conform entirely to American behavior, particularly with regard to gender roles. Simultaneously, she loved the California climate as much as her huge salary and the freedom to enjoy it—yet she complained about almost everything, and almost constantly. Hollywood was impressive in its technical efficiency; Hollywood was dreadful, and she never felt at home there. She appreciated her many American friends; she decried the informality of their lives. She enjoyed the abundance and variety of food and the opulence of restaurants; she criticized American cuisine and said she preferred to cook German-style at home. She disliked the social arrogance of many Germans in Hollywood; she dined at least once weekly at the Blue Danube restaurant, where old friends like Joe May kept the Old World alive in High German conversations. Of such contradictions was the immigrant temperament comprised before 1941—by which time American citizenship had bonded most of them forever to their adopted countrymen, whom they fervently joined against Hitler.

In October, Dietrich was back at Paramount with von Sternberg, then completing the scenario for what would be one of the

---

* Among the most notable: architect Walter Gropius; designer Marcel Breuer; philosophers Hannah Arendt, Paul Tillich, Herbert Marcuse, Erik Erikson and Claude Lévi-Strauss; conductors Otto Klemperer, Fritz Reiner, George Szell, Erich Leinsdorf, William Steinberg and Bruno Walter; composers Arnold Schoenberg, Hans Eisler, Erich Wolfgang Korngold, Kurt Weill, Alfred Newman, Béla Bartók and Paul Hindemith; writers Bertolt Brecht, Thomas and Heinrich Mann; scientists Albert Einstein, Hans Bethe and Edward Teller; filmmakers Fred Zinnemann, Fritz Lang, Kurt (later Curtis) Bernhardt and Detlef Sierck (later Douglas Sirk).

most curious movies in history. First called *Her Regiment of Lovers,* this was a wildly imaginative account of Sophia Frederica, the Prussian princess brought to Russia in the eighteenth century by the Empress Elizabeth to marry her halfwit son Peter. Learning every political and sexual tactic of ambition and exploitation at the Russian court, Sophia—renamed Catherine (and later "the Great")—accedes to the throne after the death of Elizabeth and the murder of Peter. Soon retitled *The Scarlet Empress,* the design of the production proceeded under von Sternberg's complete control—each tiny detail of scenery, paintings, sculptures, costumes, story, photography and acting gesture. The film became, as he said, a relentless excursion into style. The credits claim the story is based on the diary of Catherine II, "arranged by Manuel Komroff"; in fact it emerged whole from von Sternberg's most ardent inventiveness.

No matter that the narrative only vaguely nods at historical accuracy, the director's goal was a presentation of something unique in the annals of film: the twisted world of nightmare, a tissue of almost pathological fantasies. Inspired by German expressionism and its use of distorted perspective to suggest mental derangement, *The Scarlet Empress* and its lacerating, perverse wit totter so often on the edge of satire that the appropriate response to almost every scene is problematical. Hyperbolic in design, the sets and props impede the players, Dietrich herself included (not to say the thousands of extras employed for crowd scenes), and von Sternberg's vision emphasized an astonishing collection of brooding, expressionist statues and vast ikons that everywhere dwarf the characters. Equally grotesque were explicit scenes of torture, rape and pillage (production just preceded the application of the newly drafted Motion Picture Production Code that set standards for acceptable language and behavior for the first time in Hollywood's history).

This florid production featured everything beyond human scale, from the vast oversize palace corridors to doorhandles twelve feet off the ground, requiring half a dozen characters to manipulate them. Amid a delirium that could have come from Edvard Munch, Dietrich as Catherine was swathed in ermine, white fox and sable, wrapped in fog and smoke, a creature looming from a demented social miasma and finally transformed into a half-mad sybarite. For

*A*s Amy Jolly in *Morocco*, 1930, with von Sternberg's radiant key lighting.

*A*t the premiere of *Morocco*, with friend Dimitri Buchowetzki and Rudolf Sieber.

NATIONAL FILM ARCHIVE, LONDON.

NATIONAL FILM ARCHIVE, LONDON.

*E*xploiting a photo opportunity with Charles Chaplin in Berlin, 1931.

NATIONAL FILM ARCHIVE, LONDON.

*F*ilming *Dishonored* in 1931: an obvious rival to Garbo.

*P*osing on the set in 1931 as Shanghai Lily in *Shanghai Express*, wearing one of Travis Banton's fantastic creations.

With her daughter, Maria, in Hollywood, 1932.

With actresses Suzy Vernon and Imperio Argentina at a Ladies' Night in Hollywood, 1932.

*O*n the town with Maurice Chevalier and Gary Cooper: Hollywood, 1932.

*W*elcoming an ardent cadre of the Hollywood press to her home, 1933.

*O*n the set of *Song of Songs*, 1933.

*A*t a Hollywood polo match with Rudolf Sieber, Josef von Sternberg, Tamara Matul and Maria (1934).

*I*n Hollywood, 1935.

With Douglas Fairbanks, Jr., at a London theater, 1936.

With Sieber in Salzburg, 1937.

With von Sternberg and Erich Maria Remarque, at the Hotel du Cap-Eden Roc, Antibes: July 1939.

As Frenchy in *Destry Rides Again*, 1939.

With John Wayne in *Seven Sinners*, 1940.

*A*t the Hollywood Canteen, 1943.

*W*ith Jean Gabin, 1943.

the first half of the film, she had little to do but affect a wide-eyed
naïveté; then, as the images of sadomasochism accumulate, she was
presented as a woman whose unleashed sensuality makes her a mon-
ster of ambition ("I think I have weapons that are far more powerful
than any political machine"). Amid a swirl of gargoyles with twisted
bodies and images of emaciated martyrs bearing vast candelabra, no
exoticism was left untried, and the picture became a procession of
mobile tableaux.

Ornate and vexatious, *The Scarlet Empress* was nothing like Alexander Korda's *Catherine the Great,* released the same year and starring
Dietrich's old acquaintance Elisabeth Bergner; it also had none of
that film's ultimate success. So grotesque that it never bores, von
Sternberg's film is hilariously improbable in the love scenes between
Dietrich and John Lodge, who played Alexei, field marshal of the
Russian Army. Reasons other than his role and his performance
doubtless contributed to his decision, but soon after this picture he
left films and entered real-life politics, becoming in turn a congress-
man, governor of Connecticut and ambassador to Spain and Argentina.

Typically, von Sternberg could not dissociate his art from complex feelings about Dietrich; he was in fact drawn to this historical
pageant by the situation that recurs in each of their joint pictures: a
man rejected. Despotic, sometimes downright unkind and rarely
popular with his cast, von Sternberg was more and more frequently
described as a dictator on his pictures. In this regard, he painstakingly directed Sam Jaffe in the role of Grand Duke Peter, who
emerges as nothing so much as a stencil of the director himself, a
smiling, mad dwarf commanding his toy soldiers round a "war set,"
an idiot fated to abandonment by a woman whose beauty renders
him helpless. Otherwise, *The Scarlet Empress* is notable only for the
casting of Maria in a brief, early scene as the young Sophia.

When Dietrich returned from Europe, von Sternberg was unsure of their relationship; she spent much of her nonworking time
with Mercedes de Acosta and a new circle of acquaintances in
Brentwood and Santa Monica—amusing and talented companions
like Martin Kosleck and his lover Hans von Twardowsky, German
actors who were able to work occasionally in Hollywood films.

Feeling distant from her, von Sternberg more than ever played the directorial tyrant at the studio, imprudently expressing his fear of separation by asking her to repeat difficult scenes, as if she would thus realize a kind of pathetic dependence on him. Predictably, this had the contrary effect: the more he tried to psychologically apprehend her, the more she politely withdrew—but never revealed her dismay at work. John Engstead recalled that von Sternberg required her to descend a vast staircase in her elaborate costume forty-five times; she obeyed without a single complaint. "They say von Sternberg is ruining me," she said with apparent innocence to a journalist. "I say let him ruin me. I would rather have a small part in one of his good pictures than a big part in a bad one made by someone else."

Her director was not, of course, ruining his star at all, nor did anyone seriously wager that the brightness of her publicity could be long dimmed by the fiasco of *The Scarlet Empress*. But there was a new and deep strain between them after filming completed in early 1934. It would be hard not to link some of the disconnection to the influence of Mercedes de Acosta and her friends, for by this time Dietrich was becoming more and more blunt in pursuing actresses she found attractive; among them were Paramount's Carole Lombard and Frances Dee, whose unregenerate heterosexuality did not dissuade Dietrich from her usual stratagems of flower deliveries and romantic blandishments. Lombard, a beautiful, brash blonde, was unamused: "If you want something," she told Dietrich after finding one too many sweet notes and posies in her dressing room at Paramount, "you come on down when I'm there. I'm not going to chase you." As for Dee (who had been directed by von Sternberg in *An American Tragedy*) she and her husband Joel McCrea recalled Dietrich's inordinate attentions, asking von Sternberg to treat Dee with especial care because (so said McCrea) Dietrich was in love with her—but in love, as with Lombard, to no avail.

In addition, Dietrich did not please von Sternberg (or Mercedes, for that matter) by attaching herself to John Gilbert, then thirty-eight, whose alcoholism had rendered him virtually unemployable as a film actor. "He was killing himself," according to his daughter, "and she would not have it. Marlene simply took over."

Applying every tactic of affirmation and encouragement, Dietrich persuaded Gilbert to seek medical help to stop drinking. She asked him to escort her to parties, movie premieres and art galleries; she drove him to the beach, to restaurants and to concerts. Hovering about with maternal concern, she steered him away from liquor, offering (in the felicitous term of playwright Robert Anderson) tea and sympathy—and of course herself. According to every account, her actions were benevolent; yet it was certainly not irrelevant that Gilbert was still a close friend of Greta Garbo's, who had once briefly been his lover and who also tried to help him. In a way, then, Gilbert, like de Acosta, was a link to the enduring rival Garbo, one whom Dietrich must appropriate unto herself.

The year was in fact busy with new friendships. In March, returning aboard the *Ile de France* from a one-week sojourn in Paris, she met Ernest Hemingway, whose fame made him as attractive to her as his burly macho affectations. The circumstances of their introduction were brilliantly Dietrichian. Entering the ship's dining room in a long, white, tightly beaded gown, she approached a table adjacent to Hemingway's but then she counted twelve guests already seated. Hesitating to be the unlucky thirteenth, she started to move away—whereupon Hemingway (as she may have expected) gallantly leaped forward to be the fourteenth at her table. She suggested instead a stroll round the decks.

At once Dietrich took him as something of a counselor and father-figure, calling him (as did others) her "Papa." She was most of all one of his buddies, and in this regard the relationship was perhaps unique in his life. By a kind of tacit common consent, they were never lovers—a situation that might have aborted friendship with this man who simultaneously revered and feared women. His domineering mother, frequently dressing him as a little girl, certainly helped prepare a lifelong pattern of sexual confusion, and his subsequent relations with women always bore the twin hues of fierce resentment and fantastic idealization. His "loveliest dreams," as he said, were often of Dietrich, who was "awfully nice in dreams"—a sentiment worthy of von Sternberg. With Dietrich, Hemingway could simultaneously enjoy the nurturing adulation of a beautiful and famous woman and the matey fellowship of someone who never threatened him by demanding sex; in this way, Marlene Dietrich was the ideal Hemingway heroine. He called her The Kraut.

Their correspondence flourished over the next twenty-five years, Hemingway retaining about two dozen of her letters, and she preserving his in a vault. Mostly they concerned shifts in her career, for Dietrich often turned to him for advice. "I never ask Ernest for advice as such but he is always there to talk to, to get letters from," she once said, "and I find the things I can use for whatever problems I may have." Uncertain over whether to accept a certain job, she received terse advice: "Don't do what you sincerely don't want to do. Never confuse movement with action." In those last five words, she said, "he gave me a whole philosophy." For her part, she countered by trying to introduce him to astrology, which in 1934 had recently struck her fancy and which would often occupy her for the next five decades. This he rejected, however, saying (probably unaware of the double meaning) that he did not want his life "run by the stars."

Nor, it seems, did Josef von Sternberg. The commercial failure of *The Scarlet Empress* conspired with his own gradual but ineluctable distance from Marlene Dietrich, and that autumn of 1934 he and Paramount's executives discussed terminating the six-year collaboration between them. To his relief, she agreed that they would part company after one final picture he was preparing. "She is a complete artist," he told the press, "and another director will be better for her now. We have gone as far as we can together, and now there is the inevitable mold or groove that is dangerous for us both." For the time being, he had nothing more to say, and Dietrich herself was silent.

BY AUTUMN 1934, B. P. SCHULBERG HAD LEFT Paramount and was succeeded as production chief by director Ernst Lubitsch. In 1920, the studio had realized considerable success with a silent film version of Pierre Louÿs's novel *La Femme et le Pantin (The*

Woman and the Puppet), and to this literary source von Sternberg turned as the basis for a new picture he intended as a Spanish fancy —indeed, he wanted to title it *Caprice Espagnole* (after the musical theme to be inserted into the film). But Lubitsch, after reading the outline and first draft prepared by von Sternberg and John Dos Passos, decided on the more provocative designation *The Devil Is a Woman.* The narrative concerns a cigarette-factory tart named Concha Perez (Dietrich) who seduces, ridicules and finally destroys a middle-aged officer of the Civil Guard (Lionel Atwill). He tries to dissuade a younger man (Cesar Romero) from dallying with "the most dangerous woman you'll ever meet," and their rivalry over her leads to a duel in which the older man allows himself to be wounded. Although Concha at first seems on the verge of leaving for Paris with the younger man, she returns to the muddled affair with the injured, bereft officer, a man virtually diseased by his own fatal passion for a devil of a woman.

In its final form, of course, the picture harmonized closely with the contours of von Sternberg's own tangled affective life. And so, after the veiled and historicized presentation of his star as an ambitious empress with a regiment of lovers, von Sternberg began what would be the most personal, most dazzlingly exquisite of their films —"because I was most beautiful in that," Dietrich said bluntly. (Since he had at last been formally admitted to membership in the American Society of Cinematographers, the director proudly thus affiliated himself with this craft union in the credits of the finished film—"directed and photographed by Josef von Sternberg, A.S.C.")

The recognizable, usually mundane and often tawdry settings of *The Blue Angel, Morocco, Dishonored* and *Blonde Venus* had borne the stamp of expressionist flamboyance in *The Scarlet Empress:* here, however, every visual detail is drenched in the hyperbole of madcap carnival, hysterical with the atmosphere of a romantically daffy jubilee. The picture opens with a six-minute scene of carnival revelry in Spain, circa 1890, amid a dizzy, serpentine panoply of confetti and ultrachic costumes. And then there is an odd reprisal of the situation in Rouben Mamoulian's *Song of Songs,* as if von Sternberg wished to appropriate that picture for himself by creating a narrative with the same players. Just as in the earlier film, von Sternberg's surrogate

(Lionel Atwill, made up and lit almost as a twin, complete with moustache) buys Marlene Dietrich from Alison Skipworth.

"I told her mother that I loved Concha," he says to Romero in words that precisely echo the relationship between director and actress, "and although there were certain ties I could not form [that is, marriage], I wished to provide for her, take charge of her education, in other words make myself her protector."

Concha was never, to the dismay of the officer, a faithful, loving companion, and when he finally confronts her treachery—"You're not going to play with me anymore!"—she screams: "This is superb! He threatens me! What right have you to tell me what to do? Are you my father? No! Are you my husband? No! Are you my lover? No! Well, I must say you're content with very little!" To which he cries, "Am I?" and lunges at her, attacking and nearly strangling her. An uneasy reconciliation scene is later followed by his suggestion, "Let's leave this miserable place," and her reply, "But I can't—my contract!"

"That woman has ice where others have a heart. She wrecked my life—there were others as well," Atwill tells Romero. (In *Blonde Venus,* it is said of Dietrich's character, "She's the proverbial iceberg who used one man after another.") The inevitable destroyer Lola Lola has now come full circle, and all the intervening variations of the tarnished woman come together in Concha Perez.

Never had the dialogue of a Dietrich-von Sternberg film so clearly matched real life, or so closely resembled von Sternberg's ultimate resentment of the fact that their relationship had not been one of Marlene the puppet and Jo the manipulator. It had, in fact, been the reverse in von Sternberg's perception, she had been the cruel woman—*la femme et le pantin*—toying with her plaything. (The inspiration for the image is a small painting by Goya in the Prado, of four girls tossing a male puppet into the air.) The fickle woman of the film finally drains her protector of life, and just as before with Menjou/von Sternberg in *Morocco,* so for Atwill/von Sternberg here: to love Dietrich is to be condemned to a fatal melancholy.

Five years later, the man's passion is beyond patience, expressed only through humiliation and rage. *The Devil Is a Woman* is in every sense the most moving portrait von Sternberg offered of his perceptions of his sometime mistress—here an intelligent and sensitive man is helpless to free himself from the narcotic effect of her allure, ever tragically aware of what is happening to him as he pursues a woman who will never give him anything to compensate for what he is losing.

As might have been expected, there were tensions during filming. "Von Sternberg made everyone's life miserable," recalled Cesar Romero years later,

> but he was especially mean to Dietrich. He bawled her out in front of everyone, made her repeat difficult scenes endlessly and needlessly until she just cried and cried.
>
> "Do it again!" he shouted. "Faster! . . . Slower! . . ." Well, he had been mad about her, after all, and now that their relationship was ending he took it out on her and everybody else.

Nevertheless, Dietrich remained, publicly, the consummate professional, obeying each command and agonizing over every detail of her role, wardrobe and makeup. John Engstead remembered that Paramount's wardrobe chief Travis Banton designed an elaborate Spanish comb for her, and hairdresser Nellie Manley fashioned braids from Dietrich's own locks, wiring these to the comb. Each evening, Manley snipped the bands and released the comb with heavy wire cutters as Dietrich fell forward, arms and head resting on her dressing table, tears streaming down her face, exhausted from the pain of this intricate device.

Soon studio accountants were in anguish, too. Not only was the film a resounding critical and commercial failure in its American release, but there was virtually no foreign exhibition. This was due to a curious intervention by the Spanish government, which objected to the portrayal of an official mocked by an immoral woman. On October 31, 1935 , Gil Robles (Spain's war minister) announced that henceforth all Paramount films would be banned in Spain unless *The Devil Is a Woman* were withdrawn at once from worldwide circulation. By November 12, the U.S. State Department entered the fray, ordering Paramount to recall and destroy all prints of the picture, which the Spanish ambassador had called "an insult to Spain and the Spaniards," and to burn the negative (happily, it was not destroyed; it simply "disappeared" for forty years). At the time, it was rumored that a commercial treaty then being drafted between America and Spain effected the studio's quick capitulation, which amounted to little more than blackmail, but the truth was even more reprehensible. A wealthy Spanish industrialist loyal to Franco had promised to back the foundation of a major film studio in Madrid if he could be guaranteed minimum foreign competition. A quiet, quick series of diplomatic maneuvers answered his request.*

BY MARCH 1935, THE COLLABORATION WAS HIS-tory. But unlike their proxies at the end of *The Devil Is a Woman,* the von Sternberg-Dietrich collaboration ended not because she walked out on her man but because in real life he walked out on her. "I am no longer Mr. von Sternberg's protégée," Dietrich told the press that month in an astonishingly pointed revelation.

> It is Mr. von Sternberg's own wish that we should be separated professionally—not my wish. I would prefer to go on as in the past. It is so wonderful to have someone look after your interests. He wants a rest, and he feels that this is the time for me to go my way alone. At all times he has been very courageous. He prefers to create pictures as he feels, and it is not I who wished this association to be broken, but he.

"He dreaded the day I would become a star," she wrote more candidly after his death,

> for he loved the creature whose image was reflected on film. Before von Sternberg took me in hand, I was no one . . . The films he made with me speak for themselves. Nothing to come

---

* With their usual calm cynicism, French film critics rose to the occasion. "L'Espagne de von Stern-berg n'était et n'a jamais été l'Espagne," proclaimed the editors of *Inteciné* in a typical comment that year. "C'était un pays imaginaire, un pays de conte, une espèce de paradis artificiel et romantique peuplé des fantasmes carnavalesques et d'amours impossibles . . . Pourquoi ce féroce auto-da-fé?"

could surpass them. Filmmakers are forever doomed to imitate them.

That spring, Paramount negotiated a new contract with Dietrich's agent, Harry Edington, which guaranteed her a total salary of $250,000 for two pictures over the next year, with the right to approve story and director; it was the most lucrative contract in Hollywood history, and it marked the beginning of an entirely new phase of her career and her fame. It was also a triumph of negotiation, for although Edington knew as well as anyone that Dietrich's popularity was in severe decline, he persuaded Paramount that separation from von Sternberg would reverse all that; Edington added that after all they still required a glamorous European à la Garbo. ("My salary is not large if you consider it is spread over a year," said Dietrich without irony. "To rent a house with tennis court and swimming pool, I must pay at least $500 a month." Few were inclined to offer much sympathy, especially after she leased a richly appointed home in Bel-Air, an enclave of lavish estates west of Beverly Hills.)

"I AM MISS DIETRICH, MISS DIETRICH IS ME," Josef von Sternberg had said. Now at last, with each fantasy revealed —from provocation to passion to revenge—the relationship had run its course. In their art, she was the triumphant character, but in the end the artist had to act in his own interest, and so he paid "a final tribute to the lady I had seen lean against the wings of a Berlin stage," and then he quietly withdrew.

In every one of their films, an older man had been displaced or replaced in the affections of her character; consecutively, they had been played by Emil Jannings, Adolphe Menjou, Warner Oland, Herbert Marshall, Lionel Atwill, Sam Jaffe and again Lionel Atwill. Just so in real life now, for with much Hollywood hoopla and a lucrative new contract Dietrich not only survived but went on to conquer.

As for Josef von Sternberg, he left both her and Paramount, wandering from studio to project and completing only seven films over the next thirty-four years; none of them was successful, none had the emotional wholeness of the preceding septet. In a way, he was both Pygmalion and Galatea, the ultimate victim of precisely the mythical creature he had created and promulgated. Restricted and made subordinate by his own fancies, he could really only celebrate her beguilement of him. And Dietrich was both enchanter and enchanted, too—thus also a victim of her own poignant need to please, of her ambition and her longing for professional security, of her dependence on a man she had (without malice) exploited.

After the favorable reactions to *The Blue Angel* and *Morocco,* American audiences continued to find her exotic and alluring, but even they gradually agreed with critics that visual splendor alone was unsatisfying. Sometimes, to be sure, Marlene Dietrich was photographed so magnificently that she seemed to be acting, but that, too, was mostly an illusion. Forever after, the autocratic, benighted lover and his obedient, heedless beloved never spoke of the wounded passion, the shared, secret history behind these seven confessional works, incomparable in the history of film.

9: 1935–1936

THE SPRING AND SUMMER OF 1935 WERE A period of pleasant indolence for Marlene Dietrich. Rudolf Sieber visited from Paris with Tamara Matul; he pored over his wife's accounts, met with her agent and with tax advisers, and together they took Maria for a New York holiday. The friendship between them continued unbroken, if not uncomplicated.

So did Dietrich's relationship with Mercedes de Acosta, who preferred a virtual oath of fidelity from the ladies with whom she enjoyed concurrent intimacies. Such a guarantee Dietrich was too aboveboard to provide, although she cannily learned not to divulge those details of her life that might estrange de Acosta. That year the two spent several days each week together, motoring to Santa Barbara for lunch, hiking in the canyons near Pacific Palisades or reading quietly at the home of one or the other. Dietrich's domestic nature shone—she baked and cleaned and rearranged her friend's closets and planned small dinners for friends.

Basil Rathbone (among others) was invited to these parties more than once with his wife Ouida Bergere, a slightly affected and amusing lady. Many claimed that when she wed the very English Rathbone she quietly altered for the record her real name (Ida Berger), birthplace (Brooklyn) and accent (also Brooklyn). He recalled Dietrich serving champagne and caviar, then disappearing into the kitchen for an hour, whence she emerged "fragrant and cool and lovely as if she had just stepped out of a perfumed Roman bath" and summoned guests to an elegant dinner she had herself prepared. At such gatherings Dietrich made no effort to conceal the nature of her relationship with de Acosta, nor did she feel compelled to announce the banns.

But it was of course always easier for two women to have social variations on the so-called Boston marriage, which could be interpreted as simply a warm friendship; men, on the other hand, could never be so open, and their careers were jeopardized by even temporal cohabitation. Later, when Janet Gaynor and Mary Martin took a holiday together (leaving behind their homosexual husbands), the public felt it was charming for them to enjoy some time for "girl-talk." It was widely known that Cary Grant and Randolph Scott—although, like Gaynor and Martin, married—enjoyed more than simply a platonic friendship; in fact, they shared a beach house every weekend for years. But finally they were given an ultimatum by RKO: Grant had to choose either Scott or contract renewal. As so often, professional considerations prevailed.

Quite apart from her open relationship to de Acosta, Dietrich blazed a fashion trail around town, making a tuxedo and fedora the *ne plus ultra* of chic women's formalwear and enabling women to challenge another level of sexual stereotype. In this regard, rightly popularizing those freedoms long enjoyed exclusively by unconventional women, she brought a refreshing candor and dignity to life in Hollywood.

In September 1935, Dietrich began filming the comedy *Desire,* directed by Frank Borzage and produced by Ernst Lubitsch, whose *Trouble in Paradise* (made three years earlier) it much resembled. As a glamorous and sophisticated Parisian jewel thief who makes the American naïf Gary Cooper her unwitting accomplice in the heisting of a pearl necklace, Dietrich was at last allowed a chance to do more than pose statuesquely. "Permitted to walk, breathe, smile and shrug as a human being instead of a canvas for the Louvre," ran a typical review, "[she] recaptures some of the freshness of *The Blue Angel* . . . Miss Dietrich is not dependent upon stylized photography and direction but has a proper talent of her own." Her half-smiles hinted at a wily subterfuge, she sang Hollander's "Awake in a Dream" with wry self-mockery and thus Dietrich effectively created a modern, credible character from an array of charmingly improbable situations.

No longer simply an excuse for von Sternberg's fantasies, Dietrich demonstrated in *Desire* a flair for comic timing and supple expressiveness and, having learned every technical detail, she readily suggested to cinematographer Victor Milner the best camera angle and lighting configuration for herself (and sometimes for Cooper as well). "She was a perfectionist," according to designer Edith Head, then working with chief costume designer Travis Banton. Early during the shooting of *Desire,* Dietrich kept Head working thirty-six uninterrupted hours at Paramount, pausing only for three hours sleep as she anguished over the choice of the right hat for one scene.

> We sat up for hours trying on dozens of different hats, changing them, tilting them, taking the feathers off this one and trying them on that one, snipping off a veil or a brim, switching ribbons and bows. Finally we got what she wanted. I was amazed at her stamina and determination.

Similarly, photographer John Engstead recalled that weeks later, after trying forty hats submitted by New York designers, Dietrich selected a dramatic black one Lubitsch and Borzage at once realized would excessively shade her face. She tried others, wearing each one at a deliberately wrong angle until the men yielded and allowed her to wear the black. When she saw the film's rushes next day, however, she had to admit that they had been right. Persistent she may have been, but always thoroughly professional.

Her studio education filtered into her home life, as visiting photographers and journalists often learned. Arriving there, they were taken to the living room, whose major light source was a single pinpoint spot focussed above the fireplace. Eventually Dietrich glided in and moved silently into place, leaning against the mantel and raising her head until the illumination of her cheekbones was dramatically presented to her visitors. "Falling into exciting and sinuous poses is second nature to Marlene," commented Engstead.

BUT HER CONCERNS THAT YEAR WENT BEYOND THE contours of her own glamorous image. Privately, the autumn and early winter were laced with the anxiety of a real-life drama and its tragic dénouement. Still encouraging her occasional sweetheart John Gilbert (then separated from Virginia Bruce), Dietrich insisted that Lubitsch and Borzage consider him for a supporting role—that of her suave ally in crime. Despite the ravages of Gilbert's drinking and the fact that he looked much older than his thirty-six years, the test was successful and he was engaged for the film. But just before production began, while he and Dietrich were swimming in his pool at Tower Road, Gilbert suffered a mild heart attack and had to be replaced by John Halliday. Even as she worked daily at Paramount through the final months of the year, Dietrich hovered consolingly round Gilbert, and after another more serious attack in December she became virtually the night and weekend nurse. She also decorated his home for Christmas, ornamenting a tree, filling the rooms with candlelight and performing holiday chores, food and gift shopping for him and his young daughter. When she had to honor a radio commitment that month (reading scenes from *Desire* on the "Hollywood Hotel" promotional series), Dietrich paid for a trained medic to replace her for two hours.

Nor was her generosity at holiday time limited to intimates. Paramount employees who served her or were in special need because of erratic employment or personal hardship received gifts with notes of gratitude. To her makeup assistant, Dot Ponedel, she gave a pair of crystal lamps, and Jessmer Brown (her studio maid), Arthur Camp (the property master on *Desire)* and others all received presents she knew they needed or fancied. When an elderly couple who had retired from the studio fell ill with influenza that winter, Dietrich twice drove to North Hollywood to prepare hot meals and clean their home. Such gestures may have had an element of *noblesse oblige* (and somehow Paramount's publicity department was always informed of them); but the recipients were touched by her sentiments.

But Dietrich's kindly vigilance did not entirely obliterate less admirable traits that could have serious consequences. One evening she and Gilbert saw that the car pulling into his driveway belonged to Greta Garbo; it was the closest the two women had come to meeting thus far. Gilbert rushed out for a brief chat with Garbo while her enduring rival remained in the house, misinterpreting the meeting as a grand reconciliation scene that would revive the embers of an old romance. When Garbo departed and he returned inside, Dietrich flew into a rage and left at once. Her refuge was Gary Cooper, only too eager to comfort her for what she described as Gilbert's "rejection." Imprudently miscalculating the effect of her actions on poor John Gilbert, Dietrich ensured that he knew of her resumed affair with Cooper. Gilbert then fell into a black depression at Christmas, drank himself into a stupor and sustained an even graver heart attack early in the new year. On the morning of January 10, despite the efforts of the physician she dispatched to his bedside, Gilbert suffocated to death in an alcoholic convulsion.

Crushed with remorse, Dietrich cancelled *Desire*'s postproduction still photography and confided her guilt to friends. More than that, she affected the role of Gilbert's widow, collapsing at the funeral on the arm of Gary Cooper. A week later, Gilbert's twelve-year-old daughter received a bouquet with a note attached: "I adored your father. Let me adore you." This turned out to be a hyperbolic and impossible request, for the girl had her own mother, and in any case Dietrich scarcely found time even for Maria.

The Cooper affair survived until June 1, when she and Clark Gable read scenes from *Morocco* on a radio broadcast. Dietrich did not ask for Cooper to reprise his original role and he, annoyed at her courting of Gable even professionally, imitated her conduct vis-à-vis the hapless John Gilbert and stormed out of her house.

AS IT HAPPENED, THE SAD EPISODE WITH GILBERT paralleled a time of professional unpleasantness owing to Dietrich's demand for absolute authority. Her next Paramount picture was to be a tangled romance first called *Invitation to Happiness* and then renamed *I Loved a Soldier,* with recent French émigré Charles Boyer. But producer Benjamin Glazer left the project in January, complaining that Dietrich's right of script approval and her insistence on instructing the cameraman were sabotaging his own creative contributions. Anxious when Ernst Lubitsch departed for an extended winter holiday, Dietrich was no more cooperative with the new studio production chief William Le Baron, nor was she satisfied when seasoned screenwriters tried to whip the scenario into shape. By February 11, 1936, more than a million dollars had been lost on a film two months delayed, for which only a few scenes had been shot. On March 4, she simply abandoned the production, and because by this time neither Le Baron, director Henry Hathaway nor writers Grover Jones and John van Druten had much enthusiasm for it, Paramount cut their losses.*

Because of this (and perhaps also because the Gilbert affair had caused some unwelcome local talk), the studio readily allowed Dietrich to work on a loan-out deal for independent producer David O. Selznick; he paid her $200,000 for the privilege of starring her in one of the first Technicolor movies.

On March 26, Selznick announced Marlene Dietrich and Charles Boyer in his forthcoming production of *The Garden of Allah,* based on a turgid Robert Hichens novel about a sultry socialite who goes to the Moroccan desert seeking peace of soul. There she meets and marries a nervous, priggish Frenchman, a renegade Trappist monk who now tends to stagger uneasily backward at the sight of a crucifix. Predictably, neither finds heavenly solace, and on his honeymoon he virtually swoons with guilt until she delivers him back to the monastery gates. This ending was not so much spiritually edifying as it was dimwitted (and to some offensive), not least of all

* Later the film was resuscitated as *Hotel Imperial* with Margaret Sullavan, but she fell and broke her arm on the set. Two years later, the film was completed and released, starring Ray Milland and Isa Miranda.

because it implied that God can throw a jealous snit and command a rivalry worthy of a Hollywood star.

Studio filming began in April, and at first there was some trouble with Dietrich, who was insisting more and more on controlling every detail of her appearance. But *The Garden of Allah* involved the more complicated business of color, and here she was not in her Sternbergian element. "I told her about the tales around town [concerning her interference]," Selznick informed the director of *Allah,* Richard Boleslawski, in one of his notoriously protracted memos,

> and she told me this was all nonsense and that she *never* indulged in such carryings on and certainly would not on this picture . . . I told her that my one other worry was about her performance—that she had demonstrated to the world that she was a beautiful woman, but that she had failed to demonstrate, undoubtedly through lack of opportunity, that she was an emotional actress . . . She said she had been wanting to prove this for years . . . [Since our conversation] Marlene has been working extremely hard, never leaving the studio until twelve or one in the morning. I think she has done a magnificent job on the costumes—better than could have been done without her supervision.

But the harmony was shattered within two weeks. By April 28, Dietrich was convinced that the script was dreadful and the film would therefore be a downright clinker. As it happened, she was right on both counts. Peppered with pseudopiety ("In knowing you and your beauty, I have known God!") and crowded with characters who speak only Latter-day Apocalyptic ("This is the land of fire— and you are a woman of fire!"), *The Garden of Allah* offered not even an occasional oasis of sense or feeling.

Because no one would listen to her complaints or suggestions, Dietrich thought only of the impact on her own career. A telephone call from von Sternberg confirmed that yes, he would come to her rescue, and so she launched a campaign to replace Boleslawski (a Russian actor-director from the Moscow Art Theater). This she tried to engineer by attempting the seduction of twenty-seven-year-old Joshua Logan, the dialogue coach and rehearsal assistant on the film (later an important stage and screen director). In his memoirs he artfully reconstructed an awkward comic scene that reproduced the effect of Dietrich's lifelong difficulty with the letter R:

"It's twash, isn't it?" said Dietrich of the script. "Garbo wouldn't play this part. They offered it to Garbo and she didn't believe the girl would send the boy back to the monastewy. She is a *vewy clever* woman, Garbo! She has the pwimitive instincts—peasants have, you know. Look me in the eye and tell me the twuth, now. It's twash, isn't it? You're a tasteful New Yorker. Admit it. It's twash."

When Logan protested that the picture would finally look better than it read (it did not), Dietrich applied another kind of pressure when the company was shooting in Yuma, Arizona. She invited him to her hotel room, where Joseph Schildkraut awaited a prearranged evening assignation with her. Dismissing him, she spoke elaborately and frankly to Logan of her love for John Gilbert, pointing to the pictures of him that filled her room, and to the votive candles that burned before each of them. She then poured him a drink, sat on her bed and beckoned him.

"You don't weally like Boleslawski, do you? . . . He's a tew-wible man. He's Wussian. No sensitivity. He can't diwect women. Wouldn't you like to see him wesign?"

"Resign? Good God, no. I think it would be dangerous for the whole project if he left now."

"Call up Selznick wight now," Dietrich persisted. "There's the phone. Tell him Boleslawski is not the wight man . . . If he left, we could get a good diwector—like Josef von Sternberg, who just happens to be available. He's exactly wight for this, and for me."

She poured more Scotch into Logan's glass "and kept getting closer and seemingly more affectionate" until he bolted. Despite her wiles,

Boleslawski remained on *The Garden of Allah* which (although it won the Oscar for cinematography) fully justified Dietrich's anxiety.

As the horrors continued to forecast the picture's critical and popular disaster, Dietrich pressured Boyer and other players to beg for a change of script if not of director. "I AM GETTING TO THE END OF THE ROPE OF PATIENCE," ran a telegrammatic howl to Boleslawski from the now financially strapped Selznick on April 28. "WOULD APPRECIATE YOUR HAVING A FRANK HEART-TO-HEART WITH MARLENE AND WITH BOYER . . . I AM NOT GOING TO FACE SIX OR SEVEN WEEKS OF THIS NONSENSE . . . I WILL HAVE A LOT MORE RESPECT FOR YOU IF YOU TURN INTO A VON STERNBERG WHO TOLERATES NO INTERFERENCE."

Dietrich was also tampering with basic realism, as she colored, lacquered and coiffed her hair and then summoned her hairdresser between takes to reposition each strand so that even when the desert wind blew she looked unruffled. This Selznick called "so nonsensical, when you can see the palms blowing. Surely a *little* reality can't do a great beauty any harm."

But in fact nature in all its torrid reality could do just that. On May 2, Dietrich collapsed in the 138 degree desert heat and work was suspended for two days. When she returned, she was no doubt cheered by the news that Paramount had not yet found a vehicle for her next picture and so, according to an unprecedented clause in her contract, the studio had to pay her $250,000 for nothing.

WITH *GARDEN* COMPLETE AT THE END OF JUNE, DIEtrich was therefore again free to accept another offer, which she quickly did when Alexander Korda (who had employed her a decade earlier in Germany) cabled from England, where he had settled and established a production company. And so in early July, with twenty trunks, thirty handbags, two maids and Maria, Dietrich boarded the *Normandie* in New York. "It isn't that I don't like America," she had told the press, saying yet again (as she had in 1933) that she might remain abroad permanently. "It is just that America is not my country." After leaving Maria with Sieber and Tamara in Paris, she proceeded to London to begin filming *Knight*

Without Armour, for which she earned $450,000. In 1936, Marlene Dietrich was the highest paid woman in the world.

At a press conference at the Dorchester Hotel, she met with Korda, French director Jacques Feyder and her co-star Robert Donat. Filming was to begin before the end of July, but Donat's chronic asthma turned suddenly severe. After a six-week delay, Korda—overburdened by high actors' salaries and the costs of main-taining numerous exterior sets at Denham Studios—understandably considered dismissing Donat and radically reducing his role for an-other actor. But Dietrich was adamant. Although a dozen men could have easily assumed the role and she had no reason to concern herself with his career, she informed Korda that she would not re-main with the project if he dismissed the ailing Donat—even if her own part were to improve in the bargain. Her gesture was duly noted and appreciated by Donat, his wife and family, and admired by her colleagues on *Knight Without Armour.* Throughout produc-tion, she was constantly alert for Donat's well-being, covering him with her own fur coat while they waited in the autumn chill for a camera setup.

But the film could not have been saved by the healthiest men in England. As a widowed Russian countess who flees the 1917 revolu-tion with the help of a British spy, she was required to do very little but pose prettily, swathed in chiffon or bathing provocatively as soap bubbles slowly burst in the tub. She was at first delighted to work with Feyder, a respected director who observed that

> she only makes "Marlene Dietrich films," and accordingly she is concerned with one thing only: that this will be a Marlene Dietrich picture. Her image, her face, her costumes—in her estimation, only these count. Her technical experience enables her to verify if the light on her face is positioned as she wishes. You can usually hear her ordering the electricians around: "Put two more lamps on the right . . . reposition the key light higher behind me."

Feyder also resented her peculiar notions about costumes, which refused to consider the script, the setting or the character's situation:

"It all has to serve Dietrich—that's the sole reality—and if she does or wears something anachronistic, well, then, you just have to change the script to conform to her wishes." He resented her manipulations, her subtle seductions of whoever might serve her best at a particular moment during production. "The reputation she has for cooperation is remarkable," Feyder considered, "for that's really the height of her illusion. When you see the finished film you realize she's had her own way in just about everything. Marlene Dietrich indeed has *so* much charm."

Cinematographer Harry Stradling likewise recalled that, to ensure her best appearance, Dietrich once again demanded a full-length mirror beside the camera, so that if she felt too much light on her arms, or if her shoulders caught too much from a certain arc, she could instruct Stradling accordingly.★

Preparing for her bathtub scene, Dietrich had informed only her dresser that she would perform nude (without the customary flesh-covered bathing suit invisible to the camera). Production workers are not easily astonished men, but there was some commotion that autumn day when Dietrich arrived on the set, tossed aside her robe and (as a witness recalled) expertly "slipped and sprawled, spread-eagled naked before the camera crew." She laughed, winked at her colleagues and went on with the scene. It was then learned that, as she had known in advance, a correspondent for *Time* was present. On November 30, 1936, Dietrich (clothed and with a distinctly Mona Lisa smile) graced the magazine's cover. Onscreen, her bubble bath was the sole moment of interest in a picture that otherwise induced in viewers only a stupefying lethargy.

But there was also a mild disturbance when the German actress Mady Soyka, wife of Dietrich's former Berlin agent, visited her dressing room; with her was journalist Willi Frischauer, who years later recalled the meeting. Soyka had been sent by Joseph Goebbels (Hitler's propaganda minister) with an offer of fifty thousand British pounds, payable tax-free and in any currency, if Dietrich would return to Germany for just a month to make one picture. "You can have anything you want," Soyka said. "Anything!"

★ Reviewing *Knight Without Armour*, Frank Nugent commented on Dietrich's attitude of "unpardonable complacence, as though she had just turned from a mirror" *(New York Times,* July 9, 1937).

But despite her widely quoted comment that "America is not my country," Dietrich had not implied that Germany was. Compatriots by the score in the United States, France and England had been telling her what the press had now begun to confirm, and so— brilliantly exploiting her trademark brand of aloof disdain—she cast a long, appraising, head-to-toe stare at Mady Soyka and then replied flatly, "This comes as a great surprise," referring no doubt to the condemnations of her that had become commonplace in the German press since the time of *Song of Songs*. Soyka increased the pressure: "There will be an immediate reversal of the press campaign against you. The German public will be suitably prepared for your return."

The political implications of this apparently casual meeting were enormous, but Dietrich—who knew she was being used like the 1936 summer Olympic games in Germany, for propaganda and prestige—would have none of it. "Darling," she said sweetly, spinning a fantastic fiction for Mady Soyka, "how nice of you to bring me this marvelous offer. What a pity I cannot accept it at the moment. You see, I am under contract for the next two years, which takes us to the end of 1938. Then I am committed to do a play on Broadway in 1939. Shall we not return to the idea perhaps in 1940 or 1941?"

Dietrich's visitor departed swiftly. When the Nazis later occupied Paris during the war, Soyka, a great beauty celebrated for her naturally golden hair, managed a café on the Champs-Elysées. But some members of the French Resistance were offended when she ostentatiously wore gems and bracelets that had once belonged to Parisian Jews who subsequently vanished. One day in 1942, so did she: it was later determined that the Resistance had whisked her off, coiffed and bejewelled, to a swift, quiet execution as retribution for her spying on French Jews.

DELAYS DURING *KNIGHT WITHOUT ARMOUR* DID not leave Dietrich idle. In her suite at Claridge's she welcomed interviewers and in midsummer returned briefly to Paris for fittings with couturiers. But most of her private time in London for the remainder of 1936 and into early 1937 was spent in the company of the American actor Douglas Fairbanks, Jr. Son of the spirited silent-screen star, he was pursuing a movie career of his own, mostly in England, where his social connections enabled him to enjoy the company of aristocrats, statesmen and even the confidence of some members of the royal family—among them George, Duke of Kent (brother of the still uncrowned King Edward VIII) and his wife, Princess Marina of Greece. A tall, articulate, witty and strikingly handsome man, Fairbanks was then divorced from Joan Crawford and had (as he described in his memoirs) a vivid and busy romantic life—until he met Marlene Dietrich that July, at a dinner party given by Alexander Korda. Only years after their last meeting did he learn she was eight years older than he.

Soon after the evening at Korda's, Fairbanks invited Dietrich to the premiere of his new film, *Accused;* she accepted, bringing along Rudi and Tamara, who were then visiting in London. At first baffled by the openly unconventional arrangement, Fairbanks quickly learned that the Siebers were, as he said years later, "really like brother and sister. It had, Marlene said, been a marriage only long enough for Maria to have been conceived, but they remained good friends and he managed her finances." Within a week of that evening, Fairbanks and Dietrich were spending most nights together, alternately in her suite and his new penthouse flat, very near Claridge's, at 20 Grosvenor Square, Mayfair.

At first, Fairbanks assumed their affair was "only her passing fancy"—doubtless a reaction not only to her obvious independence but also to the shrine on her bedside table, with a votive candle ever burning before a photo of John Gilbert. These items remained in plain view for over two months, as Dietrich persisted (so said Fairbanks) in "maintaining the fictitious drama that John Gilbert died because of her," an assertion stoutly rejected by Gilbert's family. The memorabilia were temporarily packed away only when she abandoned her hotel suite and took a small flat on the floor below Fairbanks in Grosvenor Square. There the relationship thrived without the awkward hindrances of Claridge's, where, on mornings after a formal event he had attended with Dietrich, Fairbanks had to descend a rear fire escape in full-dress tailcoat.

Although, as Fairbanks later admitted, he and Dietrich were not really in love with each other, it was "a relationship of more sophisticated intensity" than he had hitherto known. She was not only an ardent mistress; she also responded empathetically to the strained relationship between Fairbanks and his famous, powerful and somewhat intimidating father who "rarely seemed to be more than vaguely aware of my presence . . . I failed to win any real affection from him."

Douglas Fairbanks, Jr., was, therefore, not only an appealing and socially desirable companion she could respect but also one, like von Sternberg, to whom she could extend the kind of nurturing solace that was at once manipulative, parental and even somewhat detached. While neither as isolated as von Sternberg nor as wounded as Gilbert, Fairbanks was, at twenty-six, emotionally vulnerable after the failure of his marriage to the formidable Joan Crawford. He was nevertheless serious about his career and young enough to be responsive to an internationally famous woman who had raised tender domination to the level of a fine art. In his memoirs, Fairbanks described his mother, the redoubtable Anna Beth Sully, as a woman who "longed for—but seldom got—the kind of smothering devotion that she lavished on her own loved ones." His subsequent attraction to two equally strong women (Crawford and Dietrich) is not hard to understand.

Perhaps because *Knight Without Armour* had introduced her to a few Russian words (or because it was the name of the Duke of Kent's German shepherd), Dietrich gave Fairbanks the nickname "Dushka," a term of endearment. This was not only an effective code-name for messages and notes; she also had it engraved on expensive gifts for him, among them a gold wristwatch. On weekends during film production, the lovers regularly entertained for cocktails and dinner—unless they had accepted an invitation out of town, to Lady Morvyth's country house in Hampshire, for example, or to Coppins, the Kents' residence in Buckinghamshire. Despite widespread economic hardship, 1936 was for the upper classes perhaps the zenith of England's age of lustrous (if somewhat fanciful) social elegance. Dietrich, always magnificent to escort, was also enough of a Prussian traditionalist to be a zealous supporter of the English monarchy, a posture which could only have further endeared this glamorous star to her fashionable new friends. (Some, to her dismay, were as ardent in their support of Germany as she was of England.)

So much was Dietrich a royalist, in fact, that she was roused to dramatic action by the rumors of Edward VIII's imminent abdication for the sake of Wallis Simpson in early December 1936. Distressed that the king might indeed defy the advice of his ministers and the hopes of his people, she was suddenly convinced that she— and only she—could prevent history from taking a tragic course. The first week of December, Dietrich summoned her liveried chauffeur and, determined to dissuade the king (by seducing him, if necessary) from abandoning the throne for Mrs. Simpson, she motored down to Fort Belvedere in her enormous limousine. But her arrival in such grand style was a signal to the ever present press as well as the police, and despite her altercation with the guards, Dietrich could not gain admission. Within days, Edward broadcast his news to the world—an event which, she was persuaded, would never have occurred had she been permitted a meeting with His Majesty.

As Fairbanks recalled, Dietrich basked in her new aristocratic connections and began to exaggerate her own pedigree. During that season, she even seriously weighed the potential advantages of adopting British citizenship. She was, however, embarrassed by the fact that her uncle had commanded the first Zeppelin raid over London during the war, and she feared this being known. Not so her romance with Fairbanks. With the shrewdness of a Hollywood publicist, she refused ever to confirm the affair, then or later; on the contrary, she always allowed her relationships (even those that remained platonic) to be the more excitingly surmised.

DIETRICH'S AFFECTATION OF BEING LINKED TO A NO-ble lineage was, according to Fairbanks, another of her brilliantly assumed illusions. Well trained from childhood in the requirements of a beguiling persona, she played the role of glamour queen to perfection, invariably saying and wearing the right thing. Related to this, she spoke of von Sternberg as a godlike artist precisely because this reinforced her status as his ultimate masterpiece on the pedestal to which he had raised her. But there was, Fairbanks realized, another woman in Dietrich—a *Hausfrau* who put a towel around her head, scrubbed her lover's kitchen floor and then cheerfully prepared their dinner: "In these tasks, she divested herself completely of mysterious allure and became a fun-loving European woman who wanted to enjoy life." What she gave the public, on the other hand, was the part of herself elaborated by von Sternberg, and this role she grew to covet; indeed, she contributed quite willingly to the myth.

By coincidence, the myth-maker was also in London, and several evenings in late 1936 Dietrich and Fairbanks dined with von Sternberg, Korda and his own contracted star (and soon his wife), Merle Oberon. Ever loyal to her mentor—and well aware that Korda was in deep financial trouble because of the delays over *Knight Without Armour* and the failure of his films *Things to Come* and *The Man Who Could Work Miracles*—Dietrich told Korda that if he found something for von Sternberg to direct, she would forfeit payment of the $100,000 still owed on her salary for *Knight*. This generous offer he accepted, and shortly into the new year 1937, Korda replaced William Cameron Menzies with Josef von Sternberg as director of the forthcoming epic *I, Claudius,* starring Charles Laughton and scheduled to begin in February. But Laughton clashed constantly with von Sternberg, causing major delays and increased costs. Thus, when Oberon was injured in an auto crash, Korda had the excuse he needed to shut down the hapless picture. Von Sternberg, feeling more anxious and rejected than ever, was paid off, but the collapse of this promising vehicle and the subsequent invasion of Austria pitched him into a nervous breakdown. To Dietrich's dismay, he was virtually an immobilized catatonic for over a year.

ON JANUARY 18, 1937, DIETRICH WAVED FAREwell to Fairbanks, Sieber, Matul and Maria (who was on holiday from the Ecole Brilliamont in Switzerland) from the deck of the *Berengaria* and departed from Southampton. Back in Hollywood by mid-February after a sojourn in New York, she began a week's rehearsals for her last Paramount film—*Angel,* directed by Ernst

Lubitsch. This was perhaps one of the two or three most disappointing pictures of her entire career, and in it she gave nothing like a gala farewell performance.

In this arid, talky and unconvincing romance (based on a creaky Hungarian play), she was Lady Maria Barker, the neglected and bored wife of an English diplomat (Herbert Marshall). On a Paris holiday she meets a handsome American (Melvyn Douglas) who falls in love with her, and after ninety minutes of brave sentiments, whispered protests of love and ever so polite threats of disentanglement, the Barkers rediscover their lost love and the American parvenu nobly withdraws from the family circle.

Angel promoted the career of no one associated with it, and because the director and cast soon realized they had committed to a loser, tempers were as short as the dialogue's wit. Lubitsch and Dietrich, hitherto friendly colleagues, were barely speaking by the film's completion on June 14. One typical critique said straight out that Dietrich, although beautifully gowned, was "at the root of [the picture's] evils . . . The film comes to a full stop every time she raises or lowers the artificially elongated Dietrich eyelids," which she did so often that she seemed a sphinx without a riddle.

Away from the studio, her life was happier. Mercedes de Acosta hosted several welcoming soirées; Dietrich bought a snappy new white convertible roadster (for the impressive sum of $2,245); and in March she rented a house in Beverly Hills. Having moved so often as a child and never having had a permanent home even in her adult Berlin life, she was comfortable with frequent changes of residence; this was her sixth California address.

On March 5, Maria Magdalene Dietrich Sieber applied formally for American citizenship, taking an oath of allegiance in Federal Court before naturalization clerk George Ruperich. On her papers, she provided correctly all the details (the date and place of her marriage, and of her husband's and daughter's birth)—except one. She gave her date of birth as December 27, 1904, and thus three years were neatly subtracted from her official age.

Her application was not ignored in Germany, where a photo of Dietrich with Ruperich was accompanied by a comment in Berlin's *Der Stürmer,* Julius Streicher's notoriously anti-Semitic newspaper:

Marlene Dietrich, the film actress of German origin, has spent so many years with the cinema Jews of Hollywood that she has become an American citizen. The association with Jews has made her whole character quite un-German. In the picture we see her taking the oath in Los Angeles. The Jewish judge's contempt for the legally prescribed oath is revealed by his demeanor: in his shirtsleeves he administers to Marlene Dietrich the oath by which she betrays her Fatherland.

Apart from the usual Nazi malevolence, Streicher had the facts wrong: Dietrich would not in fact win her citizenship for two years (this was an application to begin the process), and Ruperich was third-generation Bavarian Catholic.

AFTER PLAYING THE LAST SCENES OF *ANGEL,* DIEtrich lost no time preparing to depart for an extended European holiday. Paramount, she knew from her agent Harry Edington, had no idea how to remedy the disaster they expected from the film and so were disinclined to renew her contract. Except for some kind words for her subtle comic gifts in *Desire,* she had not received any really glowing critical notices since *Morocco.* Additionally, *The Garden of Allah* was a terrific disappointment and advance word on *Knight Without Armour* was discouraging. Now thirty-five, she knew the film-fan polls showed disenchantment—even uninterest—after seven years and ten films of basically insubstantial Dietrich exoticism. For the past two years, she had been the highest paid woman in the world, receiving almost half a million dollars a year for very little actual working time. But that was all about to end, and now she had no indication that her career would endure; accordingly, she decided to retreat rather than sustain the scorn Hollywood so likes to heap on those once adored.

The summer of 1937 began in Switzerland, where she collected Maria at school and planned a holiday with her, Rudi and Tamara. Dietrich then dispatched a telegram to Douglas Fairbanks, Jr., in London, inviting him to join her in Austria. Unaware that the plans included an extended family, Fairbanks arrived two days later, astonished and disappointed to find what he termed "really a rather curious ménage."

The arrangement was indeed knotty even by the most tolerant criteria, and it suggested that Dietrich's relationship with Sieber could occasionally be at least casually carnal. Even as she shared a room with Fairbanks, she extended herself liberally, leaving their bed and blithely toddling down the corridor to join Rudi and Tamara—and not only for hot chocolate. This may, in an odd way, have had more to do with the latter than the former, for Dietrich saw "Tami" as a necessary, helpful adjunct to her own life: Matul not only made Rudi happy, she also looked after Maria's needs in Europe. And because Matul (also a product of the freewheeling Berlin life of the 1920s) was not immune to feminine blandishments, Dietrich may well have known that to please her would be, in effect, to please Rudi (and by extension Maria). "This design for living," Fairbanks reflected years later (alluding to the Noël Coward play about a romantic trio), "was really not within my experience, much less my desire, and I made known my displeasure—to no avail, of course. Why did I sustain it? I was completely carried away with Marlene." In this he was not unique.

Apart from this element, which seemed of concern only to Fairbanks, the summer was passed in pleasant indolence, and mother and daughter enjoyed an unusually protracted period together. "Her devotion to Maria was very touching," Fairbanks added,

> although she was so extremely maternal one wasn't sure whether this, too, was a part she was playing. But I remember thinking that the child had not much sense of who or where she was. It seemed to me an odd way of bringing her up, but of course no one criticized. That summer Marlene was the doting mother— until she decided to go with her public image again, and then she was the distant, remote and cool Venus.

This odd quintet remained several months at a rustic, timbered chalet on a lake near Salzburg. They visited Max Reinhardt at his summer festival there, sat on benches in the sunshine and drank huge steins of beer, dined at a local inn (or at home, where Dietrich as usual prepared the meals) and listened to Tyrolean music in the summer twilight.

By mid-November, Maria had been returned to her Swiss academy, Rudi and Tamara were en route to Paris, Fairbanks to London and Dietrich to Hollywood. During a stopover in New York, she received the unsurprising news from Harry Edington that Paramount had definitely decided not to renew her contract. The woman who could so recently command the richest deal in the history of movies was now unemployed, had established an expensive and indulgent lifestyle, and—with two years of back taxes still owed—lacked any source of income.

Before Christmas, on Rudi's advice, she sped to Los Angeles, moved her clothes out of her furnished house, dismissed her maid and chauffeur, sold the car and moved to a hotel. But despite the widespread knowledge that she was in effect out of work, she comported herself publicly with the serene dignity befitting Alexandra, the exiled countess she had played so prettily in *Knight Without Armour*. Independent as ever, she refused an offer to live with Mercedes de Acosta; instead, she exploited the sheer force of her charm and prevailed on the management of the Beverly Hills Hotel to open a long-term account in her name. That Christmas, she invited fourteen friends and cooked a lavish roast beef dinner in her private bungalow.

10: 1937–1940

FROM JUNE 1937 TO SEPTEMBER 1939, MARLENE Dietrich did not receive any offer to work; her career had suddenly stopped, although she had by this time achieved international fame and unprecedented compensation.

She was certainly not without a minor but effective talent, but this had mostly to do with her relationship to the camera; she was no Duse, and she knew it. Dietrich was, however, absolutely *sui generis,* and she never indulged in the petty hypocrisies of many stars. She stamped her own trademark, lived according to her own creeds, forged an image that was a direct reflection of her own social and sexual complexity. In important ways, therefore, she was perhaps the first triumphant example of self-promotion.

The suppressed passion, the mysterious allure and the almost diffident sensuality Dietrich conveyed were regarded by audiences during the Great Depression with the same adoration offered to Greta Garbo. But styles were changing, and in surveys conducted in fan magazines and theater lobbies, moviegoers listed their female favorites as Ginger Rogers, Irene Dunne, Luise Rainer, Bette Davis, Jean Arthur and Claudette Colbert—all of them more accessible, more *real,* somehow, less elusive and illusory—and none of them radiating the fatal sensuality of Dietrich or the inviolable allure of Garbo, both of whom were more suited to the earlier conventions of deliberately artificial, more romantic films. Much of this change derived from the techniques of cinematography and lighting, which by the late 1930s were sharper, more clarified—just as audiences no longer required the ever more fantastic escapist fare popular at the height of economic disaster. None of this was part of anything like a programmed approach to the business of moviemaking. Studios continued, on the contrary, to operate as they always had, responding seasonally to the whims of audiences and occasionally risking, on order from an executive, the creation of a new star.

In 1938, Dietrich could assume that she was only in temporary stasis, awaiting a new director, a first-rate script, a fresh offer from Paramount, a return to favor—or even, as she expressly hoped, an offer to work in France for a director like Jean Renoir; or in England, where, it was rumored, Josef von Sternberg would be welcome despite the collapse of *I, Claudius.* She bided her time, and on American radio programs she read some pallid romances with actors like Don Ameche, or engaged in comic repartee with Edgar Bergen and his wisecracking dummy Charlie McCarthy (who, as some might have observed, also wore a top hat and formal dress suit).

Tax authorities continued to hound her for monies past due, and that spring (acting on a suggestion from Harry Edington) she took a brilliant counteroffensive, claiming that she had not reneged but actually overpaid. Her husband could not work in America because he could not speak English, she said; therefore she wished to refile for each year since 1931, on the basis of community property and a shared loss. The case would continue to be argued for three years.

But her hopes for a new contract to revive her fading career were dealt a severe blow in May 1938. Harry Brandt, president of the Independent Theater Owners of America, announced in the trade journals *Variety* and *The Hollywood Reporter* (and newspapers across the country soon promulgated it) that certain players no longer pleased moviegoers and were therefore undesirable at the box office. This was not merely a rude display of Brandt's personal taste, for in the case of Dietrich, for example, *The Garden of Allah, Knight Without Armour* and *Angel* were indeed crashing financial failures in the theaters. Studios were accordingly urged not to make pictures with Mae West, Joan Crawford, Katharine Hepburn, Greta Garbo, Marlene Dietrich, and a few men like Edward Arnold.

West, munching breakfast in bed at one in the afternoon, took a reporter's inquiring telephone call: "Well," she drawled, referring indirectly to one of her classic comedies, "Brandt and his little men have done us wrong. All I know is that whenever the guys in the front office want to pay their mortgage, they call me up with an idea for a picture."*

Dietrich's response to the Brandt manifesto was an icy, wounded silence. But privately her life continued more or less cheerfully. By autumn 1938, the unstable European situation leading to war had brought Maria back to California (Rudi and Tamara were still in Paris). Dietrich enrolled her daughter in a private school and engaged tutors for extra language lessons and trainers for horseback riding. (One of Maria's best friends and sporting companions at the time was a wistful, nervous fourteen-year-old whose name had recently been changed from Frances Gumm to Judy Garland.)

That same season, Douglas Fairbanks, Jr., was making a picture in Hollywood, and he and Dietrich virtually lived together, spending nights at his home or in her bungalow at the Beverly Hills Hotel. They went out but rarely, and when photographed together at a restaurant or nightclub, Dietrich (as he recalled) "took this in her famous 'world-weary' manner, and I took it with a mixture of embarrassment and pride." Despite her professional crisis, he noted no especial sadness or anxiety in her manner that year, and they went through what he called "the motions of secrecy" about their affair— though he was sometimes "in a fury because Marlene occasionally swam in the buff" at the pool parties she gave on Sunday afternoon

* In this regard, it is perhaps important to remember how much a woman's medium film is; there is considerable truth in the generalization that women provide beauty and emotion onscreen, while men supply mere action. In film, men (no matter how attractive) are very much of this world, while women are always more susceptible to the transforming effects of lighting and makeup and can be rendered almost supernaturally beautiful creatures.

at her rented Santa Monica beach house (some luxuries evidently still being necessities).

"She enjoyed having her beauty appreciated," said Fairbanks with bemused diplomacy; such had been the opinion, too, of the film crew of *Knight Without Armour,* and of John Engstead, who recalled that she often welcomed photographers and reporters to her Paramount dressing room wearing only a sheer foundation garment or the skimpiest covering. Every performer has to be a kind of exhibitionist; a few can sometimes be defined by the term quite literally. For Marlene Dietrich—always comfortable exhibiting herself—"more" often meant "less."

On June 9, 1939, however, she dressed like the movie stereotype of a grade-school librarian, wearing a grey serge suit to take her oath of American citizenship—stating on her affidavit that she was born in 1905—not, as she had previously stated on the application, 1904 (much less the truthful 1901). Everyone politely ignored her new birthdate, and that evening, she and Maria left Los Angeles for New York, where Rudi awaited; they were to proceed thence for a European holiday. "I am glad to be a niece of Uncle Sam," she told reporters as she drew a gold-tipped cigarette from a platinum case after the ceremony.

As it happened, her Uncle Sam immediately decided to extract more than the tribute of gratitude from his new niece. On June 14, the Siebers boarded the *Normandie* for a summer on the Riviera, to be financed by savings Rudi had kept jointly on behalf of himself and his wife. But in addition to the passengers and well-wishers, the ship was bustling with agents of the Internal Revenue Service, who were much more punctilious about details than the Naturalization Office. For six hours, embarkation was delayed as federal officers Bernard Campbell, J. B. McNamara and Steve Ryan presented writs, liens and attachments, arguing with Dietrich and Rudi about a tax debt of $248,000, due on her 1936 British salary for *Knight Without Armour.* Her thirty-four pieces of luggage were at first removed from the *Normandie,* returned to her an hour later, then taken away again and finally restored while Dietrich, her New York lawyer William B. Jaffe and United States attorney John T. Cahill debated whether she should be forbidden to leave the country (and perhaps even be subject to arrest) with such an array of possessions while so large a tax debt was pending. (Wisely, Sieber—who had no legal responsibility for his wife's case, since he was not a citizen and had earned no American income—kept a quiet distance.)

At last they reached an agreement, much to the relief of impatient passengers, of weary baggage handlers and of the *Normandie's* officers, who were more concerned with tides than taxes. Dietrich, perched atop her largest trunk, dipped into a large handbag and withdrew $108,000 worth of diamonds, emeralds and gold. These she offered for an escrow account held by the IRS and by her attorney Jaffe against the final disposition of the government's claims; the shipboard brouhaha was the lead story in every New York newspaper the next day. (Remarkably, the government decided in Dietrich's favor, and all the gems were returned to her in May 1941—along with more than $23,000 she duly claimed to have overpaid for 1936.)

BUT THIS ANNOYING DELAY DID NOT FORESTALL THE gaiety of the six-day crossing. With the Siebers for the summer holiday was von Sternberg, whom they invited at the last minute. Recovering from his breakdown, he was carefully attended by Dietrich throughout the journey—but not as the recipient of her amorous adoration. That was reserved for another addition to their party, a famous German writer in exile whom the Siebers had just met that week in New York.

Born in Westphalia in 1898, Erich Maria Remarque had served in the German army during the first World War and was seriously wounded five times. Discharged after the armistice was signed, he worked as a teacher, cemetery stonemason, race-car driver and advertising copywriter, and then he began to compose articles on automobiles and sports. Throughout the 1920s, he worked diligently on his first novel, *Im Westen Nichts Neues (All Quiet on the Western Front),* a powerful denunciation of war which, published in 1929, brought him permanent fame and considerable wealth, inaugurating as well a serious if uneven literary career. The film version of that book, made in 1930, earned him a small fortune and ensured the future movie sale of several less impressive novels. In 1938, Germany officially deprived him of citizenship on the basis that *All Quiet* offended his country's soldiers.

A quiet, soft-spoken man who wore a monocle and drank too much, Remarque had arrived in America in early 1939 with his wife, Ilsa Jeanne Zamboui, whom he had divorced in 1932 but remarried in 1938 (somewhat diffidently and, it seems, only to provide her with egress from Germany and entry to America). By June 1939, Zamboui was in Mexico seeking a second divorce.* Shunning literary fame and the adulation of strangers, Remarque's taste for fine food and wine nonetheless made him a regular patron of those restaurants frequented by celebrities. Certainly no womanizer, he was also, at forty, not immune to the importunate charm of someone like Dietrich.

At New York's "21" Club that June, he was therefore not unresponsive when introduced to Dietrich. She shared Remarque's interest in nineteenth-century art (although she was far less knowledgeable), and he told her of his growing collection of works by van Gogh, Cézanne, Renoir and Degas. At once she was taken with this handsome, articulate man; and he with her, as he later told their mutual friend Stefan Lorant. That first evening, Dietrich invented an affectionate pet-name for Remarque: "Boni," an old Berlin schoolgirl's version of the Latin substantive meaning "good man" or "good guy."

But Remarque was attractive to Dietrich for reasons other than cultural: he had a somewhat dispirited, rueful demeanor when discussing the rise of Nazism and the world's apparently headlong rush toward another hideous conflagration. This combination of good looks, talent, sensitivity and a kind of general sadness was again irresistible to Dietrich (as they had been part of her attraction to Kreuder, von Sternberg and Gilbert, among others). "His melancholy and sensitivity bordered on the pathological," Dietrich wrote after his death. "I was deeply moved by this trait of his personality. Our special relationship all too often, unfortunately, gave me an opportunity to witness his despair."

* In 1958, he married the American actress Paulette Goddard. They lived mostly in Locarno, Switzerland, where he died in 1970 at the age of seventy-two.

That first evening, she offered her usual brand of consolation—herself. After spending the night with Dietrich in his suite at the Sherry Netherland Hotel (where, concidentally, she and Rudi were also booked), he immediately accepted the offer to join her little retinue for a summer in France. Romantic and visionary he may have been, but Remarque was after all a European, and he did not find Dietrich's domestic arrangement indecorous; for the next two years he was her most constant and frequent lover.

During the summer, the group's social circle widened in Paris and on the Riviera, and at various times the Siebers, Tamara, von Sternberg and Remarque dined and toured the countryside with the French actor Jean Gabin, whom they met in Paris. They also gave a cocktail party for the American ambassador to Britain, Joseph P. Kennedy, vacationing with his son John; and they attached themselves to a circle round the multitalented Noël Coward, whose stylish wit enchanted Dietrich. Without ever being introduced, she had telephoned him in May 1935 from Hollywood to congratulate him on his film appearance in *The Scoundrel*. Now, pursuing his friendship as she did that of Hemingway and Remarque, she began to learn Coward's songs.

This motley group assembled for much of July at the Hôtel du Cap-Eden Roc in Antibes, where in the evenings Dietrich held court with Coward as she crooned his songs and those of Hollander in her now smoky, swooping baritone. For European society and the social press, Marlene Dietrich was, at thirty-seven, a film actress on extended holiday and the star of a small but glittering cast of worshipful international luminaries. She led her friends a merry chase, wining and dining from Paris to Cannes and back again, to the gambling casino at Monte Carlo, to bistros in Juan-les-Pins. ("Nobody knows to what extent Marlene was seen with some of her men primarily for the publicity value," as playwright Moss Hart said.)

Several days each week, however, she and Remarque slipped quietly away from the group, motoring for an evening tryst at an inn near Antibes, or for picnics in the hills of Vence and Grasse and a night in a *petite auberge*. They drank Calvados and drove (at least twice) to Paris for weekends, strolling over and under the city's bridges and through the Tuileries and Jardin du Luxembourg: "the sturdy Kraut," as Hemingway called her, could obviously play the Gallic amorist, and Remarque was now the leading man in her drama.

Passionate the romance may have been; it was also laced with mutual suspicion and the remnants of Remarque's Bavarian Catholic guilt. Confident that their affair would sooner or later end, Remarque became the kind of gloomy, jealous lover who seemed fated to pursue his own unhappiness. He had perhaps tried to counteract his own rigid past with her unfettered present, but this was asking too much of himself, for he had come to resent her independence, her freedom to pursue another amour if that suited her.

For her part, Dietrich constantly told Remarque she could not live without him. In her way, she perhaps meant this, but her way was not so profound and imbued with philosophy as his. He wanted to discuss history, the arts, international affairs with her and with their friends; into such conversations she entered, but Dietrich preferred to haul out a portable phonograph, put on her recordings and describe for the group the difficult circumstances of each one's production or the film from which it was excerpted. She appreciated (in the words Ophelia used to describe Hamlet) being the observed of all observers. Nevertheless, that summer of 1939, Dietrich much depended on a kind of fierce sexual bonding with a fellow countryman who also provided intellectual excitement.

But by August, as the threat of war loomed ever larger, there were also career developments impinging on the summer's idleness. Although she had an offer to appear in a French film under the direction of Julien Duvivier (who had made *Pépé le Moko* and *Un Carnet de Bal),* there was also a most unusual bid from Hollywood. Joe Pasternak, an independent producer contracted to Universal Pictures, sent cables and portions of a script in progress called *Destry Rides Again,* planned as a raucous musical parody of cowboy movies, but with an underlying tenderness and a clear if subtle antiwar subtext.

Pasternak wanted Dietrich for the role of Frenchy, a hardboiled dance-hall girl who falls for the gentle strength of a new sheriff named Tom Destry; she begins to mend her evil ways, discovers the proverbial true love with Tom, and finally dies, stopping a bullet meant for him and fired by her former lover. But there was one serious drawback to the contract for her services. After the Brandt manifesto, Universal authorized Pasternak to offer Dietrich only $75,000 for the picture, just one sixth of her previous price. She hesitated, and not only because of the salary and the unglamorous role; additionally, at that time Universal did not have the prestige of, say, Paramount or MGM.

But Remarque (not von Sternberg, as she always insisted later) read the outline and sample script pages of *Destry Rides Again* and urged her to accept. Ignore the salary, he said; this movie might well revive her career and even create a new dimension to it. Her co-star was to be James Stewart, much praised for having rendered an appealing performance in Frank Capra's patriotic comedy *Mr. Smith Goes to Washington;* he had been chosen for an important featured role in a forthcoming film of *The Philadelphia Story* (for which he eventually won a best supporting Oscar). Quickly rising star though he was, Stewart's name would appear in the credits after Dietrich's; it would be her picture if she could make it so, Pasternak promised. On August 16, she obtained the only remaining pair of connecting first-class staterooms on the *Queen Mary* and sailed for America, with Remarque as her companion; the others followed soon after (Rudi, Tamara and Maria settling temporarily in New York).

A few days after war broke out in September, Dietrich was safely at Universal Studios for wardrobe fittings on *Destry Rides Again.* To the press she expressed anxiety for her mother in Germany, but there was still no mention to anyone about her sister Elisabeth. Even a long-term friend like Stefan Lorant was unaware of Elisabeth's existence. "Ah, that is easy to understand with Marlene," he said when informed in 1991. "It is simply part of the myth she has created—the legend of the only child."

The rest of the legend, however—the creature so rapturously conceived and presented by von Sternberg—was rousingly and immediately dashed to pieces by her performance as Frenchy, and as it happened audiences loved it. A vulgar, rowdy singer at the Last Chance Saloon in the town of Bottleneck, Dietrich had three songs, one of which—"See What the Boys in the Back Room Will Have"

—became as much a popular signature tune as "Falling in Love Again." Only for these scenes was she attractively dressed and photographed; otherwise, Dietrich fully cooperated in her presentation as a tarty hellcat: she swilled whiskey, munched crudely on a chicken leg, stuffed cash in her bosom (muttering with a smile, "There's gold in them thar hills"*) and engaged in a wild fistfight and wrestling match with Una Merkel, who played a jealous townswoman. Kicking, punching, rolling on the floor, shrieking like a savage, throwing chairs, doused with a bucket of water and still swinging her fists, Dietrich filmed the "catfight scene" over four days, after which she and Merkel were much bruised and scratched —but still friendly, especially after Joe Pasternak and director George Marshall promised that this sequence alone would make movie history. It did. In *Destry Rides Again,* Dietrich made Frenchy the most beautiful manly woman of her career, while her swagger made James Stewart appear even more gentle, more passive and feminine than Gary Cooper in *Morocco.*

Some of this is in the script, of course. First seen with a parasol and birdcage, Stewart is carefully introduced as the pacifist lawman who refuses to wear guns and speaks with an almost fearful gentleness. In the role of Thomas Jefferson Destry (the middle name capitalizing on his recent role as Jefferson Smith, who went so effectively to Washington for Frank Capra), Stewart—never really a sex symbol in American film—is not so much an adoring man but a kind of transforming, almost ministerial one, as sexless as a plaster saint. He recoils from Dietrich's languid but aggressive manner and her coarse, exaggerated makeup, and she is so impressed by his sheer difference from other men that she wipes off her lipstick and gazes at herself in a mirror, wondering if he is right about her looks. The moment is reprised in the final scene, when she dashes in front of Stewart to shield him from a gunshot. Taking the bullet and dying in his arms, she again wipes off her lipstick with the back of her hand, begging to be worthy of his kiss at last. The moment works in spite of its rather arch melodramatics.

---

* The line was somehow approved by censors, heard by preview audiences and noted in critics' reviews. But when it was widely reported as an example of the movie's humor, it was ordered cut by Motion Picture Production Code chief Joseph I. Breen during major national release.

Dietrich is the macho gal throughout. Lawless, promiscuous, brash, a satiric study in tawdriness, she dispatched a performance that restored her to critical and popular favor and demonstrated her eagerness to find the right blend of comedy and romance in a new kind of role. By her thoroughly physical involvement, she accepted that her earlier glamorous image had become obsolete. She wanted, in other words, to be one of Hollywood's popular breed of new leading ladies—to be ranked with the likes of Jean Arthur, Rosalind Russell, and even the imported Vivien Leigh—all of them strong, active heroines coping (sometimes toughly, sometimes comically) with serious social realities and, surprisingly often, outwitting male characters much in need of maturation and taming. These women played characters who were neither weaklings nor passive ciphers, and often they had the intellectual and moral superiority in the stories.

In this regard, Frenchy is no heroine, but she is certainly the only interesting character in *Destry Rides Again,* the sole person who changes and finally makes a grand gesture, even a sacrifice. Stewart's Destry is simply the nice voice of decency, a kind of *Mr. Smith Goes to Bottleneck;* Dietrich's Frenchy, however, moves the story forward from inner transformation to outer action. Her long, slow gazes in this picture are no longer the morally indifferent affectations of a world-weary mannequin; accompanied by her oddly appropriate pauses, these looks signalled the character's fresh perceptions. Photographed by Hal Mohr with a sharp realism and minus the sanctifying diffusion favored by von Sternberg, Dietrich appears amused when others in the story are anxious, serene when they are frenzied, and at every moment she is a surprising counterpoint to the typical barroom moll. In her rumbustious manner and gun-toting singing, she had the opportunity to demonstrate her flair for comedy even more than in *Desire.* Her Frenchy conveyed an innate understanding that a hussy is not necessarily a harlot.

Produced the same year as *Stagecoach, Drums Along the Mohawk, Jesse James* and *Union Pacific, Destry Rides Again* was the second of four screen versions of the same story (inspiring some forgotten wag to call it *Destry Rides Again and Again and Again).* Inevitably overshadowed in 1939 by *Gone With the Wind, Wuthering Heights, The*

Wizard of Oz and *The Grapes of Wrath,* the picture retains a lively sassiness, but it is the presence of Dietrich (at first undesired by Universal, who wanted Paulette Goddard) that enabled the story to find its deepest logic, uniting the tensions of the western-frontier tale with the exigencies of both the musical and the screwball comedy—and giving it, in the final analysis, a credible humanity. For the first time in years, audiences adored her.

DURING A DEMANDING SIX-WEEK SHOOTING SCHEDule that autumn and winter of 1939, Dietrich was also socially busier than ever. Always fascinated by astrology, she now began to consult professional stargazer Carroll Righter on a thrice-weekly basis. No, she would tell a friend, the stars were inauspicious for a weekend trip to Palm Springs; or yes, Carroll has approved her appointment for an interview and photo session two weeks from Thursday. To friends like Hemingway, Lorant, Fairbanks and others her belief in celestial influences seemed genuine; but invariably this philosophy enabled her to live according to her convenience, while offering the unassailable argument of faith as her sure defense. The intersection of Mars with Jupiter's seventh moon somehow never dictated an inopportune duty or a troublesome engagement.

Righter, a cultured and influential homosexual with a large Hollywood clientele, was also an enthusiastic advocate of Dietrich's industrious sex life, and this, too, may have won her appreciation and helped to justify her trust in his counsel. As if she were a historic lady predestined for majestic intrigues, Righter supported her dizzy round of alternate nights with Fairbanks and Remarque and with the French actor Jean Gabin, who began visiting Los Angeles in 1940. By grave references to heavenly charts and zodiacal concurrences, and with much furrowing of his brow, Righter advised Dietrich to see Fairbanks on this evening, Remarque on that, Gabin on the other, Mercedes de Acosta on such a weekend; this advice, which she frankly disclosed to each one, was received with amusement—at least, perhaps, when desires were not too often frustrated.

But besides acting like a kind of noble courtesan under the tutelage of a popular occultist, she often resembled a character in a bedroom farce by Beaumarchais. Once after a day at the studio, for example, she had planned—on Righter's advice—an evening with Fairbanks, and in her bungalow at the Beverly Hills Hotel she was hurrying to prepare for his arrival when Mercedes de Acosta swept in unannounced and asked for a drink. This she sipped in the bathroom, chattering away while Dietrich bathed. When the telephone rang, de Acosta obligingly took the call and, recognizing the voice of Erich Maria Remarque, reported coolly that Dietrich had gone out for the evening. That was impossible, Remarque replied: he was to have visited her an hour earlier and was calling to announce he was nearby and en route. De Acosta lied that Dietrich had already departed—to which Remarque replied that he would come to see that for himself.

When Dietrich was told about the call, she suddenly remembered that indeed she had promised to listen to Erich read aloud some pages of a new novel he was writing. De Acosta, none too pleased with this ongoing male competition, then departed—but without telling Dietrich that Remarque was soon expected. Moments later, Fairbanks arrived and, typically, Dietrich brought him to her room while she dressed, intending to shuffle him out a back door with the protest of a sudden sick headache. But before she could play this scene, Remarque approached her door. Fairbanks sprang to answer the knock, and, although nonplussed, he acted with his usual grace and offered Remarque a drink. When Dietrich finally entered the room, she surveyed the awkward atmosphere and decided on a casual finesse. "I have so looked forward to introducing you two gentlemen," she said. "Now, where shall we dine?" As they gazed at her blankly, the doorbell chimed again, and there stood Josef von Sternberg, who swept her up in a passionate embrace (ironic only to them both) as if she had no other love in the world.

BUT SOON DOUGLAS FAIRBANKS, JR., GREW WEARY of being a rival for her time and attention—"not only from the more assured and intellectual Erich Maria Remarque," as he admitted, "but [also when I discovered] some intense love letters from someone I'd never heard of." The writer of these passionate documents was none other than Mercedes de Acosta, with whom Dietrich was of course still involved (most often at de Acosta's home in Brentwood once or twice a week, and sometimes for weekends at a Santa Barbara hotel). Fairbanks confronted Dietrich with the letters, and she was as resentful of his prying as he was of her bisexual philandering. Harsh words were exchanged, the relationship swiftly began to cool, and by spring 1940 Marlene Dietrich and Douglas Fairbanks, Jr., ended an affair that had blazed brightly for almost four years. After the war, a less complicated, platonic friendship resumed.

On the other hand, Dietrich's relationship with Remarque was unaffected by the de Acosta affair, perhaps because his earlier years in Germany had familiarized him with a more freewheeling lifestyle. As a student of human nature, he found Dietrich an endlessly fascinating conundrum as well as an admiring and attentive mistress. Sometimes he viewed her, as he told their friend Stefan Lorant, rather like a "sailor's daughter," an unsubtle woman of roaring ardor; when she wished, however, she was "[the goddess] Diana of the woods, with a silver bow—invulnerable, cool and fatal."

But whatever his sexual enthrallment, Remarque accepted the paradox of Dietrich's attachment even while he knew of her inconstancy. Perhaps the most perceptive and reflective among her men, he also recognized the difference between sexual passion and commitment, and Marlene Dietrich (he soon realized) was proficient at the former but apparently incapable of the latter; she was entirely a creature of whim and of the moment. Nevertheless, he became (like Fairbanks before him) a complaisant lover, and as permanent witness to this he left an encoded account of their romance in the novel he was writing at this time—*Arch of Triumph*. (Much altered, *Arch of Triumph* became a rather dewy 1947 romantic film starring Ingrid Bergman and Charles Boyer.) The published book bore no dedication, but Dietrich knew it was hers.

Set in Paris and on the Riviera in 1938 and 1939, the narrative concerns a German refugee surgeon named Ravic (surrogate for Remarque) and his tortured affair with an enigmatic cabaret actress and occasional film star named Joan Madou (Dietrich), who is described as pale and detached, "an exciting and forlorn beauty [with]

high brows . . . [and] a face whose openness was its secret. It neither hid nor revealed anything. It promised nothing and thereby
everything." Joan is "sometimes superstitious . . . and she was everything that enticement and temptation could give without love."
One scene neatly synthesized the author's ambivalent feelings about
Dietrich:

"Joan," he said slowly, and wanted to say something entirely
different, "it is good that you are here."

She looked at him.

He took her hands. "You understand what that means?
More than a thousand other words . . ."

She nodded. Suddenly her eyes were filled with tears. "It
doesn't mean anything," she said. "I know."

"That's not true," Ravic replied, and knew that she was
right.

"No, nothing at all," she said. "You must love me, beloved.
That's all."

He did not answer.

"You must love me," she repeated. "Otherwise I'm lost."

Lost, he thought. What a word! How easily she uses it. Who
is really lost does not talk . . . He knew their love would not
endure, that it would become the stale vinegar of dead passion.
It would not last.

Arch of Triumph did not reach its final form until 1945, long after
the Remarque-Dietrich affair had ended; it has both the luxuriant
guilt and the tainted wistfulness often found in novels that are simultaneously defensive and sealed with the author's regret for a failed
romance. Even while Ravic and Joan Madou manage to visit every
colorful locale frequented by their real-life models, the wine of their
love indeed turns sour. The protagonist resents both his mistress's
free love life and his own fierce passion for her. At the conclusion of
Arch of Triumph, Remarque the benighted lover clearly inspired Remarque the professional fantasist: just as his affair with Dietrich
ended when she invited actor Jean Gabin to live with her, so the
actress Joan cavalierly moves to a jealous new lover—who finally

shoots her. Ravic is summoned, but even his medical skill cannot save her, and she dies in his arms, begging forgiveness. The book remains valuable as a testimony of Remarque's tortured, ambivalent feelings for Dietrich. But judged even according to the most lenient literary standard, *Arch of Triumph* is bloodless, ersatz Hemingway; to call it unremarkable would be high praise.

THE FIRST RENAISSANCE OF DIETRICH'S CAREER HAD been inspired by Josef von Sternberg in 1930, but Joe Pasternak was now responsible for the second revival of her career. Audiences loved Dietrich's rough-and-tumble humor in a musical western, and critics admired her complete abandonment to a self-contained satire on her own demimondaine image. *Destry Rides Again* could have been marketed as *Dietrich Rides Again*.

She had, therefore, good reason for optimism at the start of 1940. The principal witness to this was Remarque, "one of the first refugees who benefited from my protection," she said rather loftily. Remarque took a room at the Beverly Hills Hotel near Dietrich's bungalow, where she lived with Maria, whom Rudi and Tamara had delivered to California before returning to settle for several years in New York (where he worked at Paramount's East Coast office). In such proximity to the glumly adoring Remarque, Dietrich could easily be very protective indeed.

Contrary to her mother's good fortunes, Maria was enduring a most unhappy period in her life. Although she had never lacked life's material necessities and had been pampered with gifts and good times by her father and (when work and affairs permitted) by her mother, Maria felt she could neither please her nor ever compare favorably with her—could never, in other words, really be worthy of so famous and glamorous a parent. "The greatest compliment ever paid to me," Dietrich said at the time, "was 'You spoil your daughter.' " But as usual the spoiling was not entirely beneficial. Dressed in miniature versions of her mother's elegant clothes, she was from the start groomed for beauty and fame; she had even been taught something about makeup and costumes the day she filmed her scene as young Sophia in *The Scarlet Empress*. Thenceforth, as she grew, Maria was (always with the excuse of economy) given her mother's cast-off designer clothing.

As playwright Enid Bagnold wrote in *The Chalk Garden,* "An only child is never twelve." For Maria Sieber, the years between twelve and seventeen were unnaturally desolate, with her father rarely present and her mother courting both her career and a small platoon of lovers. Imprudently, always offering the fear of kidnapping as reason enough, Dietrich kept her daughter home from traditional schools and engaged private tutors, thus effectively depriving the girl of normal socialization. "I had no friends my own age, and I was never permitted to leave the grounds," Maria later said wistfully. "Bodyguards were the only friends I had."

The outcome was perhaps predictable. By age fifteen, in spring 1940, Maria was bearing—to the point of almost seventy excess pounds—the burden of a lonely and troubled adolescence. Her sudden and alarming weight gain (to almost two hundred by the following year) may have derived from a subtle refusal to wear her mother's clothes and thus be a mini-Marlene, as well as from her sense of social isolation.

"I was always self-conscious because of my mother's beauty," Maria acknowledged later. "She was so beautiful that it always gave me a feeling of ugliness and unworthiness. All my life I suffered because I was terribly overweight and I felt my mother [was] ashamed of me . . . I got fat because my childhood was miserable." In this regard, Dietrich's failure to seek medical treatment or counselling for Maria is (notwithstanding her evident good intentions) not hard to understand. Actresses who depend professionally on their beauty cannot, as their children mature, deny the truth of their own inevitable aging—whatever the extent of nature's gifts or a surgeon's cosmetic remedies. More to the point, an unattractive daughter is no threat to a mother's primacy. The pattern has nothing to do with malevolence; such is often the garden variety of parent-child rivalry.

"Mother and I were never like mother and daughter," Maria added. "As I matured, I was often taken for her sister—an older sister, because I was so heavy. I have always felt the older one in our relationship." Dietrich, on the other hand, was quite oblivious to any difficulty. With no awareness of her condescending irony, she remarked that year, "Maria is as American as a colored girl."

The problem became more poignant throughout 1940 and 1941, when Maria—obviously feeling unattractive, unwanted and unloved —for a time seemed to harbor an alarming death wish. At first her obsession was merely academic, as she immersed herself in books about cancer, tuberculosis, infantile paralysis and all sorts of life-threatening illnesses. But then she began to speak occasionally of taking her own life, in which mood she wrote a morose little lyric she handed to her mother:

> *A man who was committing suicide*
> *Said, as his feet left the earth*
> *Which had grown too small for him:*
> *"How soon shall I regret this?"*

Dietrich, seeing only her daughter's inchoate lyric gifts, proudly showed the quatrain to Ernest Hemingway and Dorothy Parker (whose own grim sensibilities were perfectly matched to the young poet's); they only remarked on the child's gravity.

But Maria never acted out her darkest fantasies; instead, she began to take an interest in the theater. Her life had little comfort or stability until she contracted her second marriage (at the age of twenty-two) and began her own career. "Mommy grows younger and more beautiful every year," she said when still young, "[but] I never felt good enough for her."

During the summer of 1940, Mommy (then thirty-eight) was certainly considered beautiful and popular enough by executives at Universal that, when Joe Pasternak asked for her to star in another comedy, she was readily signed at twice the salary of *Destry Rides Again*. Pasternak had commissioned writers John Meehan and Harry Tugend to capitalize on the success of *Destry* and Dietrich's self-satire by constructing a spoof of the Sadie Thompson–South Seas epic subgenre. Accordingly they created the role of "Bijou Blanche," a torch singer of benevolent ill repute who floats from island to island, following and wreaking havoc among the fleet. They all arrive at a gin joint called—thus the film's title—*Seven Sinners,* on the fictitious island of Boni Komba, a name contributed by Dietrich and inspired by her nickname for Remarque. Among the latest naval arrivals is a tall, handsome lieutenant (John Wayne) who almost loses his career for her sake; they part, and Bijou returns to a boozy ship's doctor and a wandering life.

Pasternak and director Tay Garnett suggested the rugged, six-feet-four-inch John Wayne to play Dietrich's leading man. Although Wayne, a contract player at the B studio called Republic Pictures, had made more than eighty films since 1927, he had just appeared in *Stagecoach* and was on the brink of his mythic stardom. But his salary was still merely four hundred dollars a week, and he was supporting a wife and children. Wanting Dietrich's approval, Garnett invited Wayne to the Universal commissary for lunch and arranged for Dietrich to walk casually nearby to assess him. "With that wonderful floating walk," according to the director, "Dietrich passed Wayne as if he were invisible, then paused, made a half-turn and cased him from cowlick to cowboots, then turned to me and whispered, 'Oh, Daddy, buy me *that!* '"

According to John Wayne's third wife, Pilar (not married to him at that time), the subsequent developments were sheer Dietrich. Wayne was invited for a private conference in her Universal dressing room one day that June, after a session of wardrobe fittings for *Seven Sinners.* Dietrich dismissed the others, closed and locked the door and fixed a provocative look on Wayne while slowly asking the time. Answering her own question, she then lifted her skirt, and there, encircling her upper thigh, was a black garter with a watch. She noted the time, slowly lowered her skirt and glided toward Wayne, whispering, "It's very early, darling. We have plenty of time." That afternoon began one of the most intense affairs of their lives, "one that wouldn't burn itself out for three years," as Pilar Wayne knew: "Dietrich was more than an ideal bedmate. She was the first person in the film industry, excepting John Ford, to tell Duke that she believed in him . . . Dietrich made Duke feel like a man again, both in bed and on the sound stage."

During the two months of shooting *Seven Sinners* that summer of

1940, Hollywood insiders soon knew that Marlene Dietrich had made an important conquest. While Erich Maria Remarque sat in his hotel room nursing his romantic wounds and forcing the typescript of *Arch of Triumph,* his inamorata was photographed all over town with John Wayne, whose estranged (but not legally separated) wife, Josephine, began to make a noise that eventually terminated her marriage. The press not only documented Dietrich and Wayne at the Brown Derby, at the Mocambo, the Trocadero and at the beach; it was also announced that Dietrich had taken Wayne's financial future in hand, introducing him to her own business manager, a Swedish immigrant named Bo Roos. She cooked for Wayne in her bungalow and brought his meals to the Universal set each day; they played parlor games during shooting breaks, attended football games and prizefights, sped out of town on weekends for fishing trips to Lake Arrowhead or for quiet times in Montecito and San Luis Obispo.

With Fairbanks, Dietrich had a polished, sophisticated and compassionate gentleman for a lover; Remarque was the dour, grave intellectual she could both comfort and learn from; but with John Wayne, it seems, the matter was simpler. According to all accounts, they never spoke of marriage; they were simply buddies who bedded. And when it was over (after they had made a trio of films together), Dietrich clearly felt neither residual affection nor loyalty. "Unpleasant people, actors," she wrote curtly years later. "First of all, John Wayne. He needed money, and he begged me to help him . . . John Wayne wasn't exactly brilliant: he spoke his lines and that was all. Wayne was not a bright or exciting type. He confessed to me that he never read books, which proves you don't have to be terribly brilliant to become a great film star."

Their first picture remains their best, for *Seven Sinners* offers one of Dietrich's splendid comic portraits as well as a performance of gentle, self-knowing sadness. The action begins at the Blue Devil Café (clearly homage-by-inversion to *The Blue Angel),* where she causes a riot by simply being. Deported with her cronies to another South Seas isle, she sings "I Can't Give You Anything But Love" en route and later "The Man's in the Navy" at her new venue (the latter crooned in sparkling white navy drag). Learning that the fleet has arrived, she turns, takes in a sea of white-coated sailors and whispers, "Oh—the navy!" Slowly approaching them, she smiles, then stops everything in the room by asking, "Will someone please give me an American . . . [pause] . . . cigarette?"

Of all Dietrich's films between the last with von Sternberg (1935) and her work for Hitchcock (1949), her Bijou is—with Frenchy—one of her two best performances, for in it she perfects the art of the double-take, the wordlessly smoldering reaction, the cool ingestion of a man's intention. "How about coming to my cabin for a snack?" asks Albert Dekker as the ship's doctor. She stares at him, and he has to elaborate: "A snack is food." Her comic turns were carefully timed, her glances alternately inciting and reflective; there was, in other words, a recognizable woman, and some of each character she played was part of herself. Cunning, versed in masculine wants and feminine wiles, Dietrich was clearly in her element as Bijou. She was in this picture, as a typical review noted, "giving one of the finest performances of her career with verve and brilliance."

Pasternak and his colleagues at Universal knew they had another Dietrich success in *Seven Sinners,* and after filming was completed on September 14 they rushed through editing and scoring; the picture was released within weeks. Throughout the autumn, meanwhile, it became clear to more and more people across the country that the Dietrich-Wayne friendship was more than professional, for they were still seen as a nightclubbing couple—and not just as a duet. In a ploy to confuse everyone, she insisted that photographers snap them with Erich Maria Remarque, or her old friend Stefan Lorant, or with Douglas Fairbanks, Jr., or Jean Gabin (soon to play an even larger role in her life), or even with Mercedes de Acosta and a visiting Rudi Sieber. Indeed, that entire curious octet attended the Hollywood premiere of *The Thief of Baghdad* together in December.

Arranging a squad of escorts for the benefit of local cameramen was inspired. First of all, she knew it would be difficult for people to believe what was in fact the truth—that she would flaunt multiple, simultaneous love affairs. Second, the photograph, with a smiling

Sieber in attendance, would neatly suppress any rumors that her marriage was threatened. Finally, the image of Marlene Dietrich surrounded by so adoring a team effectively presented her as one of the most daringly irresistible women around town. No publicist could ever have promoted her more shrewdly.

11: 1941–1944

"ONE AMERICAN CRITIC WROTE THAT I had contrived to parody her," the French director René Clair said of Marlene Dietrich's role in *The Flame of New Orleans,* his first American film. "But she understood this. I didn't do it against her will. When Norman Krasna and I wrote the script, we intended that it be ironic—a romance with a sense of humor. Perhaps that's what surprised the public: they didn't know quite how to take it."

Alas, there was little to take. "I'm going back to New Orleans," said Dietrich as Frenchy toward the end of *Destry Rides Again;* that was the inspiring cue for Clair, Krasna and producer Joe Pasternak. As an elegant adventuress who courts a rich man, pretends to be her own slatternly cousin and eventually falls in love with a poor sailor, she was *The Flame of New Orleans,* and the picture was designed to be suffused with those delicate Gallic ironies for which Clair was previously admired (as, for example, in his French films *Sous les Toits de Paris* and *Le Million).* But the antic glee and appealing nonsense of *Destry* or *Seven Sinners* are absent from this mild confection, which

—only on paper—had all the ingredients of a riotous Feydeau farce.

Disliking the script ("a flop"), her director ("he wasn't exactly one of the friendliest men") and her co-star Bruce Cabot ("an awfully stupid actor"), Dietrich was bored from the first day of production in February 1941. As usual, she had a song, but it required a soubrette's range and delicacy; consequently—much to her dismay—her voice was electronically altered, the speed of the post-dubbing accelerated so her voice would sound higher. Attempting to salvage a doomed project, Dietrich assured that she was properly lighted and then simply purred her lines seductively, with a kind of dry-ice eroticism. ("There's more to being a gentleman than wearing tight pants," she murmurs to Cabot, surveying him head to foot with astonishing indelicacy.)

Pasternak and Clair had tried valiantly to satirize the world-weary romanticism of von Sternberg's Dietrich; oddly, the result was anemic—simply Dietrich *exagérée,* nearly suffocated in a profusion of rococo white ruffles and feathers. Neither critics nor audiences were much amused by its windy languor, and *The Flame of New Orleans* fizzled quickly when it was released in May 1941, just weeks after production had been completed. Because Universal had also lost money on *Seven Sinners,* executives were glad to loan Dietrich out to Warner for her next film, which turned out to be the second of three failures for her that year. The Dietrich renaissance seemed suddenly imperilled.

Not so her romantic life. In the spring of 1941, John Wayne was still meeting Dietrich regularly at the Beverly Hills Hotel, behind the locked door of her studio dressing-room, and for occasional weekends at a Santa Barbara inn. She dictated what ought to be the terms of his contract renewal, and Wayne explained to her the fine points of football and boxing. Their affair was monitored gloomily by Erich Maria Remarque, who hoped it would not long endure and so expressed himself to Dietrich, who calmly insisted on her independence. As it happened, Remarque's hope for an end to the fiery romance was fulfilled, although the embers were not completely extinguished for another year. But in 1941, Remarque had a more serious rival than John Wayne.

Dietrich had first met the French actor Jean Gabin in Paris, in 1939. Almost three years her junior, he had been an adolescent runaway and street brawler who eventually danced with the Folies-Bergère at the age of nineteen and appeared in plays and films from 1930. Then, in a series of French films (among them *Pépé le Moko, La Grande Illusion, Quai des Brumes* and *La Bête Humaine),* Gabin became firmly established as the prototype of the tough, sardonic marginal hero or the curiously sympathetic antihero. In private life he seemed to most people very like his movie-role image—sullen, moody, antisocial and blunt as a peasant. A naturally gifted actor, Gabin was nevertheless unresponsive to culture and literature and indifferent to social proprieties—especially those defining Holly-wood life, which he endured as a mere necessity; he was there only to earn enough money to rejoin his second wife and fight with the Free French. Von Sternberg was an idiosyncratic and obsessive vi-sionary, Fairbanks an amiable and attentive squire, Remarque a for-midable and romantic intellectual, and Wayne an attractive diversion. Jean Gabin, with his rough, rustic exterior, was entirely different.

But this was not *Beauty and the Beast.* As their affair began that year (while he was working in a film called *Moontide),* it quickly became evident to Remarque and to friends like Stefan Lorant that Dietrich's ardor was even more fierce than for John Wayne—and this seems to have been based, more than in any other affair, very much on her role as care-giver and emotional provider. She later wrote that Gabin clung to her "like an orphan to his foster mother, and I loved to mother him day and night."

First (as she had with Wayne), Dietrich supervised the negotia-tions for his movie contract and then proceeded to manage his fi-nances, although Gabin soon learned she was better at evaluating the first than administering the second. Although he lived mostly in her bungalow at the Beverly Hills Hotel, Dietrich selected a small house in West Los Angeles for him to rent as an official address, for propri-ety's sake, and there—because he was completely incompetent in the ordinary tasks of household maintenance—she cooked, cleaned and purchased everything from drinking glasses to bath towels. "I helped him overcome all obstacles," she claimed majestically.

In performing these chores, more was at stake than simple loving

assistance. Dietrich's lifelong inclination to assume the role of another's housekeeper may have been an attempt to be Earth Mother
as well as Glamour Queen, and her self-abasement for many men a
subtle atonement for her years of neglect of Rudi. There is a hint of
the heroic gesture that manipulates and controls even as it seems to
serve, for few gestures could arouse such gratitude and amazement as
the sight of Marlene Dietrich on her knees, a bandana round her
hair, her face smudged with dirt as she scrubbed a floor. "I am just a
simple *Hausfrau,*" her actions shouted—and so a part of her may
have wished to be. But her role as eager domestic was always assumed for the particular benefit of one she wished to impress, or
from whom she wished to exact some kind of tribute.

Helpmate and passionate companion she certainly was, but by
Dietrich's own admission the fires of the Gabin romance were
banked by her activities as "mother, cook, counselor and interpreter,
sister, friend—and more!" She found that his craggy posture was a
façade, that he was a man of exquisite sensitivity who showed to
others a mask of indifference but with her was gentle as a timid
schoolboy: "my lonely child," she called him. In pampering and
soothing Gabin, she was in a way treating a mirror image of herself,
the woman of serene control who preferred to think (as she insisted
to Remarque) that she was completely dependent on the love and
devotion of another, lost without the man she loved.

Enjoying her role as provider, Dietrich often surrounded Gabin
with compatriots like the directors René Clair and Jean Renoir,
preparing lavish French dinners and concluding the evening by leading guests in a rousing chorus of the "Marseillaise." "He called her
'my Prussian,' " Renoir recalled, "and she would reply to this by
tapping his forehead and saying in a languishing voice, 'That's what I
like about you—it's quite empty. You haven't a single idea in your
head, not one, and that's what I like.' " The insult, Renoir added,
apparently left Gabin untouched.

Also among the occasional dinner guests was the French actress
known simply as Annabella, once a leading lady for René Clair and
a co-star of Gabin's. In 1941 she, too, was making films in Hollywood, and since 1938 had been married to Tyrone Power. They
arrived at Gabin's house and were greeted by a slightly breathless but

beautiful Dietrich: "Oh, hello! Excuse me, I am cooking a ragout for *mon Jean* and I must stay in the kitchen." Gabin had not yet returned from his day at the studio, and the guests were left alone while their hostess scurried about preparing dinner. When he finally arrived, the Powers were astonished at Dietrich's welcome. After several minutes of passionate embraces and kisses, she prostrated herself before Gabin, removed his shoes, massaged his feet and lovingly put slippers on him. "Gabin glanced in [Annabella's] direction and winked," according to Power's biographer, "as if he was helpless, a victim of Marlene's adoration." After dinner, Dietrich played her musical saw for the guests.

In public, Dietrich was often seen with Gabin at the popular and lavish club Mocambo, which opened on Sunset Boulevard in January 1941. Privately, as she disclosed, her tender moments with Gabin were characterized by an overtly parental element: the seventh child of poor music-hall performers, he depended on Dietrich's strong maternal instinct. "He took the place of my daughter," she stated oddly, adding that "he was gentle, tender and had all the traits a woman looks for in a man." Or at least the traits sought by a woman with Dietrich's own tangled need to be needed: "He was a little baby who liked to curl up in his mother's lap and be loved, cradled and pampered."

Dietrich often signed her letters to Ernest Hemingway "from Mama." But no one ever had more maternal sustenance from her (nor, perhaps, was any man ever more dependent on it) than Jean Gabin. "The mothering is more important than the sex," Dietrich said (to her daughter) about her relations with men. ("She is mother as sex," said her next movie co-star, Edward G. Robinson.) In the 1950s, Dietrich, Sieber and Lorant were discussing her many liaisons. "Who do you think I loved more than anyone else?" she asked them without a trace of irony. "Jean Gabin?" suggested Rudi. "Gabin, yes," she replied. "Certainly, Gabin." And in 1963, when Attorney General Robert Kennedy met Dietrich at a Washington luncheon and asked who was the most attractive man she had ever met, she replied, "Jean Gabin."

Ursula Petrie, who knew Dietrich well in the early 1940s, was one of many who noted that with Gabin on the scene, "almost overnight, Dietrich's interest in Remarque waned." This may have been at least partly owing to the fact that even for a woman with Dietrich's prodigious energies it must have been difficult to make three films in one year while simultaneously maintaining ardent affairs with one woman and at least three men. But there was another issue, as Dietrich later wrote: Gabin was "stubborn, possessive and jealous." He soon learned, however, the common lesson of everyone close to Dietrich: it was futile to demand exclusivity.

This became clear to Gabin when she began her assignment at Warner in late March—a tedious business called *Manpower,* in which she played a tough floozy opposite Edward G. Robinson (who had top billing) and George Raft as electrical linemen whose dangerous job is nothing compared to their rivalry for her favors. Robinson and director Raoul Walsh later recalled that Dietrich was as usual obsessed with her hair and makeup, placing a mirror near the camera and supervising her own lighting and photography—"so subtly and sexily," according to Robinson, "that no one was offended and she got precisely what she wanted . . . [She had] arrogant self-assurance and was sexy, temperamental, demanding . . . and rough and tough."

Such must also have been the reaction of Gabin, who could do nothing to prevent Dietrich's indulgence with George Raft during the six weeks of filming that spring. Tough and cynical like him (although presented onscreen with a sleek menace), Raft fascinated Dietrich with details of his underworld connections to racketeers and gangsters. Their brief affair, according to a few friends like Ursula Petrie, had a rather bizarre beginning when Raft took Dietrich (apparently in the mistaken notion that she would be shocked) to a notorious downtown venue where live sex shows were performed. But Raft had not taken into account her years in Berlin, for Dietrich was not only unfazed but downright amused.

The trysts with Raft, which occurred with little discretion in various Warner studio dressing rooms, aroused sufficient ire in Gabin that he, too, resolved to dally, and by the time *Manpower* was completed at the end of May, Dietrich feared that her nonchalance had jeopardized the primary relationship of her life at the time. Lunching with Raft at the studio, she telephoned Gabin from their table and conducted a long and obviously amorous conversation in French (later translated for Raft's benefit). Had Gabin enjoyed the previous evening with his girlfriend? Would they be dining together that evening? Did he still love her? The conversation over, Marlene reached for Raft's hand: "I was advising Jean about his career," she said without blinking. "Oh, Georgie, it is too bad you are taken by Betty Grable [another leggy transient in Raft's busy schedule]. I am so lonely." She was not, of course, bemoaning the lack of anything more permanent with Raft; Dietrich simply did not sustain rivalries as calmly as she caused them. Once their film was completed, her co-star waved farewell, after presenting her with a gold bracelet— engraved with "George" on one side and a tiny raft on the reverse.

The dismal picture called *Manpower* was an immediate failure and marks the lowest point in Dietrich's career. Everything in it seems unreal: relationships, dialogue, sets, costumes—even Los Angeles, where the story occurs, is beset year-round by fierce winter tempests, hail and ice storms.

That the resuscitation of Dietrich's professional fortunes had indeed been only temporary was clear to her and to just about everyone in Hollywood when she had a third critical and box-office loser in a single year. At Columbia Pictures, under the direction of Mitchell Leisen, she played (for a salary of $100,000) an unmarried Broadway star who encounters legal obstacles after she sweeps up a neglected Manhattan baby and tenderly brings him home for adoption. *The Lady Is Willing* was planned as a warmly touching comedy about a woman whose heart is broken open by maternal love, but the only fracture that summer was to Dietrich's ankle. Tripping over prop toys on August 25, she whirled round awkwardly and, to prevent injury to the infant in her arms, took a terrible fall.

Rushed to Cedars of Lebanon Hospital, she was soon encased from toe to thigh in a plaster cast, requiring her to be photographed only in close-up for the remainder of the film, further restricting a weak script. On October 29, the company moved to New York for location shooting, Dietrich's ankle now almost healed and simply taped. "Watch Mama make the front pages of every paper in New York," she whispered to a press representative as they stepped from the train at Grand Central Station. She then appropriated Leisen's

decorative walking stick and, cannily aware of every excuse for publicity, stood for photographers and described in excruciating detail
her baby-saving accident.

But back in Hollywood for the final scenes, she could not so
easily win the attention she craved from two people. "She couldn't
understand why [her co-star] Fred MacMurray wouldn't fall madly
in love with her," said Leisen some time later, referring to Dietrich's
traditional ploy of seducing her leading men, the better to assert her
authority over them for the course of their collaboration. "I said,
'Listen, Marlene, Fred's so happily in love with his wife, he couldn't
care less about any other woman, so you lay off. Just make the
picture.' " She had no more luck, soon afterwards, trying to woo
young Ann Miller, then a rising musical performer who was as cool
to Dietrich's blandishments as Carole Lombard and Frances Dee had
been. Dietrich did not take this rejection easily, and for days she
pouted at home and at work; Gabin had not the remotest idea of the
reasons for her disagreeable mood.

CHRISTMAS 1941 WAS A CHEERLESS TIME FOR DIE-
trich, and in fact by New Year's Eve she was in an acute state of
depression. The bombing of Pearl Harbor on December 7 and
America's forced entry into world conflict frightened her and
evoked memories of her earlier hardships in Germany during the
first World War. Additionally, despite her naturalization she shared
the wary discomfiture common to immigrants from countries now
at war with the United States. For several years it had been too
awkward for her to play a German character in films, and so her
accent and background were ignored or she was presented otherwise.★

But there were deeper personal reasons for her anxiety. On December 27, Marlene Dietrich turned forty—a crucial moment for a
woman whose career very much depended on her ability to be

★ This was a problem from 1933 to 1945. Dietrich was a Russian in *The Scarlet Empress* and *Knight
Without Armour*, Spanish in *The Devil Is a Woman*, vaguely Middle European in *The Garden of Allah*,
English in *Angel*, and French in *Desire*, *Destry Rides Again*, *Seven Sinners*, *The Flame of New Orleans* and
Manpower. In *The Lady Is Willing*, *The Spoilers* and *Pittsburgh* the characters' national origin was simply
not specified, and she was, of all things, an Iraqi in *Kismet*.

perpetually alluring and agelessly beautiful. She calmly told the press, friends and even lovers that she was in her midthirties; the record, after all, variously stated that she was thirty-four, thirty-five or thirty-six, and this fiction was politely accepted.

The subterfuge was more comforting to the public than to herself. Privately (as Maria told her first husband), Dietrich was, at the end of 1941 and for much of the next two years, very often near panic for several reasons. First, she was aware of the indifferent and sometimes hostile reviews she was receiving in a series of wretched pictures. Second, there were (as usual) very few leading roles for those who were called "mature women." In a business that has always depended on fantasy and the promulgation of eternal appeal, she now feared for her own ability to maintain an impossible ideal.

For decades, the self that Marlene Dietrich presented to the world had been wrapped in a tissue of illusions and deceptions. Some of this had its roots in the early demands of Prussian-Victorian etiquette, the polite repression of emotions, the social and cosmetic artifices enjoined on her from infancy by society, her mother and her grandmother—a culture, in other words, that canonized appearance and propriety but courted luxury and grandeur. As a music and drama student she then created the persona of an aristocratic girl with an impressive Weimar pedigree, blithely falsifying basic truths about her family—the identities of her father and stepfather, for example, and the very existence of her sister Elisabeth. For the benefit of a carefully contrived public status, she revealed as much of her private life as was helpful to her controversial image, and so she actively altered her history and her identity, taking any means to offer a more acceptable and even a more desirable person than she may have considered herself.

In her marriage and social life, too, there were many roles and fictions that made her life a series of playlets. Dietrich cherished a persona of simple domesticity while cultivating a score of serial, often simultaneous, paramours, and although she had many lovers, there seems to have been little depth or security with them. Her affairs were little melodramas—sometimes satisfying, often tempestuous, always containing the preparation scenes of their own finales, perhaps because of her fierce independence and the nonexclusivity she demanded.

In this regard, her prodigal sex life is not hard to understand, for it was perhaps most of all her attempt to supply the missing intimacy in a life otherwise spent maintaining the image—remaining unpredictable, mysterious, even desirable by being always somewhat remote. Her lovers she tended to treat the way she did that image: by control, by meticulous management of a carefully created scenario. But in time the result would be a solitude which every public and private gesture had perhaps inevitably foreordained.

Josef von Sternberg had enabled Maria Magdalene Dietrich to become (as the press so often called her) *La Dietrich*—the beautiful, exotic, languorous creature, artificial and representing mostly his own fantasies. In some ways, of course, the Dietrich of the von Sternberg films was indeed a mannequin both sensual and detached, seductive and remote, desirable yet obviously unreal. From that time forward, with her own active cooperation, she was dedicated to maintaining the mythicizing process he had begun.

But life cannot sustain the burden of perpetual fantasy, and in a curious way the changes in public taste and the gradual depopularization of her image confirmed that. The spectral and illusory Dietrich, imagined and meticulously created by von Sternberg, coincided perfectly with the dreamlike, escapist rapture desired by Depression-era audiences. In the late 1930s, both film and the world situation altered dramatically. Lighting and lenses represented people more sharply and distinctly, and backgrounds now appeared clarified; actors were, in other words, recognizably situated. Screenplays, too, kept pace with the public's demand for fresh humor, visual realism and real if subtle eroticism. (In this regard, it is easy to understand the popularity of films like *Gone With the Wind*, *The Grapes of Wrath*, *Of Mice and Men*, *Mr. Smith Goes to Washington*, *The Letter*, *The Little Foxes* and *The Maltese Falcon*.)

THE APPROACH OF WAR SUDDENLY MADE AT LEAST temporarily obsolete (or unfashionable) many of the conventions and genres of earlier films—screwball comedies, heroic westerns, tales of mere urban gangsters. But even at the end of 1941 Marlene Dietrich was still unprepared and unwilling to accept the fact that she had come from a particular era, that she was of a certain age, that she stood for a vanishing ideal: the lessons of *Destry Rides Again* had apparently been forgotten. And so, just as she had dedicated herself completely to the manufacture of illusion, so she became one of the first unwitting victims of the price it extracts—a loss of emotional balance and of purpose, a spiritual vacuum at the core of herself and her life. She spent New Year's Eve alone, pacing in her bungalow, and (as Maria recalled) during the following months she suddenly and without apparent reason broke down weeping. Von Sternberg, Fairbanks and Remarque were no longer available to her, Mercedes de Acosta had gone to Europe, Jean Gabin spoke daily of returning to France. There seemed nothing for her to cling to, nothing substantial, secure or solid to reassure Marlene Dietrich that her life had any meaning at all.

SHE HAD LITTLE CHOICE OR REFUGE OTHER THAN her craft, and in the first two months of 1942 at least she could work, again with John Wayne; he both adored and bored her, but at least she could count on the raw comfort of their affair. Attempting to capitalize on the Dietrich-Wayne chemistry in *Seven Sinners* and her Frenchy in *Destry Rides Again,* Universal cast them in the fourth screen version of Rex Beach's novel *The Spoilers,* about crooked gold mining claims during the Alaskan boom of 1900. Dressed, photographed and given dialogue sprinkled with double meanings that recalled Mae West, Dietrich played a saloon proprietor, strutting uneasily between Wayne and the smoothly villainous Randolph Scott. Destry was supposed to ride again; no one, alas, even trotted.*

In the finished picture, Dietrich looked as she really felt off-screen—almost stiff with ennui. When production was complete, she was so depressed she fell ill, and after staying home for a week was driven to a desert inn at La Quinta, southeast of Palm Springs.

---

* Such period films were popular escapist fare during the 1940s, since the narrative could blithely omit any mention of the war. Also, the roles "masked" popular stars whose accents indicated nationalities unpopular at the moment. From 1939, the German Dietrich was conveniently hidden in the American West, the South Seas, New Orleans, Alaska, Pittsburgh and Baghdad.

Compounding her dejection that season was the news, on January 11, of Carole Lombard's death in a plane crash; the actress had been returning from a tour, using her fame and appeal to help sell war bonds. From her retreat, a distracted and disaffected Dietrich announced that she would soon abandon Hollywood and return to the theater for a New York revival of Oscar Wilde's *An Ideal Husband;* when the producer reneged on the offer, she simply said to the press, "I'm not thinking of the stage now. Time enough for that later, when you get older and harder to photograph."

That spring, she asked Gabin to come with her for a brief holiday in New York, where they went to the theater and visited old acquaintances. To cheer herself, Dietrich spent three afternoons with the couturiers at Lily Daché, where she went into a paroxysm of buying—ninety-eight items, including a Persian lamb jacket, a two-hundred-dollar scarf, a one-hundred-fifty-dollar white turban, a silver possum muff, purses, and fur gloves and accessories more suited to the Russian tundra than Southern California. But she was not happy when she received the bill for almost $5,000, and by late summer the store had to sue for nonpayment; her account was not balanced for almost a year.

That summer, Dietrich accepted an invitation from Bette Davis, who had helped organize the Hollywood Canteen, a place where entertainment and meals were provided for servicemen during the war. Dancing with soldiers and sailors and preparing dinners and cakes, she "not only contributed glamour out front," as Davis later wrote, "but backbreaking labor in the kitchen." In the spirit of her friend Carole Lombard, Dietrich then joined colleagues like Linda Darnell and Dorothy Lamour on a nationwide bond tour, exploiting her fame (and in her case underlining her opposition to Germany) by raising funds for the War Department.

Just about this time—the late summer of 1942—Dietrich received visitors from New York, who had come to discuss her appearance in a Broadway musical. Composer Kurt Weill and producer Cheryl Crawford (who had collaborated on the 1936 musical *Johnny Johnson)* hoped to follow Weill's *Lady in the Dark* with a show based on *The Tinted Venus,* by F. Anstey (pseudonym of the English writer Thomas Anstey Guthrie). *One Touch of Venus,* as it was eventually called, was a comic variation on the Pygmalion-Galatea myth. It tells the story of a barber who places an engagement ring on a statue of the goddess of love, who promptly comes to life and pursues him. But when she discovers what sort of life the typical housewife leads, she returns to Mount Olympus.

At the core of the musical comedy in progress was a character that seemed conceived for Dietrich, and so Weill and Crawford visited her to describe the story and ascertain her interest in a New York stage debut. According to the producer, Dietrich appeared attentive and interested, "but she also had an odd, rather remote quality—whether she wanted to seem as mysterious as her image, I couldn't know, but Marlene was certainly elusive." The visitors were not given more certitude when, after they had described their theatrical plans, Dietrich brought out her musical saw and accompanied herself in the Brecht-Weill song "Surabaya Johnny" from *Happy End*.

There were three or four such meetings. Weill and Crawford mapped out the plot, the musical numbers, the staging, the lush possibilities for a magnificent wardrobe. Dietrich listened, she nodded gravely, and then she inevitably entertained them on the musical saw. They were getting nowhere very fast indeed. In a final attempt to gauge some idea of Dietrich's willingness to commit to the show, composer and producer invited her and Gabin to the Cock and Bull, a popular steak house on Sunset Boulevard. "There was very little talk about our project," Crawford added, "but Marlene and Gabin were delightful to watch, two such beautiful people in love with each other." At the end of dinner, coffee was ordered—to the horror of the two beautiful people: "We wouldn't think of it!" they cried in unison. "It will keep us awake!" And that, said Cheryl Crawford and Kurt Weill later, shattered the romantic fantasies they were entertaining about Dietrich and Gabin. A last-ditch stab at the topic of *One Touch of Venus* was deflected when Dietrich told Crawford not to worry, she would soon be in New York for further discussions. Soon turned out to be late, but since there were difficulties with the musical's book, Crawford was patient.

· · ·

BECAUSE SHE NEEDED THE MONEY AND COULD DO little else, Dietrich undertook another disappointing picture at Universal in the autumn of 1942. For the third and final time she appeared with John Wayne, in a project of monumental tedium called *Pittsburgh.* He and (again) Randolph Scott played coal mine "hunkies" who climb to the top of the industry, brawl over Dietrich, fight over principles and finally knuckle down to a patriotic effort after her stout speech for the unity of labor and management during wartime. When the filming was over in late October, so was her romance with John Wayne; he did not like her incessant chatter about Gabin's great acting talent, while Dietrich finally found Wayne simply too morbidly dull. What had begun as a torrid diversion concluded from a chill distance, as his telephone calls to her went unreturned and his flower deliveries unaccepted.

IN FEBRUARY 1943, IT WAS HER TURN TO ACCOMpany Gabin to New York, whence he was to return to France by way of Morocco. But first they would have a New York holiday. At the same time, Dietrich wanted very much to appear in a stage version of Vera Caspary's popular novel *Laura,* but the author finally decided simply to sell the rights to a Hollywood studio, and the stage version was unproduced until 1947.

That spring, however, the matter of *One Touch of Venus* came to a head, and Dietrich was apparently eager to make a Broadway musical debut. After a preliminary meeting with Crawford and Weill, she made daily visits to the Metropolitan Museum of Art, where she studied various paintings, statues and engravings of Venus. She also ordered vast quantities of grey chiffon and invited the producer and composer to her suite at the St. Regis Hotel, where she stripped (at least once in their presence) and draped herself in the fashion of the Venus she had seen that day. "She modeled," Crawford recalled, "she struck poses, and she asked our opinions. She looked divine, of course, but we couldn't figure out what this had to do with her commitment to our show. I remember that she was very keen on one Venus in particular—one with gorgeous buttocks."

After several such fashion shows, Dietrich was asked to come to the Forty-sixth Street Theater so that Crawford, Weill and company might hear her voice in an auditorium. When she arrived (with Gabin for moral support), it was immediately evident to everyone that Dietrich was very anxious indeed. When she sang Hollander's "Johnny," those in the fourth row could scarcely hear her. Unaccustomed to projecting her voice from the stage and unfamiliar with the demands of musical theater in her fifteen years' absence from it, Dietrich feared she was out of her depth and range. And when she heard the richness and complexity of Weill's songs, she was convinced this would be a mistake (as indeed it would have been for her to have undertaken, at her age, the role of the twenty-four-year-old *Laura*).

But pride kept her from a flat withdrawal, and the show's creators were convinced that with rehearsals and the proper audio doctoring Dietrich was the right Venus—but still there was no contract for her participation. Arriving the following day at the St. Regis with legal papers in hand, Crawford was surprised to find Dietrich packing for an imminent return to California.

"You're leaving?" she asked.

"Yes, my darling," Dietrich said with a deep sigh, "and I have the most terrible headache." But Crawford had not become a successful Broadway producer without some education in the ways of stars. She promptly produced a modest quantity of a stimulating drug, and moments later Dietrich was gloriously exuberant. "Obviously she wasn't accustomed to taking stimulants," according to Crawford, "having declined even coffee that evening in Hollywood. However, I wasn't above taking advantage of my windfall." And with that, the contract was put before Dietrich, who signed it with a flourish. *One Touch of Venus* was now headed for an autumn premiere in New York. That evening, Gabin departed for Morocco and Dietrich for Hollywood, where she awaited the revisions of the show's book.

But in more sober moments, Dietrich knew she would have to renege on this commitment. She could not command a Broadway stage, nor (she knew better than anyone) had she the vocal or dramatic equipment to carry a strong musical. When, on March 16, 1943, the creators of *One Touch of Venus* telephoned Dietrich for her reactions to the new script by S. J. Perelman and Ogden Nash, she told Weill disingenuously, "I cannot play this—it is too sexy and profane." For a moment, the New Yorkers must have thought they had a wrong number, but Dietrich continued as if everyone would believe her: "You know, Kurt, I have a daughter who is eighteen years old, and for me to get up on the stage and exhibit my legs is now impossible."

"Marlene, what are you saying?" cried Kurt Weill. "Why, this play is delightful—it's intriguing, it's witty, it's sophisticated—"

"No, it is too sexy and profane," Dietrich repeated, as if she had just completed the title role in *The Song of Bernadette* and dared not sully her image. Weill became angry, scolding Dietrich for her ignorance and hypocrisy, but Dietrich was adamant. "No, Kurt, it is sexy and profane, and I will not now exhibit myself in that way." And rather than take their reluctant star to litigation, the creators of *One Touch of Venus* dissolved her contract. That autumn, the show opened with a leading lady named Mary Martin, who became a Broadway sensation.

THERE WAS, THEN, NO IMMEDIATE WORK FOR MARlene Dietrich and so, by default, only her daughter claimed her care and attention. But Maria—who had faced the problem of her obesity and was slowly but consistently losing weight—had begun a social life and career of her own, and she neither understood nor appreciated her mother's sudden, intense consecration of time and attention. That spring, in fact, Maria was taking serious steps to claim her independence; among them was the assumption of the professional name Maria Manton.

For almost a year (with her mother's encouragement), she had also been taking drama classes at the Jack Geller Workshop, on the site of the former Max Reinhardt school at the corner of Wilshire Boulevard and Fairfax Avenue. There Maria met a handsome and talented twenty-three-year-old actor named Dean Goodman, who had received a medical discharge after military service. He was an assistant to the legendary acting teacher Maria Ouspenskaya and had appeared to good notices in plays locally and throughout the

West (most notably in a production of the thriller *Love from a Stranger).*

Years later, Goodman recalled that he (among others) felt shy with the daughter of so famous a woman, and although they met casually and occasionally dated, there was at first nothing romantic about the friendship. But like her mother, according to Goodman, it was a challenge for the daughter to make people like her. He found Maria pretty, bright and talented, and by June they were engaged.★ "Maria was the aggressor in our relationship," according to Goodman, "and only later did it become clear to me that she wanted most desperately to get away from home and mother. She was also very adamant that I not meet Marlene, and she admitted why: she said she was afraid every man she brought home would eventually be found in her mother's bed."

Goodman understood that there was a tense balance of love and enmity between the two women. On the one hand, Maria longed for her mother's approval but resented her unstable childhood. Never secure in Dietrich's affections, she had been isolated from her peers and put in the care of various tutors, and then sent away to school in Europe—always feeling that she was entirely subordinate to her mother's career and lovers. For her part, Dietrich was never overtly cruel to Maria; but there had been a pattern of neglect. Now Dietrich realized that Maria was no longer a child but an attractive and talented young woman, and this apparently aroused all sorts of tangled rivalries and unacknowledged fears in Dietrich—for one, that Maria might find a good man and have a stable life of her own without the necessity of her mother's protection. In addition, Maria's maturing was a sure sign of Dietrich's inevitable aging. That these were subtle if unacknowledged reactions was evident from her mother's summary rejection—sight unseen, man unmet—of everyone Maria said she liked, Goodman included.

At the time, Goodman's friends (among them the actress Lillian Fontaine, mother of Joan and Olivia de Havilland) urged him to reconsider what was becoming a rush to the altar with Maria. "But Maria was convinced she was in love with me," according to Good-

★ Earlier, Maria had been engaged very briefly to the actor Richard Hayden, a bachelor almost twenty years older.

man, "and I thought I was in love with her. Right up to the wedding—because I didn't want to seem like an opportunist or a starstruck fan—I didn't insist on meeting Marlene, she had no desire to meet me, Rudi simply wasn't around, and Maria wasn't eager for me to meet either one! It was a very strange and swift courtship." A wedding date was set for late August.

Dietrich, meanwhile, swung into action with every stratagem to prevent the marriage. First, she investigated Goodman's credit and character but could turn up only favorable reports; furthermore, to supplement his acting income and support his future wife, he had taken a part-time job as a warehouse clerk. Then Dietrich made a more desperate attack, as Maria told Dean: she asked her daughter if she had considered what it would be like to have Jewish children? This surprising objection was repeated in a meeting called by Dietrich's lawyer, to whom Goodman simply replied that if he were Jewish he would not be ashamed. But even the fact of his gentile family background did not affect his worthiness, for Dietrich then flatly asserted that Dean Goodman was a fortune hunter (something she herself told him in a brief telephone conversation).

Neither of the Sieber parents attended the wedding on August 23, 1943, at the Hollywood Congregational Church; only a few friends were present. The newlyweds moved into a small apartment, to which Dietrich one day shipped pieces of furniture from her own collection in storage. And one evening the Goodmans returned home to find it scrubbed and cleaned, new curtains hung, the windows washed and the place banked with fresh flowers. "Marlene had done it all herself," Goodman recalled. "The building manager and our neighbors had thought the woman in bandana and work clothes was a hired domestic."

NO ONE MADE THAT MISTAKE IN HER ONLY TWO FILM appearances late in 1943. Wilhelm Dieterle, who had directed her in Berlin two decades earlier in the silent picture *Der Mensch am Wege,* had also emigrated and was directing in Hollywood as William Dieterle. Metro-Goldwyn-Mayer had given him that old chestnut of an Arabian Nights fantasy *Kismet* to enliven, with Ronald Colman,

Technicolor, the full resources of the studio's costume and set departments and a budget of over $3,000,000—surprising for those years of wartime restrictions. Again, Marlene Dietrich's name appeared after the leading man's and after the title, a small difference for audiences but, in the carefully negotiated scheme of things in ego-conscious Hollywood, a matter of considerable significance. She was seen briefly as Jamilla, the harem queen in the castle of the Grand Vizier in old Baghdad, romancing a beggar disguised as a prince (Colman).

Slinking none too voluptuously with layers of chiffon and veils, hairpieces carefully looped, braided and wired a yard above her head, Dietrich had the opportunity to do her first dance onscreen. In the only one of her four scenes lasting more than a minute, Dietrich attempted a five-minute wriggle, her legs sprayed with four layers of gold paint as she ambled, glided, swooned, waved her arms and tried (mostly with the help of judicious editing and the use of a double in long shots whenever there is dancing) to suggest something like a dance. Surely nothing like this—or much in the picture, for that matter—was ever seen in the Levant, for this is after all MGM's Arabia, a salad of Balinese dancers in Chinese costumes left over from science fiction serials, a studio fantasy combining what seems to be Brazilian high fashion with the latest accessories from Bullock's on Wilshire Boulevard.

From her arrival that autumn, she was in bad humor.

"Do you have a side of your face?" she asked Ronald Colman breathlessly. "A left side or a right side that's better on camera?"

"Well—yes," he replied.

"Darling, you are so lucky. I have none! I have to face the camera!"

This was really a warning, as Colman soon learned and later recalled: "She played every single scene looking straight ahead," effectively ignoring her co-star and stealing the audience's attention. This did not, however, effect a particularly flattering image, for (quite apart from the ridiculous wardrobe, hairstyles and sets) Technicolor was not kind to Marlene Dietrich. In *The Garden of Allah*, *Kismet* (and later in Fritz Lang's *Rancho Notorious*), she looks glossy and garish, her face flat, masklike, without affect, nuance or subtlety.

Like a number of actors, she needed cinematic chiaroscuro, the infinite black and white shadings of a master like von Sternberg to evoke and highlight her expression.

That same season, Dietrich was outfitted just as hilariously for her cameo appearance in an all-star Hollywood revue produced by Universal and starring mostly its own studio talent. The picture, at first called *Three Cheers for the Boys,* was an orgy of self-praise with songs, dances and skits featuring actors and dancers who had spent time entertaining troops at home-training camps and near the action abroad—among them George Raft, Sophie Tucker, Jeanette Mac-Donald, Dinah Shore and W. C. Fields. (The film's considerable profits went not to servicemen or for wartime aid, but to Universal Pictures.) One of the scenes was to feature a portion of Orson Welles's famous Mercury Wonder Show, a magic act he was staging that year in a tent on Cahuenga Boulevard. When Rita Hayworth, the actress soon to be Mrs. Welles, was enjoined by Columbia Studios' Harry Cohn from appearing in Welles's show, Dietrich stepped in and then agreed to do the brief film scene, in which (with the sloppiest special photographic effects in history) she was to be sawed in half.

At the same time, Dean Goodman returned home from acting in John Carradine's Shakespeare tour, only to be told by Maria that she considered their life together a mistake and that she was leaving after four months of marriage. "But my parents never divorced," she said airily, explaining her refusal to grant Goodman's obvious request, "and like them we can have our freedom and the respectability of the contract." (Three years later, when she wished to remarry, Maria changed her mind on the matter of divorce.) Of this brief and clearly miscalculated union, Dean Goodman said, "I liked and admired Maria—her talent, her energy, her perseverance, her cheerful personality despite the unhappiness and the difficulties she'd overcome." Maria, on the same subject, was forever after more guarded: "I don't want to talk about that. It never existed."

Predictably, Dietrich was pleased at the news of Maria's separation and urged her to get on with her career. But there was no time for maternal fussing. After nearly four straight years of professional disappointments and a long period of depression, Marlene Dietrich knew that she would have to take drastic steps to alter her destiny. Films were failing her; lovers had departed; age was an unavoidable fact.

During her bond tour, Dietrich had learned more about an important venture involving actors in the war effort, and to this she now turned her full attention. The United Service Organization—always referred to simply as the USO—had been founded in 1941 to provide off-duty recreational, social, welfare and spiritual facilities for the American military at home and abroad. Originally a consortium of social services (the YMCA and YWCA, the National Catholic Community Service, the National Jewish Welfare Board, the Salvation Army and the National Travelers Aid Association), the USO became a war agency after the Japanese attack on Pearl Harbor that precipitated America's entry into World War II. In towns near military posts as well as near battle lines in Europe and the Pacific, volunteers offered servicemen entertainment, meals and often dances. Its New York branch, the Stage Door Canteen, attracted Broadway actors to such volunteer work, and the Hollywood chapter (under Bette Davis, Orson Welles and many others) did likewise.

By 1945 there were over twenty-five hundred USO Clubs, and the USO Camp Shows were an important feature: supported by voluntary contributions, more than four thousand Americans went to posts and hospitals round the world and served more than a billion persons. Among the Camp Show entertainers were many celebrity performers popular in the 1940s who gave time and talent to appear for the armed forces (often at considerable personal risk near battle lines); their number included Jack Benny, Joe E. Brown, Bing Crosby, Betty Grable, Frances Langford, George Jessel, Jo Stafford—and Bob Hope, whose officer jokes and risqué wit made him a particular favorite, and who subsequently made troop entertainment a primary adjunct of his career.

The only pleasant interval in Dietrich's life recently had been one day's filming of Welles's magic act, before a live audience of servicemen. That picture's name had just been changed to *Follow the Boys,* and as the bells rang in the New Year 1944, that was precisely what she decided to do.

12: 1944–1945

O N MARCH 20, 1944, MARLENE DIETRICH entertained more than twelve hundred soldiers based at Fort Meade, Maryland.

Wearing an elegant long-sleeved, flesh-colored net gown with gold sequins, she was every inch the elegantly sultry Hollywood star the men in uniform recognized. She sang "See What the Boys in the Back Room Will Have" (from her 1939 film *Destry Rides Again)* and her signature tune, "Falling in Love Again" (from *The Blue Angel).* She then played "Pagan Love Song" on the musical saw. After that, Marlene Dietrich's accompanist, a thirty-year-old nightclub entertainer from Michigan named Danny Thomas, assisted her in a mental telepathy act she had learned in Hollywood from Orson Welles. She recruited soldiers from the audience, engaging them in the trick and exchanging racy anecdotes. The crowd went wild, and her tumultuous reception confirmed Dietrich's resolve to go abroad to the front lines, to entertain as many young men as she could.

From Fort Meade, Dietrich proceeded to New York, where

final papers were put in order for her to entertain troops in Europe; accordingly, she spent the last of her savings on a chic tan hat from John-Frederics and, from Franklin Simon, a fashionable olive gabardine suit with beige scarf. The colors may have been military, but the outfit was strictly Beverly Hills/Park Avenue. Dietrich had no intention of disappointing the boys she was following to camp. She also learned at this time that she would have the simulated rank of major in the United States Army: USO entertainers were routinely given rank so that, if captured, they might hope to be treated like officers. (Danny Thomas was merely captain.)

While in New York, she also learned a great deal about live performances from Thomas, an expert showman who taught her the fine points of phrasing and breath control for singing and the right comic timing for her repartee. All this was new to her. "He taught me everything," Dietrich said later of Thomas; "how to deal with an audience, how to answer if they shout, how to play them, how to make them laugh. Above all, he taught me how to *talk* to them." Together the pair continued to refine and rehearse what quickly became her one-woman show: Dietrich at the microphone singing, Dietrich playing the saw, Dietrich trading jokes, Dietrich telling stories, Dietrich encouraging the troops, Dietrich hosting a telepathy act.

At this point in her wartime service, her wardrobe, her array of cosmetics, her musical preparations—everything in her possession and attitude, in fact—indicated that she was indeed preparing to establish herself as a solo entertainer, to disprove those who claimed that her string of movie failures from 1940 to 1943 spelled the end of a career.

In this regard, Dietrich's volunteer service is easy to understand, for many actresses and singers performed USO work—especially those not under contract or committed to a specific film. But in her case this was not only her way of demonstrating good citizenship, it was also a means to gain the male attention she thrived on and the public adoration she required.

As a star, too, there was something of *noblesse oblige* in this, as in all her menial efforts for others: in this case, she was the queen mother (if not quite any longer regnant), visiting her men in action.

In another sense, of course, it was the logical extension of her "manly woman" role, which had long conjoined her own character with those she played in the von Sternberg films. She was, then, at last becoming one of the boys, the ambiguous and ambivalent woman-in-drag, the masculinized female who identified with men, loved them for themselves and as surrogates of herself, the woman of an embattled era who was striving to be all things to all men and women. Some of this psychospiritual medley was perhaps commingled in the murky depths of motivation as she entered the USO, claiming she wanted only to help the boys in battle. There had been no precedent in her character for such single-minded, altruistic sacrifice, after all. And human psychology is never so simple as to admit of a single basis; "only God is Love straight through," as Thomas More said. And whatever Dietrich's primary, conscious intentions, her purpose and her courage would soon be tested—in an ordeal worse than any devised by a tyrannical movie director.

ON APRIL 2, MARLENE DIETRICH BOARDED AN AIRplane for the first time in her life—a C-54 transport she took from New York with Danny Thomas and a little troupe who would perform supportively in their act: comedienne and harmonica player Lynne Mayberry, pianist-guitarist Jack Snyder and Milton Frome, a "straight man" for the humorous repartee. Not until they were airborne, huddling together for warmth and drinking steaming mugs of coffee to fight the cold, were they permitted to open a sealed envelope with their destination: Casablanca. They might have imagined themselves a road company banding together for a reprise of the previous year's popular movie romance with that city's name for its title—until a fierce electrical storm raged round the plane, tossing the passengers like so many rag dolls for several hours. Everyone was desperately ill except the star, as Lynne Mayberry recalled. Dietrich covered the soldiers with blankets, poured Danny Thomas and herself tumblers of smuggled scotch whiskey (which he promptly threw up) and distracted her companions from the unpleasant flight by telling stories of Berlin in the twenties. Her protective instincts had perhaps never been so beneficially demonstrated.

With stops for refueling in Greenland and the Azores, the flight to North Africa took twenty-two hours. They finally reached Casablanca, Morocco's chief port, at night and (because of the blackout) without benefit of runway lights. The poorly heated airplane had given Dietrich a chill, and she was exhausted after only three hours of fitful sleep. Casablanca was no idyllic spot, however, nor were there attractive characters like Ingrid Bergman, Humphrey Bogart or Paul Henreid greeting them in sparkling white suits. An eerie calm had settled over the city, site of the previous year's Anglo-American Conference that had planned the Allied bombing offensive known as "Pointblank" in preparation for the invasion of Europe. Everywhere were military units and English, American and Canadian soldiers on the exacting rounds of their duties.

The Camp Show volunteers, separated from the GIs, were then bundled into a hastily requisitioned Red Cross convoy truck. Officers from the American base charged with the show had been misinformed of their arrival date, and there were no quarters for them. Finally a bungalow was found, for which modest would be too extravagant a word—it was a damp, cold, putrid hut near soldiers' barracks. Without a word of complaint, Dietrich settled into a single room with her five companions. She had not come expecting much comfort, she told Danny Thomas, and with that she found the crude latrine, then returned to the group, pushed her hair under her cap and, curling up in her uniform and a regulation bomber jacket, tucked herself in for the night. Four sequined evening dresses, intended for her show, were wrapped in a knapsack; these she used for a pillow.

The next afternoon, Dietrich and company performed their first show. To cacophonous whistling and hooting, she stepped onto a makeshift platform behind an outpost of the Free French, sang a medley from her films and began her mind-reading routine. But the success of this telepathy stunt depended on a careful set of signals between her and Danny Thomas, and as she tried to make her way through the first few rows of the audience she was whirled around, asked for autographs, a kiss, an impromptu dance and a view of her famous legs. The act was sabotaged, but no one seemed to care.

From Casablanca the troupe proceeded, hugging the North African coast to Rabat and then Tangiers. Dietrich performed twice daily for gatherings of American and Allied forces along the road, coping constantly with short supplies of water and soap, erratic microphone systems and sudden windstorms. There were, of course, neither limousines nor gourmet cuisine—no comfort of any kind, in fact: Dietrich travelled in open jeeps and ate regulation tinned food. Nothing could have been in greater contrast to her comfortable life in California, but she was in her element—one of the lads, indeed. "Wherever I went to entertain troops, there were frankfurters and sauerkraut," she told a foreign correspondent. "Frankfurters and sauerkraut, all over. And always outdoors. Even when there was an indoors, we ate outdoors, often in the rain, with rain on the food and cold grease running down. We didn't mind. It was food, and millions were perishing of starvation in Russia." At the Strait of Gibraltar, Dietrich asked the driver to stop. She jumped out, saying she had a dear friend in France, and stood tearfully for several moments, gazing across the water. Her thoughts for Jean Gabin may have been clear and tender, but geography was never her strong suit.

After a stopover in Oran, they arrived in Algiers on April 11. To Dietrich's surprise, Gabin was there to greet her, for his transfer into France had not yet been arranged. The couple, according to Danny Thomas, "attached themselves to each other so amorously that the GIs cheered for at least five minutes while they clutched and kissed in full view of everyone." They had a day-and-a-half reunion before Gabin finally left Algiers.

At the Opera House, the wail of air-raid sirens interrupted her performance several times, and she had to be hauled offstage and pushed to the floor by Thomas and Mayberry ("I was more afraid about my teeth than my legs!" Dietrich said). Later, she stood with soldiers and civilians on the waterfront, peering at flashes of orange and yellow light which, they were told, were airfire from Allied Beaufighters as they shot down three Junker 88s and a Dornier 217 only a few miles offshore. Flying from bases in Occupied France, the Germans were attempting attacks on convoys like hers moving along the North African coast. "It was my first real air raid," she said next morning, "although we had practices at home when I was a girl.

But I didn't feel at all frightened." Although by every account she remained calm throughout, Dietrich must have summoned her old Prussian reserve, for the terrifying air battle garishly illuminated the sky until dawn.

Next morning, she went to a makeshift hospital and could scarcely suppress her horror at the sight of so many boys wounded, limbless and blind. Trying to hide her emotion, she visited each bedside and, when one ward would not stop cheering her, she unpacked her musical saw and improvised "Swanee River," "Oh, Susanna" and "My Darling Clementine." There was, as reporter Louis Berg remembered, scarcely a dry eye in the room.

Such an emotional response from soldiers to Dietrich is easy to understand—not only because she was a warm, maternal figure bending over them with loving concern, but precisely because she was a beautiful, somewhat remote and glamorous Hollywood *star*. Her customary array of cosmetics, powders and rouges had to be abandoned, and there was no key light to accent her features just so. Instead, colleagues and soldiers were surprised to see a short, weary woman over forty, with lines of exhaustion and anxiety clearly traced around her mouth and eyes. Star performer she may have been, laying the foundation of her future one-woman show, triumphant abroad in a way she had not been recently in Hollywood. But for this—and for them, she made it clear—Dietrich was disdaining safety, rejecting special treatment and risking her life. Additionally, she was a naturalized German who loudly sided with the men fighting against her native country.

But she also flirted outrageously, according to Danny Thomas; she doffed her khakis, slinking around whenever she could in a form-fitting gown without underwear. He called her the Golden Panther.

Throughout April and early May, the show toured from Tunis, through Sicily and up the Italian coast, while Dietrich set her cap for Danny Thomas. In Naples the company stayed briefly at a small hotel, and one afternoon she asked Lynne Mayberry to send him to her room, ostensibly to ask why he refused to be photographed with her. "I went in," Thomas recalled, "and there she was, stark naked, sunning herself on her balcony."

"Come on now," Dietrich said. "Don't be such a baby."

Thomas, then married and a father, tried to resist, but Dietrich was insistent. "You don't like me," she continued.

"That's not true. I love you."

"Then why don't you want to have pictures taken with me?"

Thomas explained that he preferred not to exploit the war or his USO service for publicity purposes (as, he could have implied, she did so readily). She replied that he was a very unusual man—a reaction that may have had more to do with his carefully preserved chastity than his ideas about photographic self-aggrandizement. And with that, according to Danny Thomas, he promptly left Marlene's room.

SOME OF THE MOST SAVAGE FIGHTING OF THE ALLIES' push toward Rome was in progress when Dietrich's convoy reached Cassino, a major Nazi stronghold. The siege centered on the hill near the ancient monastery that could trace its origins back to St. Benedict in the sixth century. From a mile away, she and her comrades—part of a small splinter group that had accidentally taken an alternative road toward the assigned camp—watched through field glasses as British and Polish troops backed up the Americans, whose most powerful mobile gun, the 240-millimeter howitzer, eventually destroyed the abbey and the entire town in days. The Nazis then moved into the monastic ruins, which provided them with an excellent defensive position.

The area was thus particularly dangerous when Dietrich and her troupe could not relocate their division on the evening of May 15 and began to wander, lost in a no-man's-land near enemy territory. Their jeep broke down, and during a cold and terrifying night they listened to the gunfire while huddled in a grove. Eventually a truck drove up and a group approached them. This turned out to be a detachment of Free French soldiers, among whom was the actor Jean-Pierre Aumont.

"I am Marlene Dietrich," she said in French after hearing their language.

The reply was instantaneous and sarcastic: "If you are Marlene

Dietrich, I am General Eisenhower." But with a flashlight, Dietrich proved her identity.

Aumont then found himself responsible not only for his comrades but for a wandering band of American performers. "Being made prisoner wasn't a very agreeable prospect for me," he reflected later.

> But to be responsible for Marlene's capture! In the eyes of the Germans, she was a renegade serving on behalf of the American army and against her own people . . . Under the veneer of her legendary image, however, I saw a strong and courageous woman. There were no tears, no panic.

Instead, she tried to ignore the danger to them all, commenting on the peculiar odor from Aumont's uniform. He explained that he had just had his first sleep in days, under a tank, next to the corpse of a Senegalese soldier. Eventually they found the French camp and hours later they located the Americans, who were not at all pleased at the temporary absence of Dietrich and her companions. By this time commanding officers had become accustomed to seeing her as a feisty, peripatetic den mother, Joan of Arc mustering her troops. She always obeyed orders, but when they were contravened by circumstances beyond her control she remained unperturbed and unapologetic.

Worse anxiety awaited everyone as they moved north toward Rome. On May 23, the Allies began a drive on the Anzio beachhead and soon the German stranglehold on Italy was definitively broken. On roads secured by the Allies there were large, leggy drawings of Dietrich—illustrated directions by amateur military artists, pointing the way to her unit. She insisted that her show must go on despite the evident danger of being so perilously close to the site where fighting had not yet ceased.

Surrounded by a protective ring of tanks, the Camp Show began the night of May 25, and as she sang "I Can't Give You Anything but Love, Baby," hundreds of soldiers provided the lighting by pointing their flashlights on the performing area. The effect was almost cinematic, as the shimmering, shifting lights sought her out and her low voice broke through the darkness. At that moment she thought (as she told a reporter next day), If they don't like my act, all they have to do is turn off their flashlights! But the lighting remained —as haunting as anything ever devised by von Sternberg. "I felt," she said, "as if I had passed the toughest test of my career."

Several days later, Dietrich came down with viral pneumonia, but she continued to perform; eventually, however, she collapsed, dangerously close to delirium with fever and dehydration. She was sent to a hospital tent, treated with injections of penicillin and five days later resumed two shows daily from Naples to Bari, entertaining groups of from fifty to twenty-two thousand. "Anyone who has played for soldiers overseas," she said later, "is not going to be satisfied with another kind of audience for a long time. The boys are full of generosity and never gloomy."

On June 4, the Allies broke through into Rome, and when Dietrich and her companions arrived a week later the street battle was still fierce. Fanning out through the city, soldiers fought a Nazi rear guard at the Forum, an armored convoy near Trajan's column and snipers round almost every corner. Dietrich and her troupe then wheeled dozens of the injured to a large hall, where she sang and joked until darkness. "It gave me the opportunity of kissing more soldiers than any woman in the world," she said later. "No woman can please one man; this way, you can please many men."

Before the end of June, her ten-week assignment completed, she was in New York, fulfilling her obligation to appear at the premiere of *Kismet.* Urged during publicity and press conferences to comment on what seemed the imminent collapse of the German Reich, she spoke frankly: "The Germany I knew is not there anymore. I don't think of it. I suppose if I did, I could never do these tours."

Telephone calls to her agent confirmed what she suspected. Her absence had not made Hollywood's heart grow fonder; on the contrary, she was out of sight and therefore not much in their business minds. Despite her two-picture contract with MGM, the studio could not find a suitable project for her after *Kismet,* and so she returned to the USO Camp Shows. Leaving New York at the end of August, she again performed twice daily at bases in Greenland and

Iceland, with a new troupe of musicians and a new accompanist replacing Danny Thomas.

BUT THE SPIRIT OF JOAN OF ARC HAD NOT ENTIRELY taken possession of Marlene Dietrich, and during this second (and, as it happened, longer) tour, she seemed to eyewitnesses quite conscious of her legendary status and fully prepared to exploit it for her present and future.

This she did first in London. Dietrich arrived in September, briefly met another old flame, Douglas Fairbanks, Jr., and then attached herself securely as a regular visitor to the headquarters of the European Theater of Operations—which by an odd coincidence happened to be housed at 20 Grosvenor Square, the former apartment-hotel where she and Fairbanks had lived six years before. With the regal grace worthy at least of a princess, she toured the apartment she had once occupied, showing Commanding General Jacob Devers, his officers and the press what could be stored in which cupboards, and how the rooms might be best furnished. "Only the door to [the] fuchsia bathroom had to be closed when visitors arrived," according to Colonel Barney Oldfield. He had been a journalist and publicist before the war, and was then entrusted with the complex job of managing military press and public relations throughout the European campaign.

Oldfield, a commissioned officer for thirty years, was known for being (as newsman Charles Kuralt later called him) "the king of the press agents." But he was also a sharp strategist and tactician, and General Floyd L. Parks, the first American commander in Berlin in 1945, confirmed that he did nothing during the first days of occupation without Oldfield at his side. Oldfield became a dutiful guardian and occasional facilitator for Dietrich throughout the next year, tasks required on her behalf by top-ranking American officers. Among them were Generals Mark Clark, Omar Bradley and George S. Patton—and especially the handsome, enigmatic and controversial Major General James M. Gavin, commander of the 82nd Airborne Division, who took the offer of Marlene Dietrich to be his company's mascot and friend, and eventually his lover.

"Dietrich was a very strong-minded lady," Oldfield recalled many years later. "She could be glamorous and she could be earthy. I saw her gnaw on a German sausage like a hungry terrier, but of course she could make a grand entrance that would upstage a reigning queen. She could be as authoritarian as Caesar, and she could pout as prettily as a six-year-old whose lollipop was stolen after only one lick."

During her time in London early that autumn of 1944, Dietrich made several propaganda appearances on ABSIE (the American Broadcasting Station in England), on a program aptly called "Marlene Sings to Her Homeland." In these transmissions, beamed to all of Germany, she sang songs from her films as well as familiar beer-hall melodies and German airs, always dedicating them to the Allied soldiers who were "about to meet up with you boys and destroy the Reich." These broadcasts, and her outspoken rage against Nazi Germany made her extremely unpopular—indeed, very much reviled—in her homeland, both during and after the war.

Dietrich's greatest concern, as the Allies proceeded to sweep across Europe toward Germany, was the fate of her mother, Wilhelmina Felsing Dietrich von Losch. As Oldfield remembered, this was the topic to which she turned in every conversation with officers, journalists, pilots and paratroopers. She intended to enlist every kind of aid in learning if Wilhelmina, whom she had not seen since 1931 (and from whom there had been no letters since 1938), was alive or dead.

In October, Dietrich arrived in Paris (liberated since the end of August) and decided that henceforth she would make this the headquarters for her own European Theater of Operations. She would still present her one-woman show as close to the front as possible, still contact the most important officers for needs and favors, and still risk safety to secure the hearts of all-male audiences in the last brutal campaigns of World War II. But whenever possible she retreated to the relative comfort of the Ritz where, among other notables, she enjoyed the company of Ernest Hemingway.

As a journalist, Hemingway had made his way to London and managed to fly several missions with the Royal Air Force before crossing the Channel with American troops on D-Day. Attaching himself to the 22nd Regiment of the Fourth Infantry Division, he fought in Normandy, participated in the liberation of Paris and, although officially a newsman, was highly respected as a skilled strategist for intelligence activities and guerrilla warfare. Dietrich sat on the edge of his bathtub at the Ritz, exchanging war news while he shaved, and telling him of the ardent hours she had just spent with General Patton, who had given her a pair of his pearl-handled pistols. Indeed, she said quite calmly, she and Patton had already shared the same bed more than once in London and in Paris.

The intervals at the Ritz in 1944 and 1945 remain examples of Dietrich's canny abilities with the officers during these difficult times, for whenever she was present there were somehow ample supplies of liquor, champagne, cocktail food and caviar. Much of this turned up anonymously (the black market thrived), much of it was sent with the compliments of this officer or that general— especially her great admirer General Patton, called "Old Blood and Guts" by his men.

There were the usual rivalries around Dietrich, this time with *Collier's* war correspondent Martha Gellhorn (the third and soon to be ex–Mrs. Hemingway) and with Mary Welsh (his current mistress and soon to be fourth wife). "Both were strong women," Barney Oldfield said of Dietrich and Gellhorn,

> tenaciously determined, probably in the land of the Amazons, and [acted like] opposing warlords. There was always the impression that each resented the other and denigrated her. To Gellhorn, Marlene was "that actress," while Marlene thought of her as "that writer." These two women jousted for the attention of General Jim Gavin . . .

. . . as they did, for different reasons, for the attention of Hemingway himself.

As for Mary Welsh, Hemingway was obviously in love with her, although time had not diluted his fascination with Dietrich. He proudly squired both women to official meetings and receptions in Paris at the end of the year, showing them off and boasting of their social help in his suite—which, he said, was "the Paris command post for all veterans of the 22nd Infantry Regiment." Although the relationship of these two women to Hemingway differed, neither suffered gladly the other's presence. No one more than Dietrich coveted the attention of men—by the thousands in an audience or individually in friendship or affair.

To obtain and keep that attention, almost nothing was beyond her caprice. William Walton, the highly respected journalist then working for *Time* magazine (and later for the *New Republic),* was subjected to the full Hollywood-party treatment. He, too, was billeted at the Ritz that year, and met Dietrich through Hemingway.

Walton had bought a chic Paris hat for a sweetheart in New York, which Dietrich insisted on modelling for all who came to her room. One evening, she passed Walton's open door while he was working and awaiting friends. She stopped, walked back to her own room and returned—completely nude—wearing the hat at a rakish angle. "Don't I look cute?" she asked innocently. Walton replied calmly, as if she were also wearing the latest Paris frock, and Dietrich had to attempt a dignified retreat. On another occasion, as Hemingway's biographer documented, Dietrich wore the same hat and calmly used Walton's toilet (taking a page from Tallulah Bankhead's stylebook), not interrupting her conversation with him while he shaved. In some ways it seems remarkable that generals and war correspondents within her emotional-ballistic range managed to conclude the war.

The discipline of conduct in war never affected the part of Dietrich's character that was calmly exhibitionist. She dangled naked legs from truck platforms before sighing soldiers, and more than once she burst in on a soldiers' camp shower to bathe as if no one else were present—actions which could not have been as beneficial to morale as she may have intended, and which led more than one angry officer to label her a cruel tease. Jean Renoir recalled that his wife Dido was so often asked by Dietrich to accompany her to the ladies' room of a restaurant that Dido feared an imminent proposition. "But Marlene simply wanted to show off her legs," according to Renoir, "and [she] took Dido with her on the pretext that she needed to be protected against the women who assailed her. It was simply the enactment of a ritual."

. . .

THAT AUTUMN AND DURING A VICIOUSLY COLD WIN-
ter, Dietrich divided her USO entertainment duties between divi-
sions of the Third and Ninth armies in eastern France, Belgium,
Holland and at last in Germany. To banish shaking chills in the town
of Nancy, in Lorraine, she drank Calvados (to which she had been
introduced by Erich Maria Remarque). Imbibing on an empty
stomach, she vomited constantly, "but I would rather vomit than be
hospitalized," she wrote later of that time. "Otherwise, what am I
afraid of? Of failing . . . of being unable to endure this way of
living any longer. And everybody will say, smiling, 'Of course, of
course, that was an absurd idea [for her to go to war] in the first
place.' "

With the ruthless, proud and independent Patton, Dietrich and
her performance troupe moved north in December from Nancy
into Belgium—precisely at the time of the Battle of the Bulge, from
mid-December 1944 to mid-January 1945. She frequently traveled
and dined with this tough tactician, and on at least one occasion she
fell asleep in his office. He carried her to his car, drove her to her
barracks, and when she awoke next morning he was still by her side.

Whether she bestirred herself at some time before dawn is not
clear, but members of Patton's staff—like his aide, Frank McCarthy,
who produced the film *Patton*—later confirmed that there was an
intense affair between Dietrich and the general all during the time
of her attachment to his army.

"She charmed her way onto more airplanes than Bob Hope—
and with an entire troop," according to Barney Oldfield. "She
could commandeer a jeep and driver and all sorts of privileges, and
these were accorded to her as if she were a queen in the eyes of those
she dealt with." Dietrich was, as she later said, frequently summoned
to Patton's quarters on the pretext of his needing a report on her
shows or to inquire about her willingness to accompany him on a
hospital tour. (When director Billy Wilder later asked her if her
affair had not indeed been with Eisenhower instead of Patton, she
replied, "But, darling, how could it have been Eisenhower? He
wasn't even at the front!") During this critical time of the conflict,

Dietrich managed to brace Patton as she did his men. Needing an official password for her, he decreed "Legs," in her honor.

Accompanying Patton all through the hostilities in the Ardennes, Dietrich suffered severe frostbite that plagued her for the rest of her life and exacerbated her later arthritis. Her twice daily song-and-joke shows continued during this last great German offensive on the western front in southern Belgium. While Allied aircraft were impeded by wretched weather, Nazi Panzers advanced toward Antwerp and the German Fifth Army completely surrounded Bastogne. Nazi Field Marshal Karl von Rundstedt then demanded that Brigadier General Anthony McAuliffe surrender the city; his response was the legendary "Nuts!" Only when Patton barrelled into Bastogne on December 26, with Dietrich at his side, did the situation begin to alter; the First Army joined them a week later, and with that the Germans began to retreat.

For the morale of troops in the thick of the fighting, the USO pitched camp two miles from the German-Dutch-Belgian border and performed in Maastricht, Holland—the first town in that country to be liberated from the Germans. "Like the rest of us that winter, she had to wear long, woolly, drop-seat underwear, heavy trousers and gloves," according to Oldfield, who was there with a press corps, "but she ignored the weather and changed into nylon stockings and a sequined evening gown—and in this glamorous outfit she stuck the musical saw between her legs and played for her cheering audience."

Seeing her discomfort in the severe cold, war correspondent Gordon Gammack (then with the *Des Moines Register and Tribune*) recalled that in Maastricht he gave Dietrich a small coal stove for warmth, which she willingly accepted. Several years later, he approached Dietrich as she strolled with her grandchildren on a New York street. He introduced himself politely as the man with the stove from Maastricht, and said how much he had enjoyed her brave performance during the war. "Thank you for the stove," she said unsmiling, with a chill that recalled that winter of 1945. "Thank you and goodbye."

Aachen, twenty miles from Maastricht, had been the first large German city to fall (on October 20, 1944); it was on the route to

Berlin when the Allies and Dietrich's USO camp arrived at the end of January 1945. Acting now as interpreter for the American army, she was asked to tell the frightened inhabitants to evacuate the streets so that tanks could move through; to her surprise, she received a warm welcome from these Germans: "they couldn't have been friendlier, even though they knew I was on the other side." But Aachen bestowed another, less clement memory, for there the entire company contracted an infestation of body lice. With no showers, soap or medicine, the situation was grim until Dietrich selected a soldier from her audience and, to the accompanying hoots of his comrades, asked that he report later to her tent behind the truck. The young man's subsequent report to his waiting friends has not been documented, but he was only invited to offer Marlene Dietrich delousing powder and instructions for its use.

The next stop was Stolberg, a few miles from Aachen, where she met a correspondent with the International News Service. "I am through with Hollywood," she told reporter Frank Conniff, perhaps more from her doubts about her career possibilities than from a settled moral conviction about Hollywood. Gazing at the wreckage of the city, she added, "I hate to see all these ruined buildings, but I guess Germany deserves everything that's coming to her."

FROM FEBRUARY THROUGH JUNE 1945, DIETRICH shuttled from Germany to Paris, alternating shows for both Allied and enemy wounded soldiers with long intervals at the Ritz, usually with Patton. And that spring, through Hemingway, she scored an important strategic victory for herself and ultimately for her mother. Because Patton then proceeded eastward through the Saar toward Berlin and the USO was deployed on a slower, more circuitous route, his contact with Dietrich was subsequently diminished. In fact he was replaced, for her attention was then lavished almost exclusively on General Gavin, and their affair affected both lives in important ways.

In 1945, James M. Gavin was a slim, six-foot-two-inch, dark-haired, boyish gentleman who looked almost a decade younger than his thirty-seven years. The youngest general in the history of the army, Gavin had lied about his birthdate to enter military service without a high school diploma, and from his first years with the army he impressed superiors with his thorough dedication and serene, methodical approach to supervising men and solving problems. Zealous in his duty as a paratrooper, he commanded the parachute combat team that first invaded Sicily in 1943, and by the time he landed at Normandy on D-Day had risen to the rank of brigadier general and soon commanded the entire 82nd Airborne Division. Because he was known to be a man of extraordinary valor (he fought for a month with a broken back, earning himself the Silver Cross and the Purple Heart), and because his military prowess was combined with a gentle, courtly manner, women—and some men as well—found him fascinating, even seductive. As Barney Oldfield recalled, "Gavin was a very glamorous figure, not only respected but much talked about by everyone. Many strong-minded women, including Mary Welsh and Marlene, were attracted to him."

Dietrich and Gavin met when Hemingway invited the general for drinks at the Ritz and Dietrich was among the guests—to the chagrin of Mary Welsh, with whom (as Barney Oldfield recalled) Dietrich had an immediate standoff for Gavin's attention. The Dietrich-Gavin affair, conducted with the utmost discretion, began that night in Gavin's suite and continued when Dietrich followed him back to Germany. Although for obvious reasons he made no explicit reference to Dietrich in his later account of that time, Gavin did describe an allusive incident in his book *On to Berlin*. As the 82nd was taking German soldiers prisoner, his men found a concertina and sang the German tune "Lili Marlene," which—although as familiar to Allies as to the enemy—had become, at Gavin's insistence, the anthem of the 82nd Airborne Division.

There were several reasons for Dietrich's attraction to Gavin. Because she was close to him, as she was to Patton and Hemingway and a number of journalists and correspondents, she shared the knowledge of Operation Eclipse, the Allied plan to storm Berlin—a strategy which was to feature Gavin's 82nd Airborne Division (and a tactic which was eventually abandoned). Since Gavin was to be the first commanding officer entering the German capital, he would be the man Dietrich could enlist in the search for her mother. Ever conscious of the power of her glamour and allure, Dietrich was certainly willing to exploit them in this matter.

There had always been a distant antagonism between the bombastic, egocentric Patton and the sedate, reserved Gavin. "Patton seemed to be getting all the publicity," Gavin wrote years later, "[but] the record now shows that it was the First Army [not Patton's Third] that took the brunt of [the German attack on Bastogne] . . . Yet when *Stars and Stripes* arrived daily, it was full of stories about Patton and his Third Army and how the defenders at Bastogne [not the counteroffensive First Army] were winning the Battle of the Bulge."

The younger general could not have been displeased, therefore, to find himself the object of Marlene Dietrich's ardor under any circumstances, and his resentment of Patton may have added to the satisfaction of his affair with her. And on Dietrich's side there was even more complexity, for in associating with the generals she was in a sense rediscovering the aloof officers of her childhood—her own uniformed father and stepfather—whose emotional endorsement she had long ago been denied.

GERMANY SURRENDERED ON MAY 7, AND MOST USO shows were disbanded by the end of June. After a sojourn in New York that summer, Dietrich returned to Paris, where Gavin contacted her with the news she had so long awaited. He, Colonel Oldfield and Lieutenant Colonel Albert McCleery were in the first American column to enter Berlin on July 1. While Gavin and Oldfield saw, respectively, to military and communications matters, McCleery located Wilhelmina Dietrich von Losch at the address Marlene had left with Gavin. Frightened, living in desperate poverty with an older sister, Wilhelmina did not at first understand McCleery's news; indeed, because Goebbels had put out the fiction that London was totally destroyed, she presumed that her daughter (whose propaganda broadcasts she had heard) had been killed.

Oldfield then arrived with a car, an interpreter and two photographers. Wilhelmina was gently persuaded to accompany them to the Tempelhof airfield where, on September 19, Dietrich arrived on the military shuttle flight from Paris. The airplane door opened and she stepped out carrying a briefcase and her musical saw, her uniform crisply pressed. After a tearful reunion, mother and daughter spent several days together, and through Gavin the most liberal rations were sent to Frau von Losch. Ten days later, Dietrich—obviously emboldened—directly approached the formidable Marshal Georgi Zhukov, commander-in-chief of the Russian occupying forces in Berlin, at his headquarters. Rudi Sieber's parents, she had learned, were interned in a Czech camp. After a long private meeting, Zhukov arranged for the Siebers to be relocated to Berlin and given hospitality appropriate to the family of the international star; generous ration cards were supplied to them, too.

The reunion of Dietrich and her mother happened none too soon, for Wilhelmina's health was frail and that autumn she declined rapidly. Finally, in Friedenau, the American sector of Berlin, she died in her sleep of heart failure on November 6 at the age of sixty-nine. From Paris, where she received the news, Dietrich at once telephoned Gavin, who was then attending an important press reception in London. Because of the strict regulations regarding non-fraternization between Americans and Germans, Gavin himself departed at once for Berlin with Barney Oldfield, to supervise the funeral details. But their plane encountered a blinding storm and they had to set down at Schweinfurt instead of Templehof.

At that point, Gavin received bad news of his own: the 101st Division had been selected over his now legendary 82nd as the regular army's postwar airborne unit (a decision later rescinded). This immediately involved Gavin in a flurry of calls, interviews and memoranda. He had not, however, forgotten the reason for his trip to Berlin: "Do everything you can for her," he said quietly to Barney Oldfield before hurrying to attend to his own complicated business. That night, Wilhelmina's coffin was carried from her apartment to a small cemetery, where Oldfield hurriedly arranged for a grave. Finally, Dietrich arrived from Paris, accompanied by William Walton. The final formalities were brief. "Miss Dietrich was heartbroken and wept constantly," Barney Oldfield remembered.

13: 1945–1949

After she returned from Germany to Hollywood at the war's end, Marlene Dietrich was the guest of Orson Welles and his wife Rita Hayworth, at their home on Carmelina Drive in the Brentwood section of Los Angeles. Several film projects failed to reach even serious negotiations with Dietrich, and for several weeks she turned to managing the household chores and social calendar. After a few hints and then a blunt request, she prevailed on Welles to arrange an introduction to Greta Garbo, whom she had seen only from afar and longed to meet. According to him, Dietrich simply adored Garbo; others had the impression that she wanted to see how Garbo looked after several years' absence from the screen, and that she also wanted to meet the woman whom Mercedes de Acosta had once loved, perhaps because Dietrich's affair with de Acosta was also history by this time.

And so a party was arranged, at the home of Clifton Webb in Beverly Hills. Welles introduced the two women, and Dietrich gushed that she was thrilled, calling Garbo divine, a goddess, an immortal muse and inspiration. Garbo, who hated flattery as much as crowds, managed only a tight smile and a curt acknowledgment designed to end the conversation, but Dietrich persisted, her praise rising like religious veneration. Garbo, too, persisted, replying nothing but muttering distracted thanks until the exhausted worshiper finally withdrew. En route back to Carmelina Drive later that evening, Dietrich said to Welles, "Her feet aren't as big as they say." But the topic was not closed. Over drinks at the house, she insisted that, contrary to popular lore, Garbo certainly did wear makeup: "She has beaded eyelashes! Do you know how long it takes to have your eyelashes beaded?" Welles had no idea, but the matter was not further explored. In any case, Marlene Dietrich and Greta Garbo had met at last; there is no evidence they ever did again.

BY CHRISTMAS 1945, LA DIETRICH WAS IN PARIS with Jean Gabin. The war had aged him: his hair had gone to grey, he had gained too much weight despite military service, the facial lines were deep, and his normally dour expression seemed graver. She, however, kept her hair a lustrous, lacquered blond and her waistline slim, and the few lines round her mouth and eyes were artfully concealed with the best cosmetics. Gabin looked at least a decade older than forty-one, while Dietrich seemed five years younger than forty-four.

Their disparate appearances would perhaps have been meanly discussed in Hollywood, but in postwar Paris Dietrich and Gabin made an attractive Continental couple. "She is the only married actress whose romance is discussed openly by columnists, magazine writers and herself," noted an American reporter. "There is nothing hush-hush about her and Gabin. She is married to Rudolf Sieber, but they have an understanding. So much so that he has accompanied her on dates with Gabin." It was still to Rudi's advantage to make himself agreeable, of course, since the bulk of his income came from Dietrich's career (however inactive).

Thus happily reunited but each without work, Gabin and Dietrich decided to look for a movie they could make together to subsidize her protracted sojourn in Paris. To the rescue came the great Marcel Carné, who had directed Gabin in two prewar pictures and during the war had made *Les Enfants du Paradis (Children of Paradise)*, which was, then and forever after, generally regarded as one of the finest films of all time. With his screenwriter Jacques Prévert, Carné was preparing a kind of fatalist, allegorical romance about occupied Paris called *Les Portes de la Nuit (The Gates of Night)*, whose leading roles he immediately offered to Dietrich and Gabin.

In her statements to the press in 1945 and 1946, she insisted her USO tours had taught her much about "real life," about courage and commitment, life and death and basic values. Dietrich said she could never return to Hollywood and her former custom of glamorous moviemaking. This was an appetizing morsel of self-promotion designed to suggest the New Dietrich, changed and chastened by the horror of war, and America swallowed it whole. But as Carné recalled, it certainly did not alter her approach to her first postwar film project in January 1946:

> Marlene had stipulated in her contract that she would not have to do the picture until she had approved the script, and she began to review it with us, scene by scene. She was, shall we say, less than enthusiastic and began to make a thousand suggestions —each one of which seemed, to Jacques and me, utterly absurd. One example: she wanted to play a night scene completely out of character, descending from a cab and paying the driver by taking the money from the top of her stocking!

Director and writer stood firm, and not even Gabin could convince Dietrich that her role as a benighted wife in war-torn Paris simply must not be prettified. She was equally adamant, and so—"deeply hurt at seeing her talent misunderstood" (thus Carné, with light sarcasm)—she refused to do the picture.

Within days (before the end of February), producer Marc Pelletier contacted her with an alternative project, to be directed by Georges Lacombe. *Martin Roumagnac* was based on a novel about a high-class prostitute whose passionate affair with her building contractor ends when he learns about her profession, kills her, stands trial, and is then murdered by one of her former lovers. Neither the actors nor the director could enliven the dreary script, and when the film was released (in America as *The Room Upstairs)* it was dismissed as a languid, unconvincing bundle of clichés, notable only for the many shots of Dietrich's legs and the Sternbergian lighting—all of this unofficially supervised by herself. But she was consoled for its failure by her fee, which was then the equivalent of $100,000.

Despite an arduous production schedule and much evening reshooting, Dietrich insisted that she and Gabin make themselves available to Parisian social and cultural life whenever possible. She sang at a gala revue honoring the Royal Air Force, and on March 15 the couple dined with Noël Coward, whose plays and films she had admired for over a decade, and whose friendship she vigorously cultivated; Coward, on the other hand, had the unenviable task of trying to mediate a Dietrich-Gabin argument that raged throughout the meal. According to Coward, Dietrich "looked lovely but talked about herself a good deal"—her favorite topic of conversation, as he and others learned.

The dispute apparently concerned Gabin's resentment over Dietrich's resumption of her affair with General Gavin. For one thing, the names of Gavin and Gabin confused Parisian gossips and journalists, who reported that Dietrich was seen somewhere with Gavin when she had actually been at another place with Gabin, and vice versa; at one point, it was rumored that Gavin would be her co-star in a forthcoming film. Public confusion or no, Dietrich demanded (as always) her independence. But when Gabin countered that he would, therefore, pursue another actress he had met, Dietrich was furious. As usual, she could not approve her lover's dalliance. Referring to Sarah Bernhardt, she insisted, on the contrary, that it was the prerogative of a woman artist like herself to have a lover (even, presumably, simultaneous lovers).

Coward was not the only witness to the troubles. The writer Max Colpet (formerly Kolpe), whom she had known earlier in Berlin and recently met again, was also in Paris, and in the middle of one night his telephone rang:

"Are you alone?" she blurted, without introduction.

"Yes, why?" Colpet replied, recognizing her voice.

"Can I stay overnight at your place?"

"Of course. What's happened?"

"I'll tell you when I get there."

The matter was simple. Dietrich had had a terrific fight with Gabin when she was preparing for an evening with General Gavin. She took refuge with Colpet, prevailing on him to escort her for her rendezvous with the general at Monseigneur, a faded old romantic nightclub overladen with Russian artifacts. In such movie-set surroundings, filled with the sound of a strolling gypsy orchestra, Gavin looked very much the young, heroic leader, recalled Colpet, who added that he "had the impression that she had protracted her affair with Gavin in order to demonstrate her independence from Gabin, who was very possessive." She also needed good contacts, superb references, and access to quick transport to London or New York, where she had possible film work pending. For all these reasons— and because Gavin was the perfect, glamorous escort and an adoring admirer—the affair continued through 1945 and much of 1946.

But Dietrich's cavalier independence and the role of lover *primus inter pares* was finally too much for Jean Gabin; within the year he married the French actress Maria Mauban. This was a devastating blow to Dietrich, who could never understand why a man she still loved (or ever had loved) would commit to another woman. When Robert Kennedy asked her, at a Washington luncheon in 1963, why she said she left Jean Gabin, she replied, "Because he wanted to marry me. I hate marriage. It is an immoral institution. I told him that if I stayed with him it was because I was in love with him, and that is all that mattered. He won't see me anymore. But he still loves me."

Josef von Sternberg's postwar marriage was an equivalent shock to her. (An aphorism frequently on her lips was: "When I devote myself to someone, no one can undo it.") So far as she was concerned for herself, the Sieber marriage was a sensible model anyone could follow: one married once, for the protection it provided from other, overeager lovers; one married once for the social status and for the children's legitimacy—and then damn the torpedoes, full speed ahead.

This attitude was for a time inherited by her daughter. Not until 1946, when Maria wanted to become engaged to a New York scenic and toy designer named William Riva, did she yield to Dean Good-man's request to terminate their marriage, which had been in name only since the end of 1943. As Maria might have expected, Dietrich again disapproved of the man she chose and strongly discouraged another precipitous marriage. But this second engagement lasted a year, by which time the couple decided to marry (on July 4, 1947) with or without Mama's blessing.

On January 11, 1946, the night before the Victory March in New York, Walter Winchell announced that Marlene Dietrich and "a certain very young general," who were both in town for the parade, would soon marry. Informed of this embarrassing (and un-true) development by a phone call from Barney Oldfield, Gavin coolly said the story was of no concern to him. His wife, who had known of the affair for some time, reacted differently, and within two years she was granted a divorce. "I could compete with ordinary women," she said privately, "but when the competition is Marlene Dietrich, what's the use?"

AFTER SEVERAL WEEKS IN PARIS THAT SPRING AND summer, the Gavin affair ended. Dietrich now had no prospects of European film work and therefore accepted an offer from Holly-wood to appear in a film called *Golden Earrings*. "I must call the general in Paris" were her first words as she stepped off the airplane and was met by the director Mitchell Leisen.

"But you've just come from Paris!" he said.

"He made me promise I would call him," Dietrich replied, "be-cause he was worried about me. He wants me to marry him, but I can't be an army wife." Leisen was an expert filmmaker but a poor keeper of confidences, and within hours Hollywood buzzed with the news of Dietrich's romance with a military hero. Nonsense, insisted the most alert gossips: it was *Gabin* she would eventually marry; there was no one in her life named *Gavin*.

Because she had been absent from Hollywood three full years (and had not starred in a successful film since 1939), Leisen had to convince Paramount that Dietrich was the right choice to play Lydia, a vulgar but seductive Middle European gypsy who helps a

British intelligence officer smuggle a poison-gas formula out of Nazi Germany just before the war by disguising him as her peasant husband. When she was first offered the role, Dietrich was still in Europe and visited gypsy camps to see how the women looked, dressed and behaved. Now at the studio for wardrobe and makeup tests, she assured Leisen she would play Lydia with complete fidelity to realism—to European neorealism, in fact, which flinched at nothing.

This she did astonishingly well, for although Dietrich could not of course completely abandon her pretension to youthful beauty (nor would the studio have desired it), she dispatched the role of a greasy, sloppy gypsy with the kind of fresh comic panache not seen since her Frenchy in *Destry Rides Again.* As a sex-starved wench, she swoops down on the stuffy hero played by Ray Milland, supervising his transformation into a Hungarian peasant. Munching bread, gnawing on a fish-head supper, spitting for good luck, diving for Milland's lips and chest, she is the complete, man-hungry virago—at once crude, funny and sensuous throughout the aridly incredible narrative. "You look like a wild bull!" she whispers to Milland after she has finished with his disguising makeup, pierced his ears and clipped on the golden earrings; then she nearly growls, "The girls—will—go—*mad*—for you!" Often resembling the seductive young Gloria Swanson, Dietrich does not simply breathe in this picture; she seems to exhale fire.

But the appealing comic nonsense of the completed *Golden Earrings* did not apply to the rigors of production, for there were bitter feuds. Milland, who had just won an Oscar playing an alcoholic in Billy Wilder's harrowing film *The Lost Weekend,* disliked Dietrich and feared she would steal the picture (which she handily did). He also found her commitment to realism somewhat revolting—especially in the eating scene, when she repeatedly stuck a fish in her mouth, sucked out the eye, pulled off the head, swallowed it and (after Leisen had shot the scene) promptly stuck her finger in her throat and vomited.

To make matters even more awkward for Paramount as they considered her option, the finished film was condemned by the watchful Legion of Decency, which disdained both Dietrich's sexually seething characterization (she could not keep her hands off Milland) and this pair of unmarried gypsies romping lustily in the woods. The Legion's censure was officially an acute embarrassment for the studio, although it was also splendid free publicity: the picture returned three million dollars in the next two years. After filming was completed in mid-October, she scrubbed off the four layers of dark makeup for the last time, tossed aside the greasy black wig, treated herself to an array of new suits and promptly departed for an extended holiday in New York.

On January 4, 1947, Dietrich embarked for Paris and a film deal that never materialized. Reunited with Rudi, she tried to obtain a visa so that he could visit his aged father in Germany. Then, to ease his disappointment when they were unsuccessful, she gave him half the profits on a sale of the Felsing jewelry stores in Berlin, which she inherited that spring when they were finally returned to the family after the liquidation of Nazi control of private businesses. Rudi was able to send his parents a large portion of the share he received from Dietrich, and thanks to her their final years were much more comfortable.

Neither of her parents replied to Maria's announcement of her plan to marry William Riva that summer, although Dietrich sent a refrigerator to their tiny apartment at 1118 Third Avenue. Only after she realized that the marriage was indeed a happy and apparently permanent one did she (somewhat reluctantly) endorse the union. The birth of John Michael Riva on June 28, 1948, made Marlene Dietrich a grandmother, and by 1951 she was sufficiently resigned to the marriage to take $43,000 from a tax refund and buy the Rivas a town house on East Ninety-fifth Street.

From Paris that summer of 1947, Dietrich wrote to her Paramount hairdresser, Nellie Manley, that she was "living quietly at the Hotel Georges V, cooking whatever can be cooked. The attitude and the feelings of the people are not as good as they were during the war. It is depressing, but not hopeless. We must all see to it that this is changed and things are better."

Her own fortunes improved that August, when Billy Wilder stopped in Paris to visit her after filming exterior shots for a forthcoming "black comedy" about life in occupied postwar Berlin; he offered Dietrich the role of Erika von Schlütow in the picture, to be called *A Foreign Affair.* At first she rejected it, hesitating to play the German mistress of an American army officer who loses him to a winsome visiting congresswoman and is then taken away by military police after her Nazi past is revealed. Nor was she persuaded by the Frederick Hollander songs commissioned for her. Dietrich agreed to the job only when the director showed her screen tests made by two American actresses whose performances she considered hilariously bad. By the end of October she was packing for the trip to California.

But there was a good reason to stop in New York, for on November 18 she was awarded the Medal of Freedom, America's highest civilian honor (at the time conferred only by the War Department). At a ceremony at the United States Military Academy, West Point, General Maxwell D. Taylor read the somewhat inaccurate (and breathless) citation:

> Miss Marlene Dietrich, civilian volunteer with the United States Service Organization Camp Shows, performed meritorious service in support of military operations in North Africa, Sicily and Italy from April 14 to June 16, 1944, and in the North Atlantic Bases in Europe from August 30, 1944 to July 13, 1945, meeting a gruelling schedule of performances under battle conditions, during adverse weather and despite risk to her life. Although her health was failing, Miss Dietrich continued to bring pleasure and cheer to more than five hundred thousand American soldiers. With commendable energy and sincerity she contributed immeasurably to the welfare of the troops in these theatres.

The allegation that the Medal of Freedom was unofficially sponsored by Patton or Gavin has never been confirmed. However, the fact that she deserved the award seems undeniable.

A week later she stepped from the train at Union Station and accepted a bouquet of flowers from her new director. Wilder, who had known her in Berlin even before *The Blue Angel,* had co-authored screenplays in Germany, France and America (among them Garbo's *Ninotchka,* written with Charles Brackett) and had begun directing in 1942. By 1947, *Double Indemnity* and *The Lost Weekend* were praised as remarkable excursions to the frontiers of human perversity; *Sunset Boulevard, Some Like It Hot, The Apartment* and many more were yet to come. With his patented brand of acerbic moral cynicism, Wilder had prepared *A Foreign Affair* as a satiric criticism of widespread military corruption amid the ruins of Berlin, of the Allied involvement in a shameful black market, and of the self-righteous abuse of German civilians by occupying American soldiers. When filming began in December, Dietrich's co-star as the prissy, investigating congresswoman was Jean Arthur; the leading man was John Lund; and the pianist in the cabaret was none other than Hollander himself, invited in tribute to his long association as Dietrich's composer.

Like Pasternak, Wilder understood the value of deglamorizing Dietrich. Her first appearance in *A Foreign Affair* goes beyond anything in *Golden Earrings:* her hair is unbrushed, her face smirched with toothpaste, water trickles from her mouth as she brushes and gargles. This character is no Amy Jolly, no Concha Perez. As the story proceeds, it becomes clear that Erika can manipulate American officers as easily as she did Nazis, one of whom was her lover and all of whom she easily attended as a fashionable companion. But she has suffered privately, socially and by postwar deprivation for her guilty past; her act at the Lorelei cabaret, singing "Black Market" and "The Ruins of Berlin," expresses her cool cynicism, her distrust of any nation's claim to moral supremacy and her necessary, fearful suspicion of everyone. The role was perfect for Dietrich, for she had been long confirmed by Hollywood as von Sternberg's icon of the tarnished woman masked with pain and capable of the sudden acknowledgment of her own need for tenderness and forgiveness— indeed, for redemption from the past. "I knew," Wilder said years later, "that whatever obsession she had with her appearance, she was also a thorough professional. From the time she met von Sternberg she had always been very interested in his magic tricks with the camera—tricks she tried to teach every cameraman in later pictures."

The film, her role in it and indeed her entire public image up to 1947 were synthesized not only by Wilder, but by Frederick Hollander, who was through long association certainly one to understand the swirling patterns of Dietrich's complex emotional history. Her singing of his touching, bittersweet "Illusions" remains certainly one of the least affected, most deeply felt recordings of her entire career, unmatched even by any of the versions of it she recorded later. In the recording studio and on the set next day—with only Hollander for her accompanist—she somehow cut through every one of her usual tendencies to make a song just a little bit more theatrical, just a bit more perfect, too *right*. As we hear "Illusions" in the finished film and see her face as she seems to sing to and of herself and her character without affectation, we feel the sting as the words become a summary of her own life:

> *Want to buy some illusions,*
>   *Slightly used, second-hand?*
> *They were lovely illusions,*
>   *Reaching high, built on sand.*
> *They had a touch of Paradise,*
>   *A spell you can't explain:*
> *For in this crazy Paradise,*
>   *You are in love with pain.*
>
> *Want to buy some illusions,*
>   *Slightly used, just like new?*
> *Such romantic illusions—*
>   *And they're all about you.*
> *I sell them all for a penny,*
>   *They make pretty souvenirs.*
> *Take my lovely illusions—*
>   *Some for laughs, some for tears.*

Later, Marlene Dietrich spent decades cutting her way through hundreds of renditions of (among many other concert pieces) "Where Have All the Flowers Gone?" and "I Wish You Love" and endlessly repeated choruses of "See What the Boys in the Back Room Will Have." From 1953, and for twenty years thereafter, her one-woman nightclub and theater performances would be meticulously planned, artful presentations of herself *as she wanted to be known*—a woman triumphant who, quite on her own, had successfully stopped the march of time. She would be a creature forever desirable because she perpetually withholds something promised; she is a person whose cool mastery of all she surveys—swathed in sequins and ermine and bathed in pink light—places her in a position of emotional supremacy over all those who dare to draw near. Her many recorded theater songs thus often convey the universal experience of romantic loss. But somehow they remain overrehearsed exercises in technique, and so they rarely communicated the spontaneous, humbling, personal, acute distress of the first recording of "Illusions" for *A Foreign Affair,* in which she so eloquently sang a woman's painful confession.

Nonetheless, there can be no doubt that Dietrich herself, the woman of so many private affairs and such assertive, prodigal professional and erotic energy, was indeed represented in the polished theatrical stance, in her attitude of controlled distance and detachment. But just as she was amusingly seductive, almost girlishly playful while singing "You Little So and So" and "I Couldn't Be Annoyed" (in *Blonde Venus),* nervously desirous during "Johnny" (in *Song of Songs)* and confidently alluring for "Awake In a Dream" (in *Desire),* both her voice and her sentiment were deeper for "Illusions." She was by this time, as Billy Wilder said, "a strange combination of the *femme fatale,* the German *Hausfrau* and Florence Nightingale."

It is not surprising that Marlene Dietrich should have access in early 1948 to such feelings about artifice, and the means to communicate her sentiments. The death of her mother, the end of her affair with Jean Gabin and the permanent departure of James Gavin, the news of her daughter's pregnancy, her difficulty in finding the contours of a future career, her compulsion to have a face-lift that year (at the age of forty-six)—she was certainly not unmindful of the inevitable encroachment of time. Only one who in a quiet corner of herself had assessed the meaning of her depressions and solitude could have brought to "Illusions" the muted remorse, the confessional simplicity and the unadorned wistfulness. She was in the business of selling illusions, and she knew it. The cabaretist knew whereof she sang; Lola Lola had grown up.

A FOREIGN AFFAIR WRAPPED PRODUCTION IN FEB-ruary, and Dietrich sped to New York. "I'm doing the chores while Maria's pregnant," she said. "The daily woman's no good—Ameri-can women have no idea of how to keep house." The birth of her first grandson that June prompted *Life* magazine to put her photo-graph on its August 9 cover, with the caption "Grandmother Die-trich," and so began the designation of her as "the world's most glamorous grandmother." In this real-life role she in fact excelled, doting on Maria's baby and, later on, his brothers. Her only profes-sional assignment for the rest of the year was in Fletcher Markle's film *Jigsaw* (made in New York that summer), in which Dietrich is glimpsed for only a few seconds as she leaves New York's Blue Angel nightclub. "No, no, no—I'm not interested. Some time later, perhaps," she says to her escort (Markle). To what she refers we are given no hint, although it is tempting—because Markle was a televi-sion producer—to assume they were discussing his real-life offers for her to appear in the new medium; this offer she repeatedly rejected because, as she said, she could not control the key light needed to present her to best advantage.

But she was very much interested, in 1949, in assuming a major role in an Alfred Hitchcock picture, to be made that summer in England. Dietrich would have second billing to the recent Oscar winner Jane Wyman, but the featured part would provide her with an aptly enigmatic personality à la von Sternberg, a Christian Dior wardrobe, sojourns in London and Paris, two songs (one written for her by Cole Porter) and a weekly salary of £7,000 for ten weeks. As usual, she consulted with her astrologist, Carroll Righter, for ap-proval of her transportation and departure day, and by mid-April was in Paris for fittings at Dior.* In France, she resumed her friend-

---

* Over the next two decades, Dietrich would continue her regular offer to have Carroll Righter draw up her colleagues' astrological charts. Typical of many such attestations was that of Richard Todd (who appeared in her next film, *Stage Fright*): "When she heard that I was engaged to be married, she asked me for details of my birth date and also Kitty's, saying she would send for a horoscope for us. It was just

ship with Maurice Chevalier, although now the relationship was strictly platonic.

Dietrich also met the legendary French singer Edith Piaf, whose life had been wretchedly unhappy since childhood, and whose history of destructive love affairs and addictions were much the stuff of her plangent songs and raw delivery. Their relationship began when Dietrich heard Piaf's signature tune "La Vie en Rose" and asked Hitchcock to secure the rights to it for her in the forthcoming film. Piaf, in the midst of one of her many near-suicidal depressions, welcomed both Dietrich's admiration and her strong emotional support: "She made it her duty to help and encourage me, taking care never to leave me alone with my thoughts," she wrote in her memoirs. Dietrich also, it seems, coveted the role of care-giver to this forlorn singer, often visiting her backstage after a performance and bringing along Chevalier as her escort. Just barely opening the door of Piaf's dressing room when journalist Robert Bré knocked, Dietrich asked, "What can I do for you, monsieur? I am Madame Piaf's secretary." But he was not to be fooled: "Ah, I didn't know! And I suppose she has engaged Maurice Chevalier as chauffeur!"

AFTER MORE THAN A MONTH IN PARIS, DIETRICH arrived on June 27 at London Airport, where she denied the waiting photographers a shot of her legs: "I am not a chorus girl," she said with a tight smile. "I have nothing to show." This was not typical of her, journalists noted—and indeed Hitchcock had a stipulation in her contract that throughout the term of her employment with him she was to be presented to the press only as he approved. She was not pleased, but this approach was consistent with the mysterious woman he wanted to create and not the glamorous grandmother easily lifting her skirt. But here, in the realm of the artist-fantasist, any comparison between Hitchcock and von Sternberg ceased, for her new director certainly entertained no romantic notions about himself and Marlene Dietrich, nor was he personally obsessed with her. His concern was the character of Charlotte Inwood in *Stage*

---

as well I did not share her obsession, because when the horoscope reached us, it was a terrible one, forecasting no good at all for Kitty and me."

Fright—not Lola Lola or Amy or Frenchy but an extremely sophisticated, astonishingly self-possessed actress of a certain age now doing musical star-turns and able to goad a young admirer into killing for her.

There was no formal introduction to the press (this was deferred to a luncheon at the Savoy several days later); instead, Dietrich was at once whisked off to Elstree Studios for meetings with her director, crew and fellow players. "Everything is fine," Hitchcock told a reporter two days later with bemused irony. "Miss Dietrich has arranged the whole thing. She has told them exactly where to place the lights and how to photograph her."

Hitchcock, who suffered no rivals for absolute authority on his productions, was at first considerably dismayed over Dietrich's presumption, for after studying the dialogue, production designs and scene requirements, she met cinematographer Wilkie Cooper early each morning and simply dictated where she would stand, how she would be lighted and framed, how she or the camera would move. She also designed her own makeup and chose her own costumes from the Dior outfits paid for by the production company. "Marlene was a professional star," Hitchcock said later, as usual selecting his words with utmost caution but elaborating her considerable influence. "She was also a professional cameraman, art director, editor, costume designer, hairdresser, makeup woman, composer, producer and director."

Such autonomy—rare in any case—was completely unprecedented on a Hitchcock set. For several days Dietrich's sovereignty caused raised eyebrows and shocked glances among the crew, and many nervous glances toward the director. But Hitchcock wanted her complete cooperation—indeed, her concrete contributions—for in fact the "Sternbergian image" of Marlene Dietrich was very much Hitchcock's intention for the role of Charlotte Inwood.

For many years, *Stage Fright* was regarded as a mediocre work by Hitchcock and a negligible moment in Dietrich's career. Few judgments about a film could be more shortsighted, for this film—although highly complex, full of demanding verbal nuances and with the multiple layers of a complicated plot—is certainly nothing less than a masterwork. As for Dietrich's acting, it remains (with *Witness*

for the Prosecution eight years later) one of her two finest late performances, perhaps because it struck so close to her own emotional
experience as a performer enduring the shifting fortunes of success.
And insofar as it was conceived, directed and released as a kind of
encoded tribute to her image, it deserves as careful an assessment as
The Blue Angel or *Morocco*.

STAGE FRIGHT CONCERNS A YOUNG DRAMA STUDENT
named Eve Gill (Jane Wyman) who pretends to be a theatrical
dresser to the stage star Charlotte Inwood (Dietrich) in order to clear
her friend Jonathan Cooper (Richard Todd) of the charge that he
murdered Charlotte's husband. Eve finally learns, however, that Jonathan (for whom she harbors a secret love) is indeed guilty, and that
he lied in saying that Charlotte killed her husband in a jealous rage.
In the process of her discovery, Eve also falls in love with Detective
Wilfred Smith (Michael Wilding), the inspector on the case. Charlotte, as it turns out, had been cruelly abused by her husband and
had exploited Jonathan's lunatic impulses by goading him to murder.
In the end, Jonathan is captured and accidentally killed, while Charlotte will stand trial for obstructing justice by not revealing her
knowledge of Cooper's murder of her husband.

From the beginning of the project (based on a novel by Selwyn
Jepson), Hitchcock, his wife Alma Reville (always closely involved
in story construction) and screenwriter Whitfield Cook had Dietrich in mind for the story's most colorful character. Hitchcock
added that "the aspect that intrigued me is that it was a story about
the theater." The structure of the finished film everywhere supports
that. The asbestos safety curtain of an English theater slowly rises
under the credits, revealing not a stage set but real-life London in full
motion; when the curtain is fully raised, the action of the story
begins.

Immediately, the distinctions between appearance and reality,
between theater life and street life, begin to blur. Everything that
follows is an interconnected series of ruses, costumes, lies and artifices, and everyone in the story plays a variety of real-life roles (a
recurring Hitchcockian motif since his 1930 talkie *Murder!*). As in

the director's darker romances, appearances and identities slip and slide. Nothing is certain in the world of disguises, performances, matinées and theatrical garden parties. And at the center of the swirling patterns of deception is Dietrich—abused and abuser, victim and victimizer. "When I give all my love and devotion and receive only treachery and hatred," she says in a final line added by herself with Hitchcock's approval, "it's as if my own mother had slapped me in the face." The event in her mind may have been her mother's slap when, in adolescence, Marlene had refused to dance with a boy she did not like. As for the "treachery and hatred" (ostensibly referring to Charlotte's husband), this was always, for Dietrich, associated with the end of any love affair.

The opening scene of flight from the police (in Wyman's open roadster) establishes the film's tripartite structure, a series of ever slower journeys until the finale. In this regard, the film is built like a geared *rallentando,* a gradual slowdown from that first car chase, to the midpoint of the more leisurely ride in a taxi (the love scene between Wyman and Wilding), to the final immobilization of Eve and Jonathan in the unused eighteenth-century stage-prop carriage. Within this framework, Wyman, a young novice actress in the story, is disabused of her belief that the theater is a glamorous life and— precisely by her success at playing multiple roles offstage—endangers herself and her family before confronting the shifting and specious nature of her own romantic illusions about art and men. And Dietrich, as the singing actress, stands at the center of that theme— virtually, as Hitchcock insisted, playing herself.

Aptly, at the end Wyman must go *under* the stage, to confront a more paralyzing fear than one could know *onstage* in a role. And there beneath the boards she invents an ingenious acting ploy whereby she disarms a pathological killer and saves herself. Real stage fright, in other words, is something deeper than mere onstage panic, demanding an improvised courage. Thus the melodramatic play Wyman is first seen rehearsing at the Royal Academy of Dramatic Art (and in which she seems to be egregiously incompetent indeed) at last becomes a "thriller" from which she must extricate herself by a superlative performance.

Besides Wyman, Dietrich and her demented lover are professional performers, and everyone in the story plays roles. "You're an actress. You're playing a part. No nerves when you're on," Todd tells Dietrich (although this exchange occurs in his mendacious flashback), just after she begs him to "draw the curtains, Johnny!" The scene points forward to the final horrific moment, when a stagehand is asked to "lower the iron curtain," effectively cutting off Todd's escape (and by implication his head). But Wyman's witty father (Alistair Sim) is also a role-player. "You're just dying to get into a part in this, and you know you are," Wyman tells him.

"A part in this melodramatic play, you mean," he replies, in the triumphant comic scene in his cottage. "That's the way you're treating it, Eve—as if it were a play you were acting in at the Academy. Everything seems a fine acting role when you're stagestruck, doesn't it, my dear? Here you have a plot, an interesting cast, even a costume [a blood-soaked dress]. Unfortunately, Eve, in this real and earnest life we must face the situation in all its bearings . . . [or else] you'll spend a few years in Holloway prison, meditating on the folly of transmuting melodrama into real life."

Wyman/Eve, we should note, is different things to different people. To Cooper she is a patient and helpful friend whose love for him he conveniently exploits, while to her father she is an apprentice actress: "You're my audience, Father! I wish you'd give me a little applause now and then"—which he later does, after she unmasks Charlotte. To Detective Wilfred Smith, Eve is an innocent actress, to Charlotte's regular maid Nellie Goode (Kay Walsh), she is a newspaper reporter eager to disguise herself to gain access to Charlotte. And to Charlotte she is Nellie's cousin Doris—whose name Charlotte simply cannot remember (she calls her Phyllis, Mavis and Elsie).

But Dietrich's Charlotte is a performer on a deeper level still; her widowhood, especially, becomes her most pointed attempt at self-glamorizing. ("Couldn't we work in a little color?" she asks about the funereal black dress. "Or let it plunge just a little in front?") And she orders others about, directs them (Eve especially) in their forms of address, their tones of voice and their wardrobes. Strangers and police inspectors are addressed as "darling." Everything, in other words, is done for effect.

Quite early, we are told (but tend to reject) the truth about Jonathan—that he is a mad killer; this Charlotte tells the police and Eve overhears. Charlotte then tries to extricate herself from involvement in the crime, but what she says of her younger lover Cooper is absolutely true (and disbelieved by the romantic Eve):

> I suppose I shouldn't have seen him as often as I did, but I didn't realize how madly infatuated he was with me. I just didn't realize. You'll never know how much I blame myself for all this. When my husband came back from New York last week and I told Johnny I couldn't see him, he kept on phoning me. He wouldn't let me alone. Oh, maybe if I'd agreed to see him he wouldn't have done this dreadful thing.

Much of her dialogue, it must be stressed, was both expanded and fine-tuned by Dietrich herself, with Hitchcock's approval.

Dietrich's focussed rendition of the Cole Porter song "The Laziest Gal in Town" is the film's clearest tip-off to the resolution of the plot: "It's not that I shouldn't, it's not that I wouldn't, and you know it's not that I couldn't—it's simply because I'm the laziest gal in town," she sings in a triumphant proclamation with multiple meanings. Our first thought about the lyrics is the obvious sexual reference, but later we realize they are also a clue to what she did with her young lover, exploiting his fanatical devotion to the extent that he killed her husband. She was just too lazy to do it herself. (Her rendition of "La Vie en Rose," on the other hand, was simply her appropriation of Piaf's signature for herself.)

Wyman's refusal to believe the guilt of the man she loves (despite overwhelming evidence) is highlighted when her affections begin to shift from Todd to Wilding, and this happens when Todd embraces her. Convinced of (what she thinks is) the ineradicable bond between Todd and Dietrich, she gazes at the piano and we (with her, from her viewpoint) remember the romantic piano melody played by Wilfred. It is additionally important, therefore, that this sequence is at once followed by Wyman's taxi ride with Wilding, accompanied by the same music; this is one of the most funny-tender love scenes in the Hitchcock canon. This ride is also psychologically acute, although audiences decades later find it a little arch and coy. Wilfred and Eve are more interested in one another than in the logic of their own remarks, and finally they are so locked in the collusion of their romantic gaze that their words meld and become senseless interphrases. Hitchcock is, at this point, one up on the sophisticates, for this is the gentlest puncture of the romantic fallacy. It is the director's quiet, compassionate little joke, a grace note to the richness of this undeservedly neglected comic masterpiece.

On its most serious level, *Stage Fright* is a typically Hitchcockian reflection on romantic illusion, with the popular ikon of Marlene Dietrich at the center—and to this she herself made important contributions as the screenplay was polished even during shooting. Central to the picture's richness is her presence, her complete blending into the role as both star-image and mysterious mover of events, for finally *Stage Fright* is about the tragic wisdom of the older performer (Charlotte/Dietrich), the concomitant cynicism, the superior experience and the ability to exploit her image to her own best advantage. Dietrich has not a false moment in this picture. Breathless with anxiety and with a cunning invented from moment to moment, Charlotte Inwood was a kind of totem of Dietrich's dark side, encapsulating the entire range of her image. She suggested her frantic first words—"Johnny, you do love me, don't you? Say that you love me!"—and we hear her voice before we see her (a great tease, Dietrich thought).

BLURRING THE DISTINCTION BETWEEN ART AND LIFE again, Dietrich took a younger lover (not Richard Todd) quite soon after filming began, just as in *Stage Fright* itself. Michael Wilding—handsome, gentle, sophisticated and artistic—was eleven years her junior and had scarcely been introduced to her when she offered herself to him, as if the way for her to feel young was to prove to herself that she could keep a young man. "I am too old for you," she said bluntly. Gallantly, Wilding tried to recall an appropriate response from lines in Shakespeare's *Antony and Cleopatra,* and when he faltered, Dietrich interrupted: "Why not just settle for kissing me?"

"From that moment," according to Wilding, "we became inseparable. In fact she would not move a step without me. She insisted that I accompany her everywhere, and she took as much interest in my appearance as she did in her own." As Hitchcock and members of his crew remembered, the lovemaking was not always discreet, sometimes conducted even in their dressing rooms on the soundstage. "But close as we became," Wilding added, "there was an unfathomable quality about Marlene, a part of her that remained aloof. Sadly, our relationship came to an abrupt end." Dietrich was again surprised at the temerity of an ex-lover when Wilding's engagement to Elizabeth Taylor was announced a few years later: "What's Liz Taylor got that I haven't got?" she asked a friend, who added that the news made her "very sad." As she had said, "When I devote myself to someone, no one can undo it"—not even, she thought, the former beloved.*

---

* At precisely this time, Dietrich's friendship with Ernest Hemingway was perhaps her great support. When she wrote to him of her romantic solitude he replied, on July 13, 1950, that after all they were two of the most forlorn people in the world; that he loved her not as a screen goddess but as a friend— the woman he first knew in a military uniform now discarded, when she reeked of all the smells of war. The exchange of letters—none of them anything like passionate communiqués—continued for years, most of them addressing one or another of Dietrich's problems with lovers. On August 12, 1952, for example (in response to her complaints about problems with her lover Yul Brynner), Hemingway invited her to come to his home in Cuba. The Dietrich-Hemingway letters are full of news, mutual affection, recipes, memories and matey advice; they remain crucial evidence that the two were indeed not lovers.

14: 1949–1953

From the beginning of her career in America, Marlene Dietrich depended on the movies to present her as an embodiment of both feminine allure and subtly masculine aggressiveness. Never cast as a blushing ingenue or a shy, virginal rose, there was, on the contrary, something tarnished and tested about the strong characters she represented; she was the shrewd, resourceful, cynical woman of the world. As for her beauty, Dietrich up to her midthirties had been meticulously photographed and always rendered as someone provocative but enigmatic, desirable but mysterious—even remote and implacable. And always, it was implied, uniquely androgynous.

But from 1939, beginning with the release of *Destry Rides Again,* both public familiarity and the shift in photographic styles had conspired to present her as earthier, more accessible, even gently satiric of her previous image. Then, when her film career stagnated dangerously in the early 1940s, she assumed a wartime role as a kind of Joan of Arc in travelling cabaret—a self-designed and self-maintained persona that effectively gave her some of the best publicity of her life and helped to clarify her future plans as a solo performer.

In 1949, at forty-eight, Dietrich found herself in the common situation of many middle-aged actresses, too old for leading romantic roles and too young for eccentric character parts. This situation clashed dramatically with what had become almost a life's work—the carefully cultivated semblance of agelessness. No wonder, then, that she simultaneously deplored her designation as "the world's most glamorous grandmother" and often and insistently rewrote history to conform to the desired illusion. "I had my daughter when I was seventeen," she said, altering the truth by six years; and speaking of Maria, who had her first child at twenty-three, she added "and my daughter waited until she was eighteen to marry and have a child. Does that make me ancient?" No, but it did not earn her points as a truth-teller. There were, after all, alternatives to claiming either perpetual youth or premature decline; one could reply (taking a cue from Auntie Mame) that there was a reality between forty and death.

Dietrich continued to require the endorsement of work as well as its financial rewards, but after Alfred Hitchcock completed filming *Stage Fright* in late summer 1949, she was again without immediate employment prospects, as she had been several times in the previous dozen years. She lingered for about a month in London, shopping, socializing with Noël Coward and attending the theater, and then she went to New York, where Maria was pregnant with her second child. As in everything else, however, Dietrich was not of the garden variety in her roles as mother, grandmother and mother-in-law. She lived luxuriously at the Plaza Hotel, spent considerable sums on restaurants, wardrobe, cosmetics and cash gifts to Rudi, Tamara and a few friends, and altogether affected the style of a fabulously wealthy star. Her financial status, too, was part of the illusion. Dietrich was in fact constantly audited by tax authorities, for she repeatedly deducted her enormous wardrobe bills as professional expenses. She was also strained by her unshakable belief that if she were contracted for a salary of $200,000 she had $200,000 to spend.

On November 16, over Perrier-Jouët brut champagne and a salver of caviar with Ernest Hemingway at the Sherry-Netherland

Hotel, she described her life in Manhattan that season. "I'm the baby-sitter," she said of a typical day at her daughter's Third Avenue flat.

As soon as they leave the house, I go around and look in all the corners and straighten the drawers and clean up. I can't stand a house that isn't neat and clean. I go around in all the corners with towels I bring with me from the Plaza, and I clean up the whole house. Then . . . I take the dirty towels and some of the baby's things that need washing, and, with my bundle over my shoulder, I go out and get a taxi, and the driver, he thinks I am this old washerwoman from Third Avenue, and he takes me in the taxi and talks to me with sympathy, so I am afraid to let him take me to the Plaza. I get out a block away from the Plaza and I walk home with my bundle and I wash the baby's things, and then I go to sleep.

With Dietrich that evening, Ernest and Mary Hemingway also entertained (among others) his publisher Charles Scribner, Sr., athlete George Brown and writer A. E. Hotchner, who recalled that Marlene dominated the conversation. When she was not speaking of herself, her USO work or her plans to make some new recordings, she proselytized on behalf of Carroll Righter. Journalist Lillian Ross was also present, taking notes for an extended profile of Hemingway that would later appear in *The New Yorker*.

"Papa, you look wonderful," Dietrich said slowly when Hemingway greeted her.

"I sure missed you, daughter," Hemingway replied, escorting her to the other guests.

Wearing a mink coat, Dietrich sighed loudly, handed the coat to Mary, sighed again, and fell languorously into an overstuffed chair. She took from her purse photographs of her grandson and passed them around, saying magnificently, "Everything you do, you do for the sake of the children"—a sentiment Hemingway boozily echoed as he refilled her glass with champagne. "Thank you, Papa," Dietrich said, sighing again.

"During the war," she continued, shifting gears, "everybody was the way people should be all the time. Not mean and afraid but good to each other. It was different in the war. People were not so selfish and they helped each other." As with everything else in her life, she had already begun the process of glamorizing the past.

JOHN PETER RIVA, MARIA'S SECOND CHILD, WAS born in the spring of 1950, and until late that summer the world's most glamorous grandmother remained in Manhattan, where she was occasionally seen pushing a baby carriage in Central Park. An offer to appear in another British film then arrived, and that September she went to Paris for wardrobe fittings. Ginette Spanier, directrice of Pierre Balmain, recalled Dietrich's arrival and her hesitation about approving a particular mink cape. "She looked at me," according to Spanier, "and, still without a smile or a 'Good morning,' said, 'I find it rather poor.' " The longest and most expensive mink stole was then added—"and, still without a smile, she said, 'I'll have that.' " She knew exactly which outfit would (in Spanier's words)

> feed the legend . . . She thinks out a whole wardrobe in terms of her various appearances. She even sees her social life in terms of star appearances. She goes straight for her needs, bearing in mind what background she will appear against, what other performers she will "top." Marlene is intelligent, ruthless and . . . knows exactly what she wants.

Indeed, Dietrich could demand a half-dozen fittings if she disapproved a seam in a lining. "First they'll look at your face," Spanier cried impatiently at her. "Then they'll look at your legs. Then maybe they'll take an interest in the story. If they have time to concentrate on the shadow of a seam in the lining of your dress, the picture must be a flop."

"You do not understand," Dietrich replied deliberately. "Everything on the screen is enlarged twenty times. If, in twenty-five years time, my daughter Maria sees the picture and notices the seam all puckered she will say, 'How could Mother have stood such a thing?' " Mother did not, of course, and her requirements often brought Spanier's sewing staff to the brink of revolution. The directrice then called for a luncheon break, and when Dietrich said gravely that she had nowhere to dine and that she would simply wander about, Spanier insisted she come to her home on the Avenue Marceau. As it happened, that was the birthday of Spanier's husband, the physician Paul-Emile Seidmann. "Marlene ate all the caviar intended as a birthday treat for my husband, and he was furious. It was an occasion that reflected no credit on either of them." Notwithstanding this debut as an importunate caviar gourmand, Dietrich was thenceforth frequently the guest of the Seidmanns.

The friendship was not uncomplicated, for from that time on, the two women were ardent lovers whenever Dietrich was in Paris or they could meet in London or New York. But her tactics with Spanier were not always well considered, and betrayed her fundamental jealousy of the Seidmanns' deep friendship and commitment to each other. When she was required to go on an American tour with Balmain some years later, Ginette—perhaps fearing her husband's dalliance as well as his loneliness in Paris—asked Dietrich to look after him and to dine occasionally with him. In New York, Ginette received from Dietrich a letter that could not have put her mind at ease:

Darling,
You were so concerned that Paul-Emile would be lonely while you are away, but you must have no fear. I have tried several times to invite him for dinner, but he is *never* available! He is the toast of Paris, it seems—out every night, God knows where! I asked him to join me and a few friends for a private movie screening—I said he could bring other friends along—but even for that he made some excuse. Imagine! Well, dear Ginette, I hope you are well . . . And to make sure you will receive this letter, I am sending copies of it to every hotel on your itinerary . . .

The end of the Dietrich-Spanier relationship years later was due in fact to Ginette's independence, which Marlene always resented. Jealous of her friend's widening fame and international social circle, Dietrich wrote a letter of abject offense, blaming the dissipation of their friendship on Ginette's indifference.

IN OCTOBER, THE FILMING OF *NO HIGHWAY* (released in America as *No Highway in the Sky)* began at Denham Studios, north of London. In the part of a film actress named Monica Teasdale, Dietrich was cast opposite James Stewart as an aerophysicist who suspects that the new airplane they travel on is doomed because of a design flaw. Successively, screenwriters R. C. Sherriff, Oscar Millard and Alec Coppel tried to infuse her role with some sparkle, but there were neither songs nor narrative credibility to support them. They did, however, provide dialogue apt for both Monica and Marlene. "My career?" she says plaintively to Stewart while disaster threatens. "A few cans of celluloid in a junk-heap some day. It's been fun, but that's about all. I would have stopped working quite a while ago if I could have figured out what to do with myself. I was married three times, but it never came to anything." Uncomfortable with this kind of nearly autobiographical confession, Dietrich nevertheless managed a performance of casual elegance, her severely chic wardrobe fitted her perfectly—and neither critics nor audiences had anything else to note.

The production schedule left her with little time for social life, but she was so eager to meet Sir Alexander Fleming, the discoverer of penicillin, that she prevailed on a studio executive to arrange a meeting. She had seen the miraculous effects of the drug on wounded soldiers and was cured by it herself when she had pneumonia during the war tour. And so Fleming and his wife found themselves, that autumn, the dinner guests of Marlene Dietrich, who prepared a tasty goulash and fussed over the Flemings like an efficient Bavarian waitress. Next day, Fleming sent her a section of the original mold from which penicillin had been cultivated; she responded with a signed photograph, a horoscope prepared by Carroll Righter and a dozen eggs (a precious commodity in 1950 England) with accompanying recipes. The acquaintance, flattering to both, continued sporadically whenever Dietrich was in London, up to the time of Fleming's death in 1955.

She also attended a more formal dinner party on November 6 with Noël Coward, at which Tyrone Power, Montgomery Clift, Gloria Swanson and Clifton Webb observed her affecting indifference to the presence of Michael Wilding, whom someone had thoughtlessly invited. Webb, elegant and puckish, asked her if she intended to be married one day soon. "Married?" she asked wide-eyed. "But I *am* married!" (Webb and the other guests could not be blamed if by this time Rudolf Sieber was, in their eyes, a forgotten spouse.)

Dietrich might have felt some nervous irritability in Wilding's presence because of the abrupt end of their affair the previous year, but she steered the discussion to the news that had just broken. Three days earlier, the government of France had proclaimed her a chevalier of the Legion of Honor—a distinction formalized a year later at a Washington ceremony (on October 9, 1951), when Ambassador Henri Bonnet pinned on her a decoration and presented a scroll detailing his country's gratitude for her wartime service entertaining troops in Africa and France.

That evening in London, she was as usual adept at centering conversation on herself, and next day those who knew her must have been amused (and some women offended) when she generalized to a reporter, "Women talk when they have nothing to say. They chatter about a lot of nonsense that interests no one but themselves. They should keep quiet and not open their mouths just because they like the sound of their voices." By a curious irony, the very same woman who had broken sexual stereotypes in fashion and conduct and always insisted on her autonomy and independence later denounced the very idea of what was called women's liberation: "It's ridiculous. I think a woman wants to be dominated by a man. Men are much cleverer than women. A dominating woman cannot be happy."

However, she was heard angrily and often in the spring of 1951, when she sued the publishers of the Paris weekly *France-Dimanche* for an unauthorized series of half-fictitious articles printed under her name and boldly marketed as "My Life"; four years later the litigation was quietly settled in her favor. Her mood did not improve much back in Hollywood that same season, when she went before the camera (for a fee of $110,000) in a disastrous film that would mark yet another clear turning point in her career. *Rancho Notorious,* as it was called, was her first American film in over three years.

Best known for a series of dark thrillers with ominous implications about society on the brink of anarchy *(Dr. Mabuse, Spies, M, Fury),* the respected German-American director Fritz Lang had for years wanted to create a film for Dietrich. With writer Daniel Taradash, he fashioned a western morality tale (originally called *Chuck-a-Luck,* after the game of vertical roulette) about a cowboy who sets out to find the outlaw killer of his fiancée. Dietrich's role was Altar Keane, a notorious, aging dance-hall queen who provides bandits with a safe house in return for a cut of their profits and who eventually falls in love with the vengeful cowboy. In a deliberate theft from *Destry Rides Again* (which it mimicked in several aspects), she is struck down by a bullet intended for another.

"Every year is a threat to a woman," Dietrich says in character in *Rancho Notorious.* Bored with herself and everyone around her, Altar should have been the perfect role for her. But the script was a tedious affair, and the collaboration with Lang was disappointing and difficult from the first day that March. "I had the foolish idea," Lang said years later, "of wanting to give Marlene a new screen image. In the script I'd described the character she played as an 'elderly dance-hall girl,' [but] . . . Marlene resented going gracefully into a little older category. She came onto the set looking younger and younger in each scene until finally it was hopeless."

In addition to this diffusion of her character for the sake of her own appearance, Dietrich constantly corrected Lang, implying that certain techniques would have been exploited otherwise by von Sternberg. Such a tactic would not have pleased any director, and Fritz Lang—a stern, severe taskmaster even in the best circumstances —was not one to be manipulated. "I am Lang, not von Sternberg," he told her bluntly, adding later that the atmosphere all through production was "very, very disagreeable . . . By the end of the picture, [Dietrich and I] didn't speak to each other any more."

As it happened, both director and star were right. The western was not an apt genre for Lang, the script was monumentally ungripping, the exterior/interior sets and painted backdrops for the western desert looked just plain silly, and Dietrich's role made little sense in her reglamorized appearance. Like the songs she was given, Dietrich's performance was listless and detached, and as she saw the daily rushes she became more and more depressed. As in *The Garden of Allah* and *Kismet,* so now in her third Technicolor film: Dietrich was not flattered by color film, nor was her appearance improved by cosmeticized youthfulness; to make matters worse, there was no budget for substantial laboratory color correction. Never before had Dietrich so bitterly resented, and with good reason, her own image onscreen.

At the same time—perhaps partly driven by the disappointment of *Rancho Notorious*—she took special pains over her appearance when asked to present the Oscar for best foreign film at the Academy Awards, held March 29 at the Pantages Theater in Hollywood. Although this annual rite of spring was not yet televised, she was told there would be 2,800 people in the auditorium and so, weeks before, she swung into action.

First, Dietrich learned that the stage sets for the show would be red, white and blue. Then she made dozens of telephone calls to agents, producers, columnists and friends, who collectively informed her that most of the women giving and receiving prizes would dress according to the current fashion—most of them in white or pastel formal gowns, some with beads and sequins, others with vast bouffant skirts. Weeks before her appearance, therefore, Dietrich decided on something radically different. She would appear with the plainest makeup and without jewelry, wearing a simple but dramatic Christian Dior black sheath, unadorned and tight from neck to toe. There would be one touch, however: a high slit up the side of the dress. "Watch Mama make the front page of every newspaper in town," she had said when about to meet the press, her ankle taped after the accident during *The Lady Is Willing.* Now, this provocative black dress would have the same publicity effect. (Dior of course needed to know which side of the sheath was to be cut open, but Dietrich could not reply until she learned from which side of the stage she would enter.)

According to her publicist Russell Birdwell, Dietrich prepared for the Academy Awards ceremony (during which she was to present an Oscar) just as she prepared for a dramatic entrance to a restaurant on any ordinary evening. She checked the Pantages lighting configuration on the afternoon of March 29, rehearsed her walk and, when introduced that evening, slithered across the stage, her famous legs revealed to the audience peek-a-boo style with every calculated step. As *Variety*'s headline story reported next day, "GRANDMA DIE-TRICH STEALS SHOW: She gave every woman there a lift by her startling denial of the fifties . . . She sauntered out with her sheath skirt slit to one knee and held 2,800 people in her instep."

Similarly, the following winter she attended the pre-Broadway tryout of Christopher Fry's play *Venus Observed* in Philadelphia, making her entrance in a simple black suit seconds before the house lights dimmed. Again, the audience was stunned, and then there was clamorous applause. By the sheer force of her personality and never promoting her wardrobe above herself, Dietrich capitalized on her legend and italicized it by a carefully studied presentation. She also used to her advantage every means of publicity—like the press luncheon she quietly suggested to honor the twenty-first anniversary of her arrival in America. The Colonial Room of the Ambassador Hotel was jammed with reporters and photographers on May 4, film clips were shown, Maria entered with her mother, and after lunch Dietrich carved an enormous cake. Except for finely rendered portraits in very few films, there had been nothing remarkable in her career for years, and so Dietrich turned herself into the object of critical acclaim, creating the image that art did not. She became, in other words, her own self-generated product.

MARIA RIVA, MEANWHILE, HAD SLIMMED TO A STAR-let's weight and, while her husband worked and taught scenic design at Fordham University, she was working under the terms of a contract with CBS–TV. During the so-called Golden Age of Television (generally the decade beginning about 1949), Maria had the leading role in over a dozen live television plays and was one of three performers seen most often (the others were Charlton Heston and Mary Sinclair). For much of the second half of 1951, Dietrich shuttled back and forth between Los Angeles and New York, furnishing a four-room apartment she took at 993 Park Avenue and frequently watching Maria at work at the studio. When completed, her living room had bookshelves lined with titles by William James, Tolstoy, Dostoyevsky, Faulkner and Hemingway, and the walls were adorned with original art by Cézanne, Delacroix, Utrillo and Corot. Also strategically positioned were personally inscribed photographs of General Patton, Jean Cocteau, Alexander Fleming, Maria Callas, Noël Coward, Hemingway and others.

During this time, Dietrich also successfully pursued the thirty-year-old actor Yul Brynner, then achieving spectacular fame on Broadway in Rodgers and Hammerstein's musical *The King and I*. His sexual relationship with Dietrich indicates how successfully she managed both her own obsession with youth and the power of her legendary status.

This affair was certainly not a case of Dietrich landing an innocent in the net of her own wiles. Brynner, born in Vladivostok, had created a fanciful autobiography and, although married at the time to the actress Virginia Gilmore, was as much a libertine as Dietrich. Throughout the 1950s they met irregularly in New York, finding one another's company physically gratifying and intellectually stimulating. Brynner was an impressive autodidact fluent in several languages, and together they spoke French, wandered into Manhattan art galleries and antiquarian bookshops, discussed the post-Impressionists and read the classics aloud to one another. Often seen publicly with Brynner, Dietrich was also invited to late suppers with him. He encouraged her return to the stage, and that year it was announced that she would appear with him in Jacques Deval's musical play *Samarkand,* a project she soon abandoned, still fearing the acting demands of nightly stage performance.

With her career now stalled, Dietrich foresaw the possible loss of her own celebrity, and neatly employed her association with Brynner to keep herself before the press; because their relationship was controversial, it could only augment her status as the ultimately unpredictable and romantic iconoclast. She would indeed be all things to as many men as possible, and simultaneously a challenge, a threat and a rebuttal to the women of her day. Advancing by her appearance and appeal the myth that women do not (indeed, *must* not) age, she publicly challenged the taboo of the older woman with a younger man.

Very much a person of her time, she had been raised and confirmed in the cultural presumptions that women were essentially inferior to men. As witness of this, she had for years been scornful of what she called the feminine mind and will and had even expressed regret that she had not been born a man—a fact she had unconsciously tried to counter by proxy during her USO tours. ("I admire men's minds," she insisted throughout her life. "They are not like women. They think things through.") But, as always, herein lies a central contradiction in Dietrich's character, for at the same time she needed to demonstrate *her own superiority* to men: thus her lifelong special attraction to the morose, brooding, weak or confused man (or one simply sick with a cold) who was—or who she thought was—in need of a gently controlling take-over.

Together, according to Brynner's son, "they could *almost* overlook the fact that Marlene was twenty years older; at least, Marlene could. She was also the most determined, passionate and possessive lover he had ever known, not in the least concerned about discretion." Just so did Dietrich dally with Frank Sinatra, with whom she had an occasional, stormy affair for two years beginning in 1955. Toward its conclusion, she noted in her diary (on September 4, 1957) that they spent an hour and a half together in bed, while she soothed his fears that he had been sexually out of practice. "But everything was fine," she concluded—although not, perhaps, in the honesty of one or the other of them.

In addition, Dietrich commandeered friends and relatives in catering to him. Among these were Rudi and Tamara, who were also in New York that year, staying several months at a hotel while

Tamara consulted neurologists and psychologists for a worsening but still undefined nervous condition (for which Dietrich paid the bills). Stefan Lorant, whose friendship with Dietrich had resumed when he, too, relocated to Manhattan after the war, recalled several occasions when she blithely rang Tamara and sent her—as if she were a servant—on a mission to a local delicatessen for a particular kind of bagel favored by Brynner.

THE YEAR 1952 BEGAN WITH A NEW ANGLE TO HER career. On Sunday evening, January 6, at nine-fifteen, after several months of negotiations with the American Broadcasting Company affiliate in New York, Dietrich announced the premiere of her own radio show, *Café Istanbul*. With Dietrich playing the manager of a Turkish haunt for spies and secret agents, the half-hour dramatic series had complicated plots frequently interspersed by her singing or humming a few measures of French, German and English songs associated, of course, with herself—like the name she chose for her character, Mademoiselle Madou, after her surrogate in Remarque's *Arch of Triumph*. (The series was written by Murray Burnett, coauthor of "Everybody Comes to Rick's," the basis for the film *Casablanca.)*

The weekly recorded series did not materialize easily, as producer Leonard Blair recalled years later. Although the idea for a Dietrich program originated when (through her agents) she contacted radio executives, she affected a certain indifference when Blair was sent to their first meeting. "Her movement and her demeanor were studied, almost calculated. In fact, she was so sparing in her enthusiasm that it wasn't at all clear she would commit to the series."

Dietrich hosted this initial conference and the subsequent story meetings at her apartment, where she insisted on cooking breakfast for Blair. Moving from refrigerator to mixing bowl to frying pan, she asked detailed questions about her character, the story line, music, sound effects, supporting roles and setting. "There was no bright green light from Dietrich; we moved step by cautious step, but with each weekly serving of scrambled eggs I could see the slow cementing of her confidence. If I was well prepared and in full command, she was polite and responsive. But if she detected an ill-considered idea or the slightest lack of preparation—or simply idle flattery—she could be pointedly tart." Self-protective and apprehensive about the series, Dietrich was virtually a one-woman creative enterprise, redrafting scripts, coaching the actors, supervising the music and collaborating on every aspect of production (except in the control booth, from which union rules barred her). The program was heard successfully for two thirteen-week seasons.

After recording several shows in advance, Dietrich departed New York in February for a brief publicity tour on behalf of the opening of *Rancho Notorious,* stopping first with her co-star Mel Ferrer at a Chicago movie theater. Not content merely to say a few polite words at the launching of a film she detested, Dietrich had arranged a surprise for the moviegoers and the house manager. She stepped onto the darkened stage and, dressed in a full-skirted, strapless gown, sang "Falling in Love Again." The audience went wild, whistling and cheering as she returned moments later, one spotlight illuminating her bare legs and black bodice as she offered three more songs. At the conclusion, she gathered up bouquets of roses, bowed humbly and slowly departed. It was her first theatrical solo in America—and in fact became the test run for a major one-woman show she was then considering.

Continuing her publicity tour for the film in Los Angeles, Dietrich learned that the actor Kirk Douglas was ill with pneumonia after the dangerous river scenes of his recent film *The Big Sky.* Although she had met him only once (through their mutual friend Billy Wilder), Dietrich immediately swept down on Douglas, offering (as he later said), "soup [and] affectionate sex. But that was less than the mothering, the closeness. Marlene is an unusual person. She seemed to love you much more if you were not well. When you became strong and healthy, she loved you less." The liaison was as brief as Douglas's illness, which kept him bedridden only a few weeks that spring; their later meetings were infrequent, cordial and much less intimate.

"She was always particularly keen on having men in her life who were sick," confirmed Billy Wilder, with whom Dietrich's relationship was strictly platonic. "This was the part of her that was wife, mother, *Hausfrau*. And during her entire life I never knew her to have an affair with a rich man. She would neither ask for nor accept any material compensation."

Dietrich could not have lingered in California in any case, since her radio show required her presence in New York, and she had also arranged with Mitch Miller (director of popular music for Columbia Records) to revive her recording career. In July, she spent several days in a studio on East Thirtieth Street, singing and resinging "Come Rain or Come Shine," "Lili Marlene," "Mean to Me" and a half-dozen others—each of them sounding like the complaints of a benighted lover, including a German rendition of "The Surrey with the Fringe on Top." She also cut a novelty record with Rosemary Clooney (one of the most popular singers of the 1950s), whom she advised, "I know you're working, Rosie, but you really *should* comb your hair!"

Preparing diligently for an important shift in her career—to become the solo star of her own nightclub act—Marlene Dietrich, true to character, proceeded systematically. First she had to assure the maintenance of a positive image nationwide, and to that end she convinced a friend at *Life* magazine to schedule a lead story on her enduring fame and endearing friendships. The article, by Winthrop Sargeant, ran on August 18, with Marlene and Maria on the cover.

But Dietrich also knew she required more than publicity: she needed a serious education in all the details and mechanics of a solo stage performance if, in her fifties, this new venture were to succeed. She began by attending Judy Garland's rehearsals for her one-woman show, and then her performance at the Palace Theater on October 16—after which she heaped praise on Garland before prying crucial information from her. Several weeks later, Dietrich arranged to be invited to a dinner party for Garland at the Waldorf Towers suite of the Duke and Duchess of Windsor. To this soirée she brought several of her own phonograph recordings from live performances during the war, corralling everyone to hear each number, pointing out the long and gratifying applause for each song.

("Wouldn't it be wonderful if I could sing, too?" she later wrote across a photo of herself in the Jean Louis gown.)

The opening night of the Ringling Brothers–Barnum & Bailey Circus in April 1953 at New York's Madison Square Garden was a charity benefit. A number of stars had agreed to appear, and it was Maria's idea that her mother's fervor for publicity would be well served by her presence, too. But one among many was not Dietrich's goal, and so she managed to land the role of mistress of ceremonies. Of the outfit she designed to show off her legs, she said, "I invented the short pants later known as 'hot pants.' I looked wonderful, with my boots and my whip." And thus attired as a combination of Lola Lola and a Berlin dominatrix, she stepped out with only a single spotlight on her red coat, diamond studs, shining boots and silk hat rakishly tipped. "Hel-loooo," she purred into a microphone. "Are you having any fun?" While Dynamite, billed as the only horse in the world able to gallop backwards, did so, thousands of spectators and thirty photographers concentrated solely on the lure of Marlene Dietrich.

Many other actresses, given so many disappointing professional developments, would—voluntarily or not—have retired. Not so Dietrich. That night at Madison Square Garden, the vagaries of the last sixteen years were forgotten—that she had appeared in only two or three memorable films, made but a short list of recordings and aged to over fifty without yet demonstrating any great gift for singing or acting, much less any newly discovered talent. Yet the third (and, as it happened, the longest) resurgence of a long career had now begun, and it owed only to the skillful marketing of herself as an ikon of perpetual glamour and feminine allure.

Actresses like Bette Davis, Joan Crawford and Katharine Hepburn sustained long careers by abandoning claims to youth and beauty and developing new facets for themselves within a wide range of roles for mature women. Marlene Dietrich, however, had to rely only on a cultivated sex appeal that was provocative but never coarse, slightly naughty but never sordid. She pleased men and women in her audience by incarnating in her roles and expressing in her songs a cynicism without acrimony—by representing the ordinary adult experience of failed romance, lost love, diminished expectations. She represented what she was—the eternal lover, tenacious, proud, destined for the cycles of fierce romance and eventual disappointment, hovering too closely, nurturing too much, rejected but unbitter, ever eager for restoration to favor. But most of all, she simply endured, and all the world loves a survivor.

15: 1953–1956

"KLONDIKE IN THE DESERT," A REPORTER CALLED Las Vegas, Nevada, in 1953. That year, seven million tourists flocked to its legal gambling tables, and a major expansion of the city's many hotels and resorts was in progress. At the Desert Inn, the Flamingo, the Sahara and the Sands, guests passed through garish foyers to reach vast casinos filled with the cries of croupiers, the endless chiming of slot machines, the snap of cards and the clatter of chips.

In the restaurant-nightclub spaces of these hotels, cabaret performers could earn astonishing salaries, although they often had to compete with animals, circus and novelty acts and a distracted audience. "A wayfarer arriving in Las Vegas during any given week has a wider choice of top banana talent than the average New Yorker," reported the *New York Times* that year. But some artists agreed with Lena Horne that "the audience is a captive one, but the thing that has captured them is the gambling. They really only come to see you in order to take a rest from the crap tables." Nevertheless, a diverse roster of celebrities was regularly billed—Jimmy Durante, Bert Lahr,

Georgia Gibbs, Ray Bolger, Ezio Pinza, Jeanette MacDonald, all of them lured by fees of $20,000 a week for less than an hour's work nightly. Some performers were contracted to movie producers or television networks, but in a town controlled by organized crime, all manner of means were found to secure the services of a big name.

Marlene Dietrich, free of studio interference, needed no doubtful company for permission to work here. Arriving in Las Vegas in 1953 to negotiate for her debut that December, she surveyed the sound and lighting facilities, gauged the effects of this position and that gesture, assessed the sightlines and inspected the dressing rooms. She also listened to other performers—among them the twenty-five-year-old singer Eddie Fisher. A smooth tenor with a shy personality, he was carefully piloted by managers and billed as one of America's most adorable teenage heartthrobs. Fisher's boyish charm also made him the darling of the grandparents, and so for agents and record producers he was that rare find, a singer popular with both audiences.

Dietrich invited Fisher to her table after his performance one night and explained her plans, but he thought of her as an actress, not a nightclub star. "Eddie," she replied, "I was singing in cabarets before you were born." That age difference (twenty-seven years) apparently made no difference to their reunion a few weeks later in Dietrich's New York apartment, to which she invited him for a home-cooked supper. Greeting Fisher in a revealing, low-cut beige gown, she served a candlelit meal and, as he recalled years later, completely took charge of the situation: "I was both excited and a little scared. But Marlene knew how to make me feel like a man. The ceiling of her bedroom was mirrored."

Predictably, the affair (conducted mostly in New York during the summer and autumn of 1953) was intense but brief. On the one hand, it was flattering to an eager young singer from Philadelphia who appreciated every personal, social and professional endorsement offered by this "remarkable woman who knew how to enjoy life, the most stimulating woman I had ever met." But as in the case of Michael Wilding, Fisher was really more important to Dietrich than she to him. Although the charms of a handsome young lover were certainly not to be disregarded, she was, as usual, attracted by the situation of nurturing as much as by sex. More vital still, she needed to know that she was attractive to and could please a new generation of admirers. What she longed for in public—the attention and love of thousands—required a private supplement. Once again, a transitory affair signalled her need to be worshipped rather than loved, although by the paradox often engendered by sex, it was perhaps simultaneously a plea for affection. But if, as she always contended, work was her cardinal value, she did not (at least past the age of forty) select lovers who would threaten that primacy; each affair had within it the seeds of its own demise.

FOR THREE WEEKS BEGINNING DECEMBER 16, 1953, Marlene Dietrich sang a half-dozen songs each night at the Sahara in Las Vegas; for this she was paid $90,000, which again made her the highest-paid entertainer in America (and very likely in the world). Half-singing, half-speaking with a strategic mutter, a purr, a wink and a flutter of her half-closed eyelids, she was more a *diseuse*—a husky, gauzy lady baritone blithely unconcerned for accuracy of tone yet somehow communicating the sly, world-weary sagacity of what the French call *une femme d'un certain âge*. Her audience clapped, whistled, stomped the floor and banged their tables after she sang "The Boys in the Back Room," "Falling in Love Again," "Lili Marlene," "The Laziest Gal in Town," "Johnny" and "La Vie en Rose," and she closed her thirty-minute set in her scanty ring-master's outfit from the circus; she was, after all, the owner of legendary legs. In a way, she had come full circle, revising for modern audiences certain key aspects of earlier Berlin entertainments—and always teasing her audiences, inviting them yet maintaining a cool distance.

But it was not Marlene Dietrich's talent as a vocal artist that was earning her headlines, feature photographs and the greatest press coverage of her career thus far. In fact, her singing was ignored by the critics; her success was in what she wore and how she was lighted—in other words it was all style. "Her voice deficiencies were neatly offset by her rather radical costume," read a typical press

report, "the most revealing gown" anyone could recall on an entertaining figure anywhere.

"My outward appearance was extremely important, since I had
no illusions about my voice," Dietrich later admitted. For that reason, she had a few Las Vegas entrepreneurs pressure the reluctant
Harry Cohn, chief executive at Columbia Studios, to loan her his
chief wardrobe designer, Jean Louis.★ He had designed a seductive
trompe l'oeil costume for Rita Hayworth's film *Salome* which con-
sisted of a thickly padded, girdlelike "living foundation" covered
with a body stocking of flesh-colored chiffon. This was then overlaid
with beads to hide the seams, and with the right lighting and camera
angles Hayworth upset the censors. Dietrich had seen the film the
previous spring and had been impressed. Jean Louis then drew up
the basic blueprint for Dietrich—furs, spangles and diamonds, she
insisted—and then, all during the autumn, fifteen seamstresses
worked on three versions of the gown, sewing and resewing the
sequins, glass brilliants, six hundred rhinestones and yards of chiffon,
tearing and refashioning according to Dietrich's alterations. According to Jean Louis, Dietrich had "almost a mania for everything to be
just right. She flew to Hollywood from New York maybe six times
until everything was perfect. And then she would move one more
bead the size of a pinhead—just an eighth of an inch to the right or
the left and back again until she was satisfied. I have never seen such
patience—and such tenacity to get just the effect she wanted!"

The notorious dress (which appeared in magazines and newspapers internationally) cost just over $6,000 and weighed about four-
teen pounds. It was a masterpiece of the couturier's artifice, creating
the illusion that—after Dietrich tossed aside her white fox stole—
there was a firm and youthful body, nude from neck to waist but for
a few scattered sequins, rhinestones and pearls. "Jean Louis's creations metamorphosed me into a perfect, ethereal being," Dietrich
said, "the most seductive there was." Not even patrons in the first

---

★ The circumstances of the Dietrich-Louis collaboration were curious. Not long before, she had
agreed to appear in a film version of the musical *Pal Joey* with Frank Sinatra, but when Harry Cohn
decided to substitute Jack Lemmon, Dietrich withdrew, claiming Lemmon would not be right as her
co-star. Cohn, still furious, at first flatly rejected her subsequent request for Jean Louis's services, but
after Dietrich complained to her Las Vegas management Cohn received cautionary telephone calls
from certain underworld figures in Chicago, and Jean Louis was soon permitted to design Dietrich's
dress. (As it happened, Sinatra eventually did play *Pal Joey*.)

row could tell she was tightly enveloped in astutely dyed layers of rubber foundation covered with a body-stocking and then chiffon. "Well," Dietrich sighed to a journalist, "this is Las Vegas. If not here, then where?"

Her act—in the Sahara's Congo Room—was a model of Teutonic detail, from her coiffure to the position of a light, from the tempo of each song to the few moments of gesture. Her recent experiences in film (with Fritz Lang especially) had been so dreadful that she had taken the idea of her wartime one-woman show a decade earlier and raised it to a precise art. At last she needed no one but herself and her audience. "Technique and control," she said, "they are all that matter. In every single bar of my music, every single light that hits me—I know it and control it. In films, [there are] too many people, too many intangibles . . . [but in my solo act] nobody cuts or dubs or edits me afterwards."*

Several nights, from one to four in the morning, Dietrich stood and sat for still photographs with John Engstead, who rushed them to a laboratory and then raced back to Dietrich with the proofs for her to approve at seven o'clock. She slept only after she had supervised every detail and Engstead and his assistant had departed for Los Angeles to do the retouching and the final printing, so that her publicist would have copies for the press that afternoon. Dietrich wanted every detail correct, Engstead recalled, and every detail was elaborated in her contract with him as it had been with her nightclub hosts. According to Engstead, she loved her own face more than any other; she was her own creation for an audience, and she required that he help her maintain that creation. George Hurrell, who also photographed Dietrich that year, remembered that she returned a number of shots with multiple marks indicating which facial lines were to be removed by the retoucher. "You don't take pictures like you did fifteen years ago, George," she said sadly. "But

* According to Jean Louis, Dietrich agreed to loan one of the three copies of her dress to a starlet scheduled to hand out a prize at a charity ball. She attached two conditions, however: offering the value of the dress as a reason, she insisted that it should not be delivered to the wearer until moments before it was to be worn; it was also stipulated that the young lady wear nothing underneath (as, Dietrich lied to a gullible press, she had worn it). "The poor girl put on the dress hurriedly and as she had agreed," Jean Louis recalled, "and of course all those sequins and bugles and everything were so heavy it just pulled the dress down, and with no foundation garments or anything sewn in, it just hung on her like wet cement." Exactly, no doubt, as Dietrich had foreseen.

Marlene," Hurrell replied with consummate diplomacy, "I'm fifteen years older!"

The occasional photographic disappointment notwithstanding, Dietrich's time in Las Vegas was triumphantly happy, for almost everyone who knew her personally came to see her show during the holidays; she was, she wrote to friends in Europe, exceedingly pleased, making lots of money and in control of her own destiny at last.

Unfortunately, her return trip, just as the new year 1954 began, broke the spell. Dorothy, Countess di Frasso, an American millionairess who had married an Italian aristocrat, had come for Dietrich's final performance and, with their mutual friend Clifton Webb, had booked sleeping compartments on the train journey back to New York. A somewhat madcap member of café society, an international party-giver and a pursuer of the Hollywood elite, di Frasso also had some doubtful (if only transiently romantic) relations with the underworld. En route from Las Vegas, Webb found her in her roomette, dead of a heart attack at sixty-six, lying fully clothed in her expensive mink coat and wearing a diamond necklace worth almost $200,000; her luggage contained as much in additional precious stones and jewelry. The event troubled Dietrich very much: Dorothy di Frasso was not an intimate, but she was nearly a contemporary, and they intersected the same social circles. Age Dietrich could try to ignore; death was unspeakable, and the death of a rich, buoyant, elegant, life-loving woman like Dorothy must have reminded her of her own mortality as nothing else had. (Mentioning a seamstress who worked for her in Las Vegas and died later of natural causes, Dietrich said flatly that her death was "unjust.")

Still more unhappiness awaited in New York, where Rudi told Dietrich that Tamara, who had suffered from vaguely defined and intermittent emotional ailments for several years, had finally been diagnosed as severely manic-depressive with occasional frankly psychotic episodes. Doctors recommended that Matul enter an asylum for several months, but because Sieber was virtually without work by this time that was not feasible. Without hesitation, Dietrich suggested that they both return to California at her expense. Before the end of that year, Rudi and the frail Tamara had gone West, where

Dietrich's money set him up in the rustic life of a chicken farmer, an idea very much his own. This he preferred to the vagaries of working as a minor film company employee, and for a time Tamara, too, seemed to respond favorably to their new environment in the heart of the San Fernando Valley.

For Dietrich, the first months of 1954 were otherwise quiet. Stefan Lorant arrived early at her Park Avenue apartment one Sunday afternoon to take her to dinner, but Dietrich was in the midst of a major housecleaning, scrubbing the floors in each room. She then excused herself and returned from her bedroom and bath "transformed into a major star" (thus Lorant). After finding the doors of several East Side restaurants closed on Sunday evening, they finally located a quiet venue, but when the host said, "Of course, Miss Garbo, I have a lovely table for you," Dietrich turned to Lorant and said, "This is not my evening." They left at once and settled for pastrami sandwiches at Reuben's Delicatessen.

She also turned up regularly at the Riva house, where Maria interpreted her mother's frequent housecleaning as an implicit criticism. Dietrich fussed over her grandchildren, bought them clothes, and insisted on doing the same for Maria, for whom she bought what she considered to be the proper shoes and accessories.

There was also the usual round of theater-going with visiting friends like Noël Coward or Orson Welles, dining with literati like Hemingway when he passed through the city, and attending a United Nations reception at the special invitation of Secretary-General Dag Hammarskjöld, whom she did not know. Dietrich also repeated her benefit appearance at the circus that April, and over the course of several transatlantic telephone calls, finalized the details for the transfer to London of her Las Vegas act. Although England could afford to pay only about half her American fee, this was prestigious new territory to conquer.

And so on June 16, Noël Coward, a crimson carnation in his blue suit and carrying a bouquet of the same mixed with sweetpeas, met her at London Airport. Wearing a grey beret, a tightly fitted grey suit with its skirt two inches higher than the year's fashion, Dietrich smiled demurely, stopped to sign a few autographs and, ignoring reporters' questions, was summarily whisked off to the

Dorchester Hotel. There she was installed in the very grand seventh-floor suite decorated by Oliver Messel (complete with a grand piano and a gold bed in a gold bedroom) and prepared, as secretly as if her task were atomic research, for her debut at the Café de Paris, Leicester Square. On Monday morning, June 21, crowds began to gather outside the dinner club on Coventry Street; the five hundred available tickets had been sold weeks earlier, but fans jockeyed for the best positions to see the elite arrive that night, and perhaps the star, too.

While the patrons dined on salmon, sole, broiled chicken and strawberry ice cream, Dietrich slipped quietly into her dressing room at ten o'clock that evening. Precisely on schedule, at a quarter past midnight, Noël Coward stepped to the microphone:

> *Though we all might enjoy*
> *Seeing Helen of Troy*
> *As a gay cabaret entertainer,*
> *I doubt that she could*
> *Be one quarter as good*
> *As our legendary, lovely Marlene.*

A single spotlight found her, at the top of a staircase, wearing the notorious Las Vegas gown and a floor-length white fox coat. The hush throughout the Café was followed by a collective inhalation of breath, then a rapturous sigh, then clamorous applause as she glided down to the stage. With another face-lift, she looked perhaps too perfect, her features almost unnaturally smooth, her expression daringly impersonal. With eyes almost closed and lips tentatively parted, she barely acknowledged the presence of her audience, and by this calculated aura of something perilously close to apathy, she announced—substituting authority for warmth and domination for intimacy—"a few songs I have sung in pictures, on records and during the war." There was absolute silence, not the lightest clink of dinnerware, not a cough in the room; had she called "Attention!" the crowd would have leaped to their feet.

Dietrich pointed an index finger at the orchestra leader and then stood almost motionless for a half-hour, hands on hips, occasionally raising an arm defiantly, crooning with amiable disdain in a voice that no one criticized for its narrow range or its vacillation somewhere between harmony and hoarseness. As usual, she asked what the boys in the back room would have; she fell in love again, never wanting to; she was the laziest gal in town and not the marrying kind. Her inflections were alternately subtle, racy, forlorn; she did not ask to be loved or admired. She defied anyone to reject her, and that night no one did. She was simply there, a memorial to discipline, a statue of Eternity.

In the final analysis, that is what people came to see—a monument made famous by transcending time; a woman representing sex, yet implying that she was beyond it; an insolent, iconoclastic grandmother; a beautiful, overpowering and utterly unapproachable being whose manner on- and offstage said at once "Come hither" and "Keep your distance." Everything about her expressed what she had recently told the press:

> It is a woman's job to sense the hungers in men and to satisfy them without, at the same time, giving so much of herself that men become bored with her. It is the same with acting. Each man or woman should be able to find in the actress the thing he or she most desires and still be left with the promise that they will find something new and exciting every time they see her again.

And so it was for six weeks, in the most successful cabaret show in postwar London. By being in complete control, never granting an encore no matter how insistent the applause, she impressed every patron of the Café de Paris and had London at her command. It did not matter that she had become an institution, almost a spectacle, a Snow Queen trapped, as Noël Coward said privately, in her own legend.

TYPICALLY, SHE ENTERTAINED AFTER HER SHOW UNtil four or five in the morning, then slept until late afternoon. To the Dorchester came old friends and new acquaintances, who cheerfully listened to recordings of her opening night. Among others was Jean Howard (the wife of Charles Feldman, producer of two Dietrich pictures at Universal), who years later recalled a meeting one afternoon. "Van Johnson and I arrived at her suite, and she put on a record. It was nothing but excerpts of the applause to her numbers! For her it was wonderful, but it hardly seemed the thing to do for guests."

There were also charity excursions—beneficial publicity, she was assured—an occasional garden party benefit for blind babies or old age pensioners. When she heard that composer Harold Arlen was hospitalized with ulcers, she kept several days' vigil at his bedside, occasionally soothing him by humming his tunes "Stormy Weather" and "That Old Black Magic." As Billy Wilder recalled, "Arlen was on his deathbed when she took care of him—just as she had cared for Kirk Douglas, and for [actor-director] Gregory Ratoff when he was sick." Her compensation was the act of mothering itself.

Dietrich then dashed to the Café, where each night a different celebrity introduced her (Jack Hawkins, Alec Guinness and David Niven, for example); the patrons at the final performance included Princess Margaret and the Duchess of Kent.

On August 17, Dietrich attended the Bal de la Mer in Monte Carlo, where Jean Cocteau and his mate, the actor Jean Marais, introduced her to a crowd as "a bird of paradise, a magnificent ship with sails unfurled, a woman whose plumes and furs seem to grow naturally from her skin. Her name begins tenderly and ends with the sound of a cracking whip—Marlene Dietrich."

She returned to Paris with Marais to visit Piaf, Chevalier and the Seidmanns, but Marais had a clear impression that she was lonely and sad after the great London triumph. Dietrich claimed to harbor an enduring love for Gabin, and over several weeks Marais had to escort her to a small bistro near Gabin's home on the Rue François. From there she gazed longingly, watching for him to emerge, waiting hours for a mere glimpse. She also asked Marais to escort her to various retrospective cinemas screening Gabin films, at which she laughed, cried, commented on his acting and reminisced about her love affair.

• • •

IN OCTOBER 1954, SHE WAS BACK IN LAS VEGAS, IN a new peek-a-boo Jean Louis creation that had fewer bugle-beads but, with the same artful foundation and construction, gave the identical illusion of nudity beneath diaphanous chiffon. For her final song, a wind machine strategically positioned offstage blew the billowing fabric round her, effecting for a moment the image of a heavenly Aphrodite, or of Venus rising none too demurely from the waves.

A week into the run of her show, she was offered contracts to return during the next two years, at $100,000 annually for four weeks work. One evening not long after that she noticed John Wayne in the audience, blew him a kiss and, when she took her bow, beckoned him to follow her backstage. This he did cheerfully, taking along his fiancée. Dietrich greeted him with a passionate kiss, but turned her back suddenly and began to speak with another guest when Wayne introduced his future wife. Her attitude about the fealty of former lovers had obviously not changed.

Nor had her mothering instincts. That winter, Harold Arlen's musical show *House of Flowers* was scheduled to open on Broadway, and during its Philadelphia tryout Dietrich, worried about Arlen's ulcers, sped to his side with cartons of milk. She also made herself the production's servant, preparing coffee for the cast, stitching wardrobe and sending for her own brilliantly deceptive costume jewelry when Pearl Bailey's real gems failed to sparkle under stage lights. But by the time *House of Flowers* came to Broadway, Arlen— simply an acquaintance flattered by her attention and her desire to sing some of his most famous songs—had clearly allowed Dietrich too much latitude as a kind of unofficial mascot. She freely offered actors and technicians so much advice and direction that there was considerable dissension onstage and off, and she had to be politely asked to keep still.

Dietrich left the company before the Christmas premiere in New York, and during the holidays she complained bitterly (to visiting friends like Coward and Hemingway) that apart from her nightclub act there was really nothing to engage her energy or talent. In a letter to her Hollywood agent, Charles Feldman, she complained that she longed to try new kinds of film, and that no one had yet "taken advantage of the worldwide publicity resulting from my initial appearance in Vegas and London. I don't think there is another film actress idol for so many years who had such a success in a new field." She received a polite but indifferent reply; it was, after all, the era of Marilyn Monroe.

At the same time, there was little emotional constancy in her life at the age of fifty-three. She lavished on her daughter and grandsons the attention she had not given Maria in childhood, but her generosity was often excessive, embarrassing and frankly smothering to the Rivas. Coward put the matter succinctly when, addressing the complaints of fortunate actresses with brittle bitterness, he described Dietrich as

> fairly tiresome. She was grumbling about some bad press notices and being lonely. Poor darling glamorous stars everywhere, their lives are so lonely and wretched and frustrated. Nothing but applause, flowers, Rolls-Royces, expensive hotel suites, constant adulation. It's too pathetic and wrings the heart.

Each item from applause to adulation was hers again in London that June of 1955, where Douglas Fairbanks, Jr., introduced her second summer engagement at the Café de Paris, and where the opening night audience included patrons as diverse as Danny Kaye, Tyrone Power and Dame Edith Evans. Even the government pursued her this time. After Dietrich was introduced to the audience on July 5 by Bessie Braddock, the formidable Member of Parliament whom opponents compared to a Sherman tank, the two met backstage. "We chatted like one working girl to another," Dietrich said and promptly accepted Braddock's invitation to visit the Houses of Parliament the following week. When she did (on July 13), members of both Lords and Commons flocked to meet her, and the ordinary business of the day was interrupted by her simple presence in the galleries.

. . .

ON OCTOBER 4, 1955, DIETRICH RETURNED FOR another engagement in Las Vegas (with a new, equally deceptive outfit), and at Christmastime she was in New York, attending the premiere of the film *Oklahoma!* with its producer, Mike Todd. They were, at the time, discussing his idea of casting dozens of major stars in cameos for his forthcoming epic *Around the World in 80 Days,* and Dietrich was readily persuaded to join the ranks: other actors passing momentarily through the picture included Noël Coward, John Gielgud, Charles Boyer, Frank Sinatra, and Ronald Colman. Dietrich agreed to appear for a half-minute as a San Francisco saloon queen (protected by bouncer George Raft), one of hundreds of colorful characters encountered by David Niven in his worldwide balloon excursion. ("I am looking for my man," Niven says to Dietrich when he needs his valet in the noisy, brief sequence. "So am I," she murmurs.)

That winter, Dietrich and Todd became quite openly known in New York as "a twosome." A good friend of Todd's and still on amiable (although platonic) terms with Dietrich, Eddie Fisher soon learned the truth of this report when he attended a Todd party and found her clothes in Todd's bedroom closet. "Mike knew of my romance with Marlene and was obviously a little embarrassed."* But neither man need have been too chagrined, for it was only a matter of weeks before the dresses and cosmetics were removed when Todd went around the world with his production company. Then, not long after her cameo was filmed, Rudi suffered a slight heart attack at his home in California. Dietrich was at his bedside daily throughout most of that April 1956, conferring with physicians and seeing that Tamara was properly attended. Not until he was fully recovered did she proceed to New York and thence for her stint in London at the Café de Paris, which she followed with four performances at a Dublin theater.

For these shows Dietrich added a second outfit, making a quick change from her diaphanous gown to top hat, white tie and tails, straight from her cabaret scene in *Morocco.* Puffing a cigarette, she

---

* In light of this brief affair, Dietrich could eventually claim that three of her former lovers subsequently married Elizabeth Taylor: in 1957, after divorcing Michael Wilding, Taylor wed Todd. A year later, Todd was killed in a plane crash, and the first to comfort the grieving widow was Fisher, who in 1959 divorced Debbie Reynolds to marry Taylor.

straddled a chair and sang "One for My Baby and One for the Road."

To the amazement of her audience, she accomplished this wardrobe change in less than a minute and without intermission. Dashing offstage, she doffed her shoes and stripped off the gown and its foundation garments while her assistant removed the jewelry and wiped off the lipstick. Another assistant handed Dietrich two hairbrushes already thick with brilliantine, and her plastered hair was stuffed under the top hat. Over her body stocking went black socks, the trousers and shirt were put on in a single piece, and she slipped into the coat and shoes. Before the orchestra had completed the introduction to the upcoming song she was back onstage, unsmiling and ignoring the applause with the affectation of stoic detachment long familiar to moviegoers.

IN AUGUST, SHE TOOK A HOLIDAY WITH NOËL COWard in Paris, at the home of Ginette Spanier and Paul-Emile Seidmann, with whom she was still on intimate terms. But Rudi's brush with death and Tamara's instability made Marlene Dietrich (then in her fifty-fifth year) both more anxious and more unrealistic about the inevitabilities of age and illness. She spoke endlessly about her past, about John Gilbert, Erich Remarque, Jean Gabin and Michael Wilding, and "with her intense preoccupation with herself and her love affairs," wrote Coward in his diary, "[she] is showing signs of wear and tear. How foolish to think that one can ever slam the door in the face of age. Much wiser to be polite and gracious and ask him to lunch in advance."

The forms of her courtesy to those nearby—essentially endless physical activity on their behalf—were often curious. At the Seidmann home, Coward continued, Dietrich was "in a tremendously *hausfrau* mood and washed everything in sight, including my hairbrush (which was quite clean)." It may not have occurred to her that such duties were sometimes ill advised.

The rationale for this sustained motif of menial housewifery, as if Dietrich were exchanging the role of Queen Mother for that of

Visiting Charwoman, is not difficult to understand. In her favor, it must be said that she certainly wanted to help, to please her friends (as housecleaning had pleased her parents and even, on occasion, lovers) and to demonstrate that she was—when she wished to seem so—an ordinary, practical woman, capable of lowly toil as well as high fashion.

But to offer such laborious assistance to someone ill or in need was one thing; to come upon Marlene Dietrich scrubbing one's bathroom floor or washing windows was another, and it must have been disconcerting. This was an odd form of self-abasement, perhaps partly motivated by a repressed neurotic guilt for the little of depth she did for others, and for the consistent attention she denied them. Her chores were thus a kind of penance that predictably embarrassed those it was meant to honor. Even her support of Rudi and Tamara and the lavish gifts to Maria and her husband must have sprung at least in part from Dietrich's remorse for past negligence. As for those she visited, her zealous housework spoke eloquently of a desire to be admired and thanked—and perhaps even to make debtors of those to whom she was, for their hospitality, obliged.

Contrariwise, once her self-imposed domestic tasks were dispatched that summer in Paris, Dietrich withdrew, reentering the Seidmanns' living room looking beautiful, crisply attired in a simple beige suit. She then sat as still as an artist's model (as John Engstead and others recalled), with her legs so perfectly posed that she seemed almost unnaturally arranged. Everything about her looked ideal, as Spanier said: "I don't know how she [held this single pose] for half an hour!" Thus did Cinderella handily assume the role of Princess Royal. Later during the visit, when friends gathered round the piano to sing, Dietrich hung back gloomily from the group; at last she went to her room, returned with a few of her recordings, snapped on the phonograph and promptly turned the evening's spotlight on herself. This was a habit she practiced regularly in her later life when visiting friends in Switzerland (Coward), London (Fairbanks), New York (Garland) and Los Angeles (her publicist Rupert Allen, who also represented Grace Kelly and Marilyn Monroe). Her friends' quiet indulgence may have at least partially derived from astonishment.

The Paris sojourn preceded her first major film role in over five years (since the dreadful *Rancho Notorious),* and every element for success seemed in place: a glamorous wardrobe (by Jean Louis), a photogenic setting (Monte Carlo) and one of the world's most respected actors and directors as her leading man (the dashing former matinee idol Vittorio De Sica, whose films *The Bicycle Thief* and *Umberto D.,* among others, she much admired).

The Monte Carlo Story was filmed there during that summer of 1956, but somehow none of the attractive constituents could counterpoise a wooden script, unappealing characters and uninspired direction. De Sica played a minor, faded aristocrat addicted to the gambling tables who decides to marry a rich woman (Dietrich) who turns out to be even poorer than he—an elegant fraud with her own designs on his dwindling fortune. According to the custom of European filmmaking, the dialogue was dubbed after photography, and in the finished film every scene is sufficiently asynchronous to make the actors seem as if they move on command.

Decked out in primary colors, Dietrich moved carefully (sometimes as if sleepwalking, it seems), and only in the relaxed, comic kitchen scene with De Sica did she appear interested or vivacious. The entire production was indeed an unhappy experience, beginning with Dietrich's irrational and singularly graceless attitude toward a young American starlet cast in the film. Natalie Trundy was a pretty blond fifteen-year-old who, after appearing on the cover of *Paris Match,* incurred Dietrich's jealous wrath simply because of the attention lavished on a young player by the press. For no good reason (and to the shock of cast and crew), the star slapped the poor girl after a scene one afternoon. The courtly De Sica was furious, referring thereafter to Dietrich as "that witch." There was more trouble when Dietrich was barred from the Monte Carlo Casino because she attended in trousers. Even a telephone call to Aristotle Onassis (who owned a major share of the place) was of no avail in that instance, and she was shocked to learn that Princess Grace and Prince Rainier were away from the principality and unable to rush to her aid. Her temper finally flared when, in her suite at the Hôtel de Paris, she hurled abuse at the manager when only a dozen roses decorated her suite: "You call these *flowers?* I want five thousand roses, not a dozen!" Her tantrum had the staff hopping, as her secretary, Bernard Hall, recalled, "and vases upon vases were rushed to her suite."

16: 1957–1960

O N FEBRUARY 14, 1957, SIX WEEKS AFTER her fifty-fifth birthday, Marlene Dietrich opened her annual Las Vegas engagement, this time at the Sands Hotel. She began her midnight act with a husky, almost bleated rendition of "Look Me Over Closely"—an apt tune in light of her outfit, a floor-length, skintight gown with thousands of tiny handsewn beads and a white, twelve-by-eight-foot wrap fashioned from five million swan feathers (which weighed less than four pounds). Dietrich had undergone yet another face-lift earlier that winter, and with expert makeup and a hairpiece designed to her meticulous specifications, there was inevitably something too studied, too exaggeratedly artful about her appearance. At odd moments when she regarded herself in a mirror, she saw (as she told photographer John Engstead) a grotesque female impersonator. One evening backstage in Las Vegas, a seam split, several dozen dress-beads clattered to the floor, and she was anxious that all of them might fall off and scatter. She could have seen the moment as metaphoric, a marker of the unravelling of that part of herself that was entirely false.

Yet to the maintenance of this fundamentally unreal personality, of a strictly created and annually recreated illusion, she dedicated herself with canny zealotry. Her avidity for this was based on a fierce professionalism and a tenacious will to succeed, but she was also imprisoned within a persona for which there was simply no replacement: in thirty years there had been only minor variations to her image as a *femme fatale*.

Although Marlene Dietrich was associated with a kind of enduring, timeless beauty and the triumph of wily, feminine allure, it was equally clear from her image (as from her life) that much of her victory was Pyrrhic, that it had left her with fame and a bank account, social access anywhere, and an often unacknowledged loneliness everywhere. She told many people some facts of her life, but no one was privy to her deepest feelings; indeed, many who knew her well (her publicist Rupert Allen, for one) felt that perhaps she had no deep feelings at all, that by middle age she had successfully inured herself against grief, loss and the demands of authentic love—that there was, in other words, no frame of reference outside herself.

In any case, there certainly seems to have been no one in whom she ever confided in a deeply affectionate way. Neither lovers nor platonic friends like Noël Coward (whose gift for true camaraderie has been much documented) ever described her with any of the empathy that characterizes mature friendship. Dietrich was thus, perhaps unwittingly, severely limited by her devotion to an exhausted, manufactured personality to which she had no alternative because she considered no choices.*

Some of this was perhaps inevitable for a woman who had not acted on the stage since 1929, and whose international fame depended on an audience's familiarity with how she had once looked; she was, in other words, something of a museum piece. But actresses were presented very differently in 1957 from the way they had been in the 1930s—and not only in hemlines, cosmetics and lighting. Of

---

* "The Danger of Being Beautiful" was the apt title for a shallow, impersonal interview for *McCall's* in March 1957, in which Dietrich discussed old-fashioned feminine wiles.

those women who had made films in the 1930s, few had careers that survived into the new world of movie entertainment, threatened by television, but saved by Technicolor, wide screens and gradually more latitude in content and treatment. The public now preferred the fey charm of Audrey Hepburn, the sheer luxuriance of Marilyn Monroe, the sensuous youth of Elizabeth Taylor, the perky audacity of Shirley MacLaine and the muted passion of Deborah Kerr. Dietrich had only a past iconography to tap, and only a present reputation for appearing on the lists of Best Dressed Women: she gave no indication of having grown into a new era or a fresh perception. It was of course fine to be the carrier of a grand history, but there was a consequent danger, and Dietrich seemed in a strange way mummified. In that regard, she was victimized by one of the most fantastic aberrations in contemporary culture, one to which she herself contributed: the futile quest for perpetual youth and the concomitant obsession with forestalling death.

AT THE CONCLUSION OF HER LAS VEGAS assignment, Dietrich hastened to Los Angeles, where in 1957 she appeared in two of her last four film roles. For Orson Welles, the star and director of *Touch of Evil,* she agreed—on two days' notice—to work one afternoon and evening, impersonating a cigar-chomping, fortune-telling bordello madam. "There was no talk about reading the script or what the part was at all," according to Welles. "She said, 'What should I look like?' I said, 'You should be *dark.*'" And that gave Dietrich her clue: tearing through cartons of her own costume remnants and scouring thrift shops, she came up with a stringy black wig, spangled shoes and a variety of tacky odds and ends that were perfect for the role and delighted her old friend the director.

Appearing in three scenes of *Touch of Evil* for a total of less than four minutes, Dietrich—perilously close to unintentional parody—advised the pathetic, vicious character played by the obese Welles to "lay off the candy bars," and then sadly informed him, "You have no future—it's all used up." For the rest of her life, she often said this brief role was "the best thing I have ever done in films . . . I think I never said a line as well as the last line in that movie, 'What does it matter what you say about people?' "

In June, Dietrich received an urgent cable from the writer and director Preston Sturges, then residing in Paris, asking her to replace Ingrid Bergman in the French production of Robert Anderson's play *Tea and Sympathy* so that Bergman could appear in a Sturges production. But she could not, for she had accepted Billy Wilder's offer to play the apparently duplicitous but actually faithful wife who is the *Witness for the Prosecution.*

In this screen adaptation of the successful play, Dietrich was Christine Vole, a former cabaret star brought from Germany to England after the war by her husband (Tyrone Power). He is accused of murdering a wealthy widow, and during a complicated trial she schemes to prove that she is untrustworthy as a witness against him. Her ploy works, and the jury pronounces her husband innocent, framed by his faithless wife; but once he is free, she reveals to his attorney (Charles Laughton) that her husband was indeed guilty of the crime, and that she has risked everything and perjured herself to free him. Greeting her husband after his release, she then learns that he is eagerly awaited by another woman; scorned, she stabs him to death, immediately earning the advocacy of the same attorney.

As a woman who plots, lies and kills for love, Dietrich put aside every bangle and bauble of her nightclub image and worked to exhaustion on a role that could have been written for her. "She was like nothing I've ever seen," according to Billy Wilder. "Marlene was always a worker, always the good trouper, but on this picture she was tireless—it almost seemed as if she thought her career depended on it." She worked daily with Wilder and into the evenings with Laughton to perfect the cockney accent she needed for her disguised character-within-the-role.

Seconds before her entrance, Laughton warns a colleague about her character: "Bear in mind she's a foreigner, so be prepared for hysterics or even a fainting spell. Have smelling salts ready." At once her voice is heard off-camera: "I don't think that will be necessary." Only then do we see her, framed in a doorway, a somewhat remote figure in a tailored suit, cloche hat and gloves. In utter simplicity,

photographed full-face in black and white, Dietrich appears as nothing like a screen goddess; her beauty is in fact severe. "I never faint,
because I'm not sure that I will fall gracefully," she says unblinkingly
to Laughton, "and I never use smelling salts because they puff up the
eyes." Alert with pretense and passion, her mouth defiant, Dietrich's
Christine was from the first moment a woman of steely self-confidence—a fascinating role played without fussy technique.

There was one concession to the legend, however—an early
flashback devised for the film so that Dietrich could belt out "I May
Never Go Home Anymore" at a German cabaret called The Red
Devil, a neat inversion of her most famous venue. For this sequence,
as homage to moments in several earlier movies, Dietrich causes a
riot, soldiers rush the stage and her trouser leg is conveniently
torn; it was the last glimpse, in film history, of this Prussian cheese-
cake.

"It is not easy to teach Cockney to a German glamour-puss who
can't pronounce her Rs, but she did astonishingly well," noted Noël
Coward in his diary on August 4 after visiting Los Angeles and
adding his own suggestions to Laughton's diction lessons. As she
worked on her accent and created garish makeup for the scene in
which Christine disguises herself, Dietrich had the idea that her
performance might win her what she thought was a long overdue
Academy Award. She had been nominated only once (for *Morocco*).
"She was desperately disappointed when she was not even nominated for the award," according to Billy Wilder. And the veteran
Hollywood reporter Radie Harris remembered "too well how
much [Dietrich] wanted an Oscar. She even went so far as to call me
from Las Vegas and asked me to please hint in my column that she
deserved [it]."* Dietrich also complained to Rupert Allen that the
publicists engaged for *Witness for the Prosecution* were not giving her
the attention she merited, nor advancing her for the Oscar sufficiently. But none of her self-promotion availed.

During production she and Wilder were, as always, the best of
friends. He and his wife included Dietrich at a dinner party that
season, and years later he recalled

---

* In her memoir, Dietrich claimed that the idea of winning an Oscar for *Witness* meant "nothing at all
to me" (*Marlene*, p. 128).

that of course Marlene was the center of attention. I began a kind of little interview, urging her to tell us all the story of her fantastic life. I asked her who was the first man in her life and she said her violin teacher. She was holding back nothing, and everyone was hanging on her words. Next I said, "Now tell us about your relations with women," and she began, "Well, of course there was Claire Waldoff, and then . . ." By this time there was a great silence in the room, and I turned to everyone and asked, "Oh! Are we boring you?"★

That autumn she was back in New York, theatergoing with Noël Coward and offering companionship to playwright Robert Anderson, whose wife had recently died. (They had met briefly when Maria had appeared in a road company production of *Tea and Sympathy.)* "I understand you're lonely," she announced on the telephone to him one day, inviting him to escort her to a play next evening. This Anderson declined, as he did any contact more intimate than a luncheon, for he did not wish to accept Dietrich's overture.

But it was really she herself who was lonely, and in the following year she embarked on a series of short trips round the country, attempting to visit almost anyone she knew on a first-name basis, as if she felt her span of life was quickly running out. In 1958 and 1959 she performed her annual Las Vegas engagements (now worth $40,000 a week for four weeks), and few in her audiences seemed to care that there was less voice than ever. Everything about her appearances, in fact, seemed more and more frozen, stylized. Her shows were expanded in those years to include concerts in Rio de Janeiro, Sâo Paolo, Buenos Aires and Paris, where she added to her repertory American ballads ("My Blue Heaven," for example), recent show tunes ("I've Grown Accustomed to Her Face," from *My Fair Lady),* and German, French and Brazilian standards.

"She looks ravishing and tears the place up," Coward noted in Paris after her show at the Théâtre de l'Etoile in December 1959,

---

★ "She always admitted to me that she preferred women to men," said Dietrich's secretary Bernard Hall after her death. "She said, 'When you go to bed with a woman, it is less important. Men are a hassle.' And she knew she didn't have to make a commitment to a woman."

"[but] she has developed a hard, brassy assurance and she belts out every song harshly and without finesse. All her aloof, almost lazy glamour has been overlaid by a noisy, 'take-this-and-like-it' method which, to me, is disastrous. However, the public loved it."

COWARD WAS ON THE MARK, FOR DIETRICH'S SHOWS (preserved on recordings) were unvarying presentations of the same songs, each introduced by her embellished, self-aggrandizing anecdotes about (a) auditioning for *The Blue Angel;* (b) coming to America; (c) making this or that film; (d) serving the troops in wartime. And on each recording the audience's applause was of course carefully and completely preserved. With Dietrich supervising the final cuts, it was also at least partly created: it was easy for her to demand (and subsequently easy for the listener to discern) the looped repetition of cycles of applause, whistles, shouts of approval. Reporters (like friends) were frequently subjected to documentations of this applause: "She plugged in a tape recorder and played me ten minutes of the uninterrupted applause which greeted her act when she was in Rio," according to a journalist from London's *Sunday Express,* "and I knew as soon as she discovered that my breathing was regular and my pupils undilated that there was no hope [that she would like or approve me]."★

As for her singing, it could hardly be called that. Nor was she properly a *diseuse* in the style of Edith Piaf or Lotte Lenya, for there was something chillingly detached and unemotional about almost everything Dietrich recorded; it was hard to believe that she was wounded by love, impossible to accept from her the lyrics about emotional devastation. She did not, in other words, communicate so much the sense of a song's lyrics as she marketed herself, and the recordings have none of the vitality or animation of those she did for

★ Few journalists were left unsubjected to recordings of Dietrich's applause. Eugene Archer described a typical newsman's meeting with Dietrich in her New York apartment: "She walked to her phonograph and turned it on. 'Listen to this,' she murmured. The recording was from [a recent opening], and the applause was both prodigious and apparently endless. 'I'd never believe that if I didn't have it on tape,' she brooded. 'I had sixty curtain calls. I sold out every performance . . .' " ("Light from an Undiminishing Star," *New York Times,* Sept. 4, 1960). This inspired female impersonator Lynne Carter, in his sendup of Dietrich, to quip, "Have you heard my latest record? It's all applause!"

films in the 1930s. Dietrich gave no indication that her heart had expanded as the voice contracted. "Let's not fool anyone," she admitted in 1959. "It takes money to be glamorous these days. Glamour is what I sell in my act, and it costs plenty. It's my stock in trade. My clothes arouse more comment than anything except maybe my figure."

She marketed herself otherwise, too, recording five-minute network radio spots of advice in 1958 and 1959 that were astonishingly vapid even according to the stricter, more conventional requirements of talk-radio at the time:

—"It is very difficult to be happy without working, without taking pride in achievement, however small."
—"Know your own limitations and be realistic about them. If you are a good carpenter, take pride in being a good carpenter."
—"Men are so easy to love. All women have to do is to orbit around them, to make them the center, the hard core of existence. The trouble with so many modern women is that they want the men to orbit around *them*."
—"Teenagers must be patient, more tolerant of our failures. We have some love and wisdom to give, and of course we all have to maintain our sense of humor."

A sense of humor failed her one night in 1958, however, when she attended Carol Channing's act at the Tropicana Hotel in Las Vegas. In a diaphanous negligée, mesh hose and exaggerated German accent, Channing devastated her nightclub audience with a parody of the queen of glamour, lying on the floor with her legs pointing to the ceiling and, à la Dietrich, chattering endlessly about herself—her songs, her films, her wardrobe, her travels, her wartime service. Then came her punchline: "But enuff about me—let's talk about *you* for a vile," she muttered throatily. "Vot do you tink of my outfit? Is it too flimsy for a grandmother?" The spotlight located Dietrich at a table as she rose magisterially and swept out. The impersonation remained in Channing's act for several years despite Dietrich's request that it be dropped.

. . .

PERHAPS RARELY HAS MERE CELEBRITY SO SUCCESS-
fully sustained itself as in the case of Marlene Dietrich. "I don't ask
whom you are applauding—the legend, the performer or me," she
told an audience at the Museum of Modern Art after a retrospective
tribute in April 1959. "I personally liked the legend. Not that it was
easy to live with, but I liked it." Tens of thousands agreed with her
in the coming decade.

Everywhere, she knew how to exploit that legend. In Rio
(part of a three-city South American tour in August 1959) a vast
throng gathered to greet her arrival at the theater and she apparently
swooned. "I didn't really faint," she later admitted, "but it was the
only way I could get inside. Besides, there were many photographers
present, and it was a good chance for publicity." But as Rupert
Allen later verified, many in the pressing crowd were paid, professional theatrical extras glad to be part of a documented mob scene.
They were present after she stormed into the local constabulary and
demanded that off-duty police attend her that evening.

Just so in Paris, where the following December she planned
every detail of her arrival: Maurice Chevalier and Jean-Pierre
Aumont were recruited to meet her at the airport. On her arrival,
she carried a small, decorated cigar box which, as arranged, finally
evoked a question about its contents when she stepped before the
waiting microphones. It was, she said with a wink, the gown for her
show. The following day (November 19) every Paris newspaper announced the imminent display of the scantiest costume outside the
Folies-Bergère.

To old friends like Coward, such tactics made her "boring and
over-egocentric, poor darling"; new acquaintances, like Paris correspondent Art Buchwald, found her curiously fascinating when she
read him her best reviews and explained the two portions of her act
—revealing gown for the first, white tuxedo and top hat for the
second (bringing to life her final costume from *Blonde Venus*):

> You could say that my act is divided between the woman's part
> and the man's part. The woman's part is for men and the man's
> part is for women. It gives tremendous variety to the act and
> changes the tempo. I have to give them the Marlene they expect

in the first part, but I prefer the white tie and tails myself . . .
There are just certain songs that a woman can't sing as a woman,
so by dressing in tails I can sing songs written for men.

Although there was, in 1959, a brief liaison with the athletically
handsome forty-two-year-old Italian actor Raf Vallone, Marlene
Dietrich by the end of the year had restricted her romantic life to
her musical arranger and conductor Burt Bacharach, then thirty—
"a man who took me to seventh heaven," as she wrote later,
often reverting to language hitherto reserved for her affair with
Gabin.

> He was the most important man in my life after I decided to
> dedicate myself completely to the stage [and] my highest goal
> until the day he left was to please him . . . I lived only for the
> performances and for him . . . With the force of a volcano
> erupting, Bacharach had reshaped my songs and changed my act
> into a real show. On tour, I washed his shirts and socks. In short,
> I took care of him as though he were my savior. And as a man,
> he embodied everything a woman could wish for. He was con-
> siderate and tender, gallant and courageous, strong and sincere;
> but above all, he was admirable, enormously delicate and loving.
> And he was reliable. His loyalty knew no bounds. How many
> such men are there? For me he was the only one . . . He was
> my lord and master.

And so Bacharach remained for several years of international
travel with her and her show. His youth, charm and talent made him
enormously attractive to Dietrich, who desperately required proof
that she could still compete with younger women, and who knew
few ways other than sex to fascinate a man she needed and to sustain
his attention. For Bacharach's part, the life of a bachelor/traveling
musician could otherwise have been dismally lonely, and his simultaneously personal and professional intimacy with Dietrich quickly
proved to be enormously valuable. Additionally, he indeed cared for
her patiently, coping with her ego and her moodiness, her self-
absorption, her constant need to be confirmed as an artist and as a

woman. Twenty-eight years her junior, Bacharach was certainly among the most estimable to her. He was also, it seems, her last male lover.

To Burt Bacharach belongs at least part of the credit for perhaps the single most dramatic period of Dietrich's seniority, for had he not encouraged and attended her she might not have returned to Germany in 1960—an event of which the success (not to say her safety) could not be guaranteed.

On Thursday, April 14 (following a three-week engagement in Lake Tahoe, Nevada), Dietrich and Bacharach arrived in London en route to Paris, where she had scheduled wardrobe fittings at Dior and Balenciaga. The German tour had just been announced, to include concerts in Berlin, Hamburg, Oldenburg, Düsseldorf, Essen, Cologne, Hanover, Wiesbaden, Munich, Stuttgart and Frankfurt (for which she would receive almost $4,000 for each performance). But when Noël Coward took her to dinner, she admitted that she had some hesitations about the journey. "She was in a dim mood," he noted in his diary, "because all is in a state of chaos [and] the German press has come out against her."

In fact the pretour publicity then being generated was a horror, and it was much to Dietrich's credit that she ignored the threats of danger and pressed on; she could, after all, have easily substituted engagements elsewhere. "If they had any character," she had said in 1952, "the German people would hate me [for my entertainment of Allied troops]." Eight years later, that torn and divided land had "character" aplenty, but much of it was harnessed against Dietrich from March to the end of April, as warnings and vilifications filled the German press:

—"The USA and Germany are long since friends, but Dietrich is still leading a private war against the fatherland she unnecessarily gave up. Obviously she does not despise the Deutsch Mark as much as her homeland." —*Kölnische Rundschau* (Cologne), March 3.
—"Who has invited this person who worked against us during the war to perform as a visiting actress? Marlene, go home!" —*Bild-Zeitung* (Berlin), March 3.

—"Marlene marched on the side of the Resistance fighters and the
enemies of everything that was Germany. She did not keep still
when Germans tried to dig themselves out of the ruins and misery and regain respect in the world. It would be better for us if she
were to remain where she is." —*Badische Tagblatt* (Baden-Baden),
March 24.

—"She donned an Allied uniform and entertained their troops!
While her actions can be understood during the Hitler regime, it
is incomprehensible why she refused to change her mind after the
war." —*Bild am Sonntag* (Hamburg), April 3.

There was some (but not much) dissent: "If she is received with
tomatoes and rotten eggs," warned Hamburg's *Die Welt,* "then our
reputation in America will decline further, and it will prove anew
that we have learned nothing from our mistakes." And newspapers
did receive a few letters like that from a woman in Düsseldorf:
"Who showed more character—Marlene, who resisted all entice-
ments to turn to Hitler and who fought uncompromisingly against
criminal Nazi Germany, or we who went down on our knees before
those wretched leaders? It's not a very far journey from 'Jews, get
out!' to 'Out with Marlene!' "

But support for the returning Dietrich was essentially as flimsy as
the chiffon of her gowns. As the date of her arrival drew near, letters
to editors proliferated and privately circulated handbills opposing her
littered every major German city:

—"An impudent wench fights for her honor by daring to come
home. Dietrich has thousands of German soldiers' graves on her
conscience. She not only fought the Nazis but the German people as well! Now she is even enlisting help from Willy Brandt
[mayor of West Berlin], the former resistance fighter. She is an
antisocial parasite and should receive deserved punishment from
us."

—"Aren't you, a base and dirty traitor, ashamed to set foot on
German soil? You should be lynched, since you are the most
wretched war criminal." —Open letter from Mayen.

"The major error of this tour," said the respected Belgian critic Jean Améry years later,

> is that she thought she was returning home triumphantly. What she did not take into account was the unexpected self-assurance of the German citizenry and especially of West Berliners. With the economic recovery of Germany, people had regained their good conscience. And a new generation had grown up, too, for whom Dietrich meant very little—as the ghosts of Nazism meant very little to them.

The outcry against her return increased when Dietrich's earlier unambiguous comments on Germany were loudly broadcast: "I was German but I refused to declare myself a supporter of a country in which such atrocities were taking place." And when asked that spring whether she felt any sentiment about returning to her former home she replied coldly, "Not one bit. I gave up my fatherland because I was ashamed of it. Home is where my family is, and my family is in America." Far from attempting to reconcile herself with her country, her return seemed more an act of defiance.

But Dietrich was not, nor had she ever been, ranked as a political person exploited as a German national or, later, as a naturalized German-American. At stake in 1960 was her adherence to a moral position from which she had never wavered a quarter-century earlier, when many of her compatriots were not at all convinced that Hitler was so bad after all. ("If I were a German," added Améry, "I would be proud of her—and of her pride.")

ON APRIL 30, 1960—FIFTEEN YEARS AFTER HER last visit—Marlene Dietrich arrived in Berlin, and on May 2 she strode into a hotel dining room and answered journalists' questions in flawless, elegant German. Wearing the red ribbon of the French Legion of Honor and carrying a bouquet of lilies of the valley, she stared around, then sat down and spoke with remarkably cool assurance: "I am singing here because singing is my business, and I have been asked by my German agents to come. Why should I say no?

With the Ninth
Army in France, 1944.

With Allied troops in Belgium, winter 1945.

With General George S. Patton, 1945.

General James M. Gavin.

With returning troops, July 1945.

Reunited with her mother at Berlin's
Tempelhof airport, September 1945.

With Danny Thomas, about 1949.

With Ernest Hemingway in New York, 1947.

With Maria in New York, 1950.

*O*pening night in Las Vegas, 1953.

*L*ondon, 1954.

MILTON H. GREENE.

*T*he famous legs, celebrated by photographer Milton Greene in 1955.

*D*uring filming of *Witness for the Prosecution*, with Charles Laughton, Tyrone Power and director Billy Wilder: Hollywood, 1957.

*W*ith Noël Coward, 1958.

*A*t the Titania Palast: Berlin, May 1960.

*C*rowds with placards urging "Marlene, go home!" outside the Titania.

*A*t the Locarno Film Festival with von Sternberg, July 1960.

*A*t the funeral of Edith Piaf:
Paris, 1963.

*W*ith her musical director Burt
Bacharach: London, 1964.

*O*utside the theater after the New
York premiere of her one-woman
show, October 1967.

On tour.

Dietrich's last screen appearance,
as the Baroness von Semering in
Just a Gigolo, 1978.

. . . Am I afraid of rotten tomatoes? No, rotten eggs would be worse, because they could not be cleaned from my swansdown coat . . . Perhaps I will do some good, you say? I don't want to do any good." She felt, she told a friend that evening at the Berlin Hilton, "as though I'm going to my Nuremberg trial when I step out on that stage tomorrow night."

On Sunday, May 1, a Berlin newspaper—in a triumph of Teutonic efficiency—announced the recovery of the certified birth certificate of Marlene Dietrich, who was about to step onto a German stage for the first time since 1929; she was born, the article proclaimed gleefully, on December 27, 1901.

On Tuesday, May 3, there were police precautions encircling the Titania Palast, after threats of riots, egg-pelting and a broadcast warning of the release of five hundred white mice in the theater aisles. Of two thousand seats, five hundred were empty for her premiere, but at prices ranging from two to twenty-four dollars the tickets were beyond the range of all but the most independently affluent Berliners. In her hotel room, Dietrich was moody and tense, impervious even to Bacharach's reassurance. "I am not particularly glad to be here or there or anywhere," she told an inquiring reporter. "All my former friends here either left Germany or died in concentration camps, and so there are none left for me to see." She did not, she added with astonishing frankness, have any happy memories of Berlin at all.

Her attitude was, in fact, very like her act, in which Marlene Dietrich affected a stance bordering on cold contempt. Asking for nothing but attention, she offered a bluntness rarely heard from visiting performers, who ordinarily (then as later) insisted how much they loved the place they were performing in, what devoted friends and precious memories were evoked, how ineffably divine the experience was, what sheer love they felt. From Dietrich there was none of this bogus sentiment, no idle palaver. She was in a sense not ending the war once and for all, she was declaring the impossibility of a truce.

That evening, affecting a bravado she almost certainly could not have felt, Dietrich asked her driver to stop several blocks from the Titania and she walked the remaining distance. Outside the theater, a small crowd had gathered—mostly people her own age who had seen her more than thirty years before. One woman who depended on a cane and had no ticket simply wanted a glimpse, and she quickened her step to greet Dietrich at the stage door. Her name was Mrs. Erich Ernst, and although the two women had never met, bystanders might have thought they were old friends. "Dear Marlene," said Mrs. Ernst, "please shake my hand." And for just the flicker of a moment, as the two women joined hands and lightly caressed one another's cheeks, a photographer captured the image—one of them smartly dressed in a tweed coat and fashionable hat, the other wearing a faded kerchief and shawl, but both of them with tears glistening.

An hour later, the houselights inside dimmed, the orchestra struck a drumroll, and the filmmaker Helmut Kräutner introduced Marlene Dietrich as "a woman who has been true to herself." And then a hush descended on the audience as she entered, wearing a form-fitting dress that gave not quite the provocative illusions customary in Las Vegas. There were no catcalls, no rotten fruit, no mice, no ungracious or rude reactions. The applause began politely and then, with Mayor Willy Brandt leading the ovation, there was a more enthusiastic welcome. Except for a few rowdies outside on the street, denouncing her as a traitor and holding signs demanding her immediate removal from the country ("Marlene, hau ab!—Take off, but quick"), there was nothing to suggest hostility.

With a nod of her head, Dietrich simultaneously acknowledged the welcome and cued Bacharach. And then she began to sing—first "Ich bin von Kopf bis Fuss auf Liebe eingestellt" from *The Blue Angel*—crooning for the thousandth time that she was primed for love from head to foot. For an hour, she offered her standard numbers—"Johnny," "The Laziest Gal in Town," "The Boys in the Back Room," "One for My Baby," some in English, others in German or French—but she never told the audience that she was singing just for them; she neither flattered nor appeased them, never asked or bestowed signs of false affection. Yet with each round of applause, the audience seemed more hers—even when she reminded them that she had not forgotten the past and would not repent a single moment of her decisions, a sign she gave by singing two songs by German Jews who had fled Hitler. These she specifically dedicated to the two composers—Richard Tauber ("a wonderful human being," she said) and Friedrich Holländer, who had written the majority of her movie songs. There was only silence in the Titania when she announced these songs, but no mention of this at all in the overwhelmingly favorable reviews next day.

The theater was only three-quarters full (and half of those had been admitted on free passes), but the fifteen hundred spectators sounded like thousands. After her final number—a wistful rendition of a sentimental ballad called "I Still Have a Valise Left in Berlin" she delivered in her white tuxedo—Mayor Brandt rose to his feet, leading a thunderous eleven curtain calls.

"She won her battle from the first moment," proclaimed *Der Abend* next day. "She stood there like a queen—proud and sovereign. According to the *Bild-Zeitung,* "Marlene came, saw and conquered," to which the *Berliner Zeitung* added heroically, "She is not only a great artist, she is a lovable woman—she is one of us. Marlene Dietrich has really come home!"

Less grandly, an elderly lady leaving the theater had said to her companion, "That's the old Marlene."

Of course it had not been the old Marlene at all—neither the saucy chorine, the plump, bored repertory player, nor even the innocent destroyer of *The Blue Angel.* But there was something of the past for those who ransacked memories or longed for reconciliation. Dietrich's now deep and reedy voice, to those who wanted to hear it so, was lined and sealed with recollections of a distant time, before an ocean of rancor and resentment separated her from Berlin. No matter how much had changed there, she had indeed come home. Without any counterfeit sweetness or phony tenderness, and after a mere one hour of song, she had rediscovered her lost role as a proud Prussian commanding both the stage and her hearers—courageous, insistently autonomous and, as her introducer had said, true to herself. To postwar Berlin, ringed with a wall, with fear, suspicion and remorse, she could have offered no greater benediction.

17: 1960–1973

OVER THE COURSE OF MARLENE DIETRICH'S two weeks in Germany and one in Scandinavia that May of 1960—and despite a superb publicity campaign—her sponsors suffered a major loss because of her nightly $4,000 salary and the inability of patrons to pay high ticket prices. But she was triumphantly content after that first night, undaunted even in Düsseldorf on May 16 when a hysterical young woman rushed up to her in the lobby of the Park Hotel, spat in her face and shouted, "I hate this person who betrayed Germany in the war!"

That moment she used for a sympathy plea in subsequent interviews, but—along with the mostly half-sold auditoriums—it also contributed to her decision "never again [to appear] in Germany . . . The Germans and I no longer speak the same language." More painful was the broken collarbone she sustained when, momentarily blinded by her spotlight in Wiesbaden, Dietrich highstepped too energetically and toppled offstage. Moments later she gamely returned in her white tuxedo for the final number with her line of chorus girls, agreeing only the next day that Bacharach could take her to a clinic. For the residual pain that afflicted her during other performances that year (in Paris, Brussels, Dallas, Los Angeles, Toronto and San Francisco), Dietrich refused anything stronger than aspirin—perhaps because of Edith Piaf and Judy Garland, whose drug addictions greatly alarmed her when she saw them that year.

A pleasanter reunion occurred with Josef von Sternberg, with whom she was honored at the Locarno Film Festival in July. His white hair, moustache and courtly manner gave him the appearance of a benevolent patriarch, but von Sternberg was, as ever, restrained and diffident. Since the end of his connection to Dietrich twenty-five years earlier, they had met only two or three times and he had completed but seven feature films. From a life of genteel semiretirement in California, von Sternberg was occasionally invited to film festivals and universities, where his extraordinary achievements in cinematography were at last beginning to be appreciated.

At Locarno, *The Blue Angel* and *The Devil Is a Woman* were screened, and after a formal dinner the press besieged director and star for comments. Von Sternberg simply expressed his gratitude, and Dietrich's terse remark was appropriately enigmatic: "As an actress, I belong to an album of souvenirs, an album that will remain silent." Reporters (Americans particularly) then encouraged them to say something warmly sentimental and to embrace for the benefit of photographers, but this request only confirmed them in their natural public reserve.

Her most satisfying appearance that year was in a way even bolder than her return to Germany. In late June, Dietrich performed in Israel, where she set a new record for encores and, even more significantly, ended the taboo against the public use of German when she asked her audience's permission to sing in that language. (Earlier that month, Sir John Barbirolli had been forced to conduct the choral parts of Mahler's Second Symphony in English.) The crowd was at once won over, she sang in her native language, and in 1965 Israel awarded her the Medallion of Valor for antifascist work during the war.

"Well, darling," she told an American reporter later that year, "there is no parallel to me in show business. There is no film actress

. . . who has the stage presence I do." Nor, apparently, the frank self-esteem.

AFTER A DISAPPOINTING TWO-WEEK ATTENDANCE AT her Boston engagement in January 1961 (due at least partly to a fierce blizzard the first week), Dietrich signed a contract with producer-director Stanley Kramer to appear in his film *Judgment at Nuremberg*, essentially a courtroom drama about the trial of Nazi war criminals. As Frau Bertholt, the widow of an executed German general, she had several scenes with Spencer Tracy, cast as the presiding American judge.

Obtaining Dietrich's participation was not easy, as Kramer recalled; she had to be assured that the character and the script by Abby Mann were emotionally honest and accurate. To that end, during production in Hollywood that April she made several suggestions, incorporating her own childhood experiences and attitudes into the text ("I'm not fragile. I'm a daughter of the military. It means I was taught discipline—not to drink when I am thirsty, not to cry when I am sad . . ."). At Dietrich's insistence, Jean Louis was engaged to design even her simple black wardrobe, and a studio artist was summoned to correct a painting of the Nazi general used in the film. "He doesn't look dignified enough," she told Kramer of the image, and so with a few deft strokes Dietrich's bidding was done. "See how easy I am to please?" she asked rhetorically.

She was not always so, however. "She came on the set each morning," according to Kramer, "looked around and said, 'No, put that light there—put this reflector here—move that screen so . . .' And of course in five minutes she was lighted to the best possible advantage. It was quite uncanny." To co-star Maximilian Schell, the thirty-year-old Viennese-born actor whose eventual work as a director later intersected her life importantly, Dietrich was

a typical Berlin woman who could handle king and beggar with equal adroitness, and she was totally open about her homosexual relationships. I had the impression that Marlene did not just converse with people she met but rather wanted to provoke them. There was a spirit of confrontation in the air wherever she was.

Dietrich's presence in this serious (and sometimes grim) picture was secured, as Schell added, primarily for the drawing power of her name. As a weary, arrogant aristocrat, she played the role with a kind of Berlin Wall round her, and because her voice was by this time thin and almost in the range of an operatic bass, much of her dialogue had to be post-dubbed—which further italicized the curious detachment in her characterization. This was a quietly nervous performance, eyes shifting left and right even as she and Tracy strolled through a dark street at night, the measures of "Lili Marlene" heard nearby, to which she hums a few bars.

But perhaps most ironic of all—and what very much displeased her when she saw the finished film—was that the meticulous care she and the cinematographer had taken over her features had an odd effect. Before beginning the picture, she had submitted to another surgical face-lift, and the result—sharp angles in her cheeks and tightness around the mouth that further limited her expression— made the once supple iconography of her face almost surreally masklike. The press, however, simply noted her austere grief in May, at the Beverly Hills funeral of Gary Cooper, who died of cancer just after his sixtieth birthday.★

As Dietrich herself approached that milestone, she chose two new projects that did not depend on how she looked in close-up. She had abandoned the idea of an autobiography, but not of some kind of book, and so in the autumn of 1961 Doubleday and Company signed her to a contract for *Marlene Dietrich's ABC*—a compendium of her opinions gleaned by Dietrich and her secretary from thirty years of press clippings. Her favorite menus (lamb chops, pot-au-feu, goulash) provided the tastiest ingredients of a book over-spiced with high-toned aphorisms but otherwise pasty and insubstantial, as these complete entries indicate:

★ During the next fifteen years, Dietrich was a frequent visitor to the famous spa and rejuvenation clinic managed by Dr. Paul Niehans at Clarens, near Vevey, Switzerland, where she subscribed to a series of injections, hormone treatments and chemical regimens. "She really believed in it," recalled her secretary, Bernard Hall, "and she thought her life could go on almost forever."

"Egocentric: If he is a creative artist, forgive him."

"Gabin, Jean: A magnificent actor without knowing the tools of the trade. Rough outside—tender inside. Easy to love!"

"Germany: The tears I have cried over Germany have dried. I have washed my face."

"Nail polish: Dark nail polish is vulgar."

"Travellers: Don't detain travellers."

Somewhat more solid was her soundtrack narration in December of a film documentary on Hitler and the rise of Nazism called *The Black Fox,* for whose pictorial horror her dry, affectless and almost androgynous voice was perfect in its clinical coldness.

MARLENE DIETRICH DID NOT MARK HER SIXTIETH birthday in December 1961; she was preparing her opening at the Sahara, Las Vegas. At least in her one-woman show she had no story to act out, no part to study and assume other than the ikon she had made of herself.

By this time she had only two or three tones in her range, and with increasing frequency in the coming years Dietrich seemed to be on a kind of automatic pilot, although audiences were overwhelmed by the sheer impudence of a legend. "The showmanship is all very calculated and deliberated," ran a typical review by 1974, "even to the point of management placing flowers to be thrown from key theater spots—but the audience is more than willing to play along with their idol."

When someone suggested that her voice was now occasionally indistinguishable from a man's, Dietrich was blunt as ever: "Well, I would have liked to have been a man, a great man." Instead, she had to be content with dressing like one, which she continued to do in her act, adding more and deeper songs to the first portion and now appearing in her bejewelled gown only long enough to satisfy the crowd's need for the traditional glamour. From 1962, the gown, at her demand, fitted so tightly that she was able to take only tiny, precarious steps, and two assistants had to support her as she moved from dressing room to stage; eventually, it was almost a lethal weapon that turned against her. Nevertheless, in Paris for her show at the Olympia that spring of 1962, she had perhaps her greatest Continental success—singing, as even the benevolently critical Noël Coward noted, "with far more authority and technique" than ever before.

And so her performances continued through much of the decade —in dozens of cities round the world (among others Tokyo, Washington, Minneapolis, Johannesburg, Stockholm, Taormina, San Francisco, Cardiff, Moscow, Vancouver, Edinburgh, Warsaw, Los Angeles, Melbourne), with the dutiful Burt Bacharach as her arranger and conductor until his marriage and career advancement took him from her. Her decision to add modern songs to her repertory—numbers like "Where Have All the Flowers Gone?" and "Puff, the Magic Dragon"—did not bring vast numbers of a new generation of admirers to her show. But when she appeared onstage with the Beatles at the Prince of Wales Theatre, London, on November 4, 1963, the quartet agreed with reporters that Dietrich was indeed one of the most elegant women in town.

And so she was. Typically, she wore designer clothes everywhere, and everywhere it was noted that they fitted her to perfection even in her sixties—simply because each dress, suit and gown were made to order. A city's most expensive tailor was summoned at two in the morning if she required a new hook or seam, and Dietrich had to see the color sample and texture of any thread used even for a minor repair. It was apt, therefore, when early in 1964 Coward asked her to appear in the film *Paris When It Sizzles,* a comedy that did not, but in which Coward co-starred with Audrey Hepburn and William Holden. In her momentary, wordless cameo, Dietrich—all in white—stepped from a white limousine into the House of Dior (not far from her rented apartment at 12 Avenue Montaigne, just across from the Plaza-Athénée Hotel). Even those who may not have known what Marlene Dietrich represented could tell that here was a handsome woman who knew how to dress.

Her life was remarkably peripatetic from 1960 to 1974, but it was also (contrary to popular misperceptions about show business on the road) grindingly monotonous. She toured from city to city with her loyal and long-suffering little retinue—a hairdresser and a wardrobe mistress; her musical conductor; sometimes her manager, Major Donald Neville-Willing, formerly impresario at the Café de Paris; a companion named Ginette Vachon; and usually her secretary, Bernard Hall, who had earlier been in the dance troupe that briefly accompanied the second half of her show. Demanding to be treated like a star in each city, she was, and the results were predictable. Marlene Dietrich was greeted, hailed, lauded and applauded, she gave press conferences and met mayors, she accepted keys to cities and pronounced weightily on any topic put to her, from international politics to medicine, from child-rearing to modern art. Besieged by deliveries of flowers, champagne and requests for autographs, she never wavered in projecting the image of a legend, which was precisely what she insisted she was not. But people do not respond warmly to those who insist on remaining legends, and so there were never simple, quiet evenings with a few friends, nor old acquaintances with whom she could relax.

Marlene Dietrich was, reflected the great designer and photographer Cecil Beaton in a diary entry,

a remarkable piece of artifice . . . All the danger spots were disguised. Her dress, her figure, her limbs, all give the illusion of youth . . . Marlene has become a sort of mechanical doll. The doll can show surprise, it can walk, it can swish into place the train of its white fur coat. The audience applauds each movement, each gesture. The doll smiles incredulously . . . Marlene has a genius for believing in her self-fabricated beauty. Her success is out of all proportion and yet it is entirely due to her perseverance that she is not just an old discarded film star. She magnetizes her audience and mesmerizes them (and herself) into believing in her. The old trouper never changes her tricks because she knows they work, and because she invented them.

"I give the audience what they want," she insisted. "In my case it is beauty." But her complete dedication to maintaining the illusion of youth and eternal allure—what she had to believe people wanted—was slowly exacting the bitter price of a terrible loneliness. This she could not yet acknowledge, although it was manifested in increasing ill temper toward her staff and even her producers—though never toward her public, whose wishes she always considered.

Her concerts in Moscow, Leningrad and Riga in May 1964, for example, were carefully planned for Russians who knew little of her on film and for whom she sang mostly popular ballads and folk songs in four languages. When Soviet journalists tried to draw her into political statements—"How have you conducted your struggle against fascism? By means of your films or with your songs?"—she neatly parried, "By myself." She also knew how to win the cold war, and for this she warmed with her monologue: "I have a Russian soul," she told the audience at the Moscow Variety Theater, offering them an intimacy she had denied Berliners. "I cannot speak Russian, which is very sad. I can tell you I have always loved you, loved you for your great writers, poets and composers and the Russian soul. And so I will learn Russian and come back to you again and sing to you in Russian." Yekatarina Furtseva, the minister of culture, and Yevgeny Yevtushenko, then the angry young man of Soviet poetry, led the cheers.

To reporters she was not quite so genial, however. "You must be an American," she snapped when one admiringly asked how a grandmother was so energetic, and to another who inquired about her wardrobe and her good looks she shouted, "That's the same kind of stupid, boring old question!" She might be Venus to her adorers, but Dietrich with the press was a daughter of Mars; she bowed low onstage, but like Concha Perez in *The Devil Is a Woman,* she knew how to make slaves of her audience. (Dietrich's tartness on the Russian tour was not ameliorated by her exhaustion after she fumigated, scrubbed and waxed her Russian hotel and dressing rooms, for she was convinced that the austerity of each signalled a perilously germ-ridden condition.)

More and more, she perceived the press as enemies. "You are the dumbest people in America," she said to a platoon of journalists and critics. "I have never heard such stupid questions." This was virtually a refrain in the last decade of her tour, but like her audience, journalists were rarely put off by her rudeness. "That horrible woman from the *New York Times* came to ask me if I like long skirts or short skirts," she complained to interviewer Rex Reed. "Fashion bores me. Why don't they ask me about important things, like women's liberation?" Fine, Reed said; what did she think of women's liberation? "Nothing. It bores me." Well, then, what about the upcoming Christmas holidays? "I hate Christmas. It bores me."

There could be, at times, a nobility to her rudeness. At a Johannesburg restaurant that July of 1964, she suddenly thought of the company chauffeur, left outside alone and hungry while the press dinner was prolonged. Informed that apartheid prevented a black man from entering the place, she cursed loudly, ordered two plates of food and promptly swept out to the car, where she ate her meal with the astonished driver.

Wherever Dietrich toured, photographers without appointments were held in as much contempt as racists. After travelling to Cannes from South Africa, she was disturbed by a flashbulb from the camera of Zsa Zsa Gabor's personal photographer, who wanted a photo of the performance. Dietrich stopped her show, demanding that the camera be turned over to her and that the offender be forthwith ejected. "So he will give you the film, darling," Zsa Zsa said to Marlene. "Anyway, he couldn't sell it for a penny." On the French Riviera, riots have begun with a less pointed remark.

Even when a photographer represented her host or producer, Dietrich could be downright bellicose if unprepared. Terrified of appearing without every cosmetic artifice that she thought could disguise her age, she interrupted a London lighting rehearsal, reacting to a camera as if it were a cross held up to a vampire: "You with the camera!" she commanded, pointing to a young woman on assignment. "Out! I will not be photographed!" (An identical scene occurred in June 1973, during her appearance at the Espace Cardin in Paris.) More complicated still was her demand that twenty thousand programs for the 1965 Edinburgh Festival be withdrawn from circulation when she disapproved of the printed portrait celebrating her appearance.

By 1975, not only was specially diffused stage lighting employed to correct the appearance of age, she also refused all personal interviews and insisted that a curtained tunnel be erected to shield her from view as she passed from her hotel suite to the elevator, and, on the lower floor, to her dressing room. She may well have longed for von Sternberg's scrims, fogs and veils to recapture the illusion. "You are all morons!" she shouted at a group of reporters and photographers greeting her in London. "Why don't you go out and get a proper job?"

Eventually, she categorically refused to meet the press. According to Vivien Byerley, then in the offices of H. M. Tennant (the company that produced her London engagements), this made tasks difficult for management, sponsors and backstage employees, who were variously the object of Dietrich's wrath if any stranger or spectator somehow managed to wander within the predefined no-man's-land around her. "It is not," Byerley said years later, "a chapter in life one wants to remember."

Producer Alexander H. Cohen felt similarly. After more than a year of thorny negotiations that took him to meetings with her on three continents, Cohen finally saw Dietrich's signature on a contract that would bring her to New York, a city whose theatrical rejection she had long feared. When at last she made her Manhattan stage debut in the autumn of 1967 (just weeks before her sixty-sixth birthday), it was clear she need not have worried. The press was benevolent and New York theatergoers, amid a singularly dreary season, bought every ticket for six weeks of performances at the Lunt-Fontanne.

For Cohen, however, that period was

the least enjoyable enterprise of my entire career. On opening night [October 9] I saw her go onstage in absolute triumph, receiving the adulation of the crowd throwing flowers at her. But it was all an extraordinary con game! There was really no act at all—she stood there and managed a few notes and everyone went mad—and for this she received $40,000 a week plus a good percentage of the receipts.

The newspapers, during her New York engagements for Cohen in 1967 and again in 1968, frequently reported near riots at the theater—fans stopping traffic, admirers thronging the streets, flowers everywhere, shouts and hurrahs before and after each performance, in the lobby, at the stage door. Marlene Dietrich seemed to have stormed the city. But as Cohen confirmed years later, all this extreme adulation was under Dietrich's astute management. Just as elsewhere (even, according to Vivien Byerley, throughout England), Dietrich herself paid for the flowers to be thrown down at her from the balcony and, through intermediaries, hired claques of professionals who—inside and outside the theater—cheered until they were hoarse.

It was important for her to be part of the current theatrical scene, too. Beginning in 1968, Mart Crowley's hit play *The Boys in the Band* was a *succès de scandale* as well as a *succès d'estime*. The first American drama to treat openly and honestly of homosexuals in a repressive society, it blended high drawing room comedy with a fierce resentment of hypocrisy and a shattering, unsentimental compassion. This Dietrich found fascinating, and she insisted that Cohen escort her to a performance. Afterwards she held court with the all-male cast backstage. "She said repeatedly that she was so envious of young actors in this smash-hit play," recalled Peter White, one of the players in *Boys,* "and she insisted that we come to her show on a Monday, when we did not perform. Dietrich also took a fancy to Frederick Combs [another of the actors]."

For Combs, the attention directed at him that night and over several weeks thereafter was confusing. It seemed clear she had no sexual agenda, but she detected (rightly) that his career had involved considerable struggle. "I told her that yes, I had had hungry days," Combs recalled years later, "and this seemed to set her into a panic. She said that I must never be hungry or needy again—that the very thought of it must be banished, and if I were ever in difficult circumstances I must call her at once."

Weeks later, the entire cast of *The Boys in the Band* attended Dietrich's show. Afterwards, apologizing for a poor performance (at which at least four of her guests thought she was slightly inebriated onstage), she ushered this entire team of handsome young actors to a prominent table at Sardi's, the nearby theatrical restaurant, for a post-theater supper. Sipping tea and then a few glasses of beer, she spoke openly about her lesbian life in Berlin in the 1920s, about her love affairs with Claire Waldoff and Ginette Spanier, among others. "I became involved with women when men found me intimidating," Peter White recalled her saying. As for Frederick Combs, whom Dietrich called at least once to escort her home after her show, she quickly lost interest when she saw that his own real-life character—confident, cheerful, intelligent, optimistic—bore little resemblance to the man he played onstage.

DIETRICH'S OBSESSION WITH MANIPULATING THE EF-fect of her appearance delayed her television debut until late 1972. For a one-hour taped special, she was paid $250,000 and the astonishing, unprecedented rights (a) to be taped in the auditorium of her choice—the New London Theatre, Drury Lane, whose technically advanced acoustics and electrical configurations she approved; (b) to have Broadway's Rouben Ter-Arutunian design a flattering pink set and its scrim; and (c) to bring to the project Joe Davis, her personal lighting director, and Stan Freeman, who had replaced Burt Bacharach as musical arranger and conductor. During the rehearsal and taping of the show, Alexander Cohen (its producer) found Dietrich "at times intolerable, without doubt the most demanding star I've ever worked with." She did not endear herself, for example (as an eyewitness recalled), by asking Cohen during a rehearsal, "Do you know what you are doing? A light is a light, an angle is an angle, and I know what I am doing. I was trained by the master—by Josef von Sternberg. *I'll* pick the shots I think are best."

No one, of course, ever upstaged her in any situation. That season in London she attended a performance of the Stephen Sondheim musical *Company* and afterwards went to the dressing room of singer Marti Stevens. When Dietrich told her that a woman in the audience had said this had been one of the most wonderful evenings of her life, Stevens replied, "How sweet of you to tell me that! It's always gratifying to know when someone has enjoyed the show."

"Oh, darling, it wasn't the show that thrilled her," Dietrich continued with absolute gravity. "It was meeting me."

As Burt Bacharach was her last male lover, so was Marti Stevens

Marlene Dietrich's last close female friend. Daughter of Nicholas Schenck (head of Loews, Inc.), wealthy, intelligent and well educated, she had been close to Dietrich since the early 1960s. Under Dietrich's tutelage, Stevens developed into a mannered blond singer who—onstage in an identical coiffure and diamanté-beaded dress— looked uncannily like her friend and mentor. Dietrich and Stevens were on several occasions the guests of Noël Coward at his home in Switzerland, and they were known to be so close that artist René Bouché celebrated them in identical drawings.

DIETRICH'S MOODS DURING THE 1960S AND 1970S were certainly, according to her staff, affected by the multiple deaths of former lovers and friends—Hemingway, Cooper, von Sternberg, Remarque, Chevalier, Piaf, de Acosta. Noël Coward, too, was dismayed at the loss of people he had known well over the years, and to Dietrich he said with black humor, "All I demand from my friends nowadays is that they live through lunch"—to which, uncomprehending, she replied, "Why lunch, sweetheart?" Later, Dietrich forgot the remark she had not caught, and when an interviewer asked if she would spend a winter holiday with Coward, she replied airily, "Oh, he could be dead before I get there"—which, she thought, might be before lunch.

Dietrich's low spirits led her, at least once, to fire without reason an employee—a maid who had come daily to her Paris apartment. The dismissal seemed capricious, and the woman, hurt and angry, devised an ingenious retribution. Four days after the maid had been sent away, Dietrich had arranged a dinner for eight friends. The woman returned to the public foyer of the apartment building and, as each guest arrived, announced sadly that Madame had come down with laryngitis and influenza and was thus forced, at the last moment, to cancel her party. The invited guests went sadly home and Dietrich was left to wonder why no one came to her dinner.

COWARD AND DIETRICH MET FOR THE LAST TIME IN January 1973 when she escorted him to a performance of a musical revue in his honor; when he died that March 26, she was deeply upset. Of Judy Garland's death in 1969, on the other hand, she had simply said with a shrug, "There was someone who wanted to die, so I was glad for her."

She had to cope, too, with the loss of Bacharach, who in 1965 had left Dietrich to marry actress Angie Dickinson and to proceed elsewhere with his career (although he returned briefly for the 1967–1968 New York engagements). For Dietrich, his departure was a personal rebuff, virtually a defection from the loyal ranks. "When he became famous," she wrote,

> he could no longer accompany me on tour round the world . . . From that fateful day on, I have worked like a robot, trying to recapture the wonderful woman he helped make out of me . . . I thought of him, always longed for him, always looked for him in the wings, and always fought against self-pity . . . When he left me, I felt like giving everything up . . . I was wounded. Our separation broke my heart.

"The issue was simple, and a little sad," said Alexander Cohen. "Dietrich was in love with Bacharach. And she thought he was in love with her. The fact of Angie Dickinson didn't faze her."

18: After 1973

O<small>N</small> J<small>UNE</small> 7, 1972, M<small>ARLENE</small> D<small>IETRICH</small> <small>SUS</small>-
tained painful bruises after falling onstage during her London en-
gagement: her beaded, body-hugging gown was so tight and her
Ferragamo pumps so high-heeled that she was thrown off balance
and stumbled, sustaining painful bruises and causing the cancellation
of the show.

An even more serious accident occurred the following year, in
November 1973. After her performance at the Shady Grove Music
Fair, near Washington, she bent over from the front of the stage to
shake conductor Stan Freeman's hand in the orchestra. But he was
standing precariously on a stool to reach her and he lost his equilib-
rium, fell and dragged her down into the pit with him. Dietrich
refused to be moved until she was covered with a blanket, to conceal
the split in her dress which revealed the intricate foam rubber "living foundation" that gave her the figure of a woman one-third her
age.

Besides the severe bruising (but no fractures), there was a deep gash along her left leg. Dietrich insisted on superficial treatment only, and by the time she had visited several other cities and arrived for a show at Toronto's Royal York Hotel she was confined to a wheelchair with a serious infection. Her condition forced the cancellation of a Carnegie Hall concert scheduled for January 1974, and she was transported to Houston, where Dr. Michael De Bakey performed a skin graft at Methodist Hospital.

The slow and painful recovery required four months in bed, and no one seriously considered her return to singing onstage. But that autumn, not long before her seventy-third birthday, Marlene Dietrich astonished everyone by keeping a contracted date at the Grosvenor House hotel, London. Wheeled to the edge of her performing area, she walked slowly but then sang robustly, receiving perhaps the most tumultuous applause of her career. She was, according to Stan Freeman, "a perfectionist, although she certainly wasn't the world's greatest singer. She could be very difficult, but she could also be generous. If she thought you were ill, she'd send to Paris for the medicine she swore by, but she could be miserable if you were well."

Photographers, of course, were forbidden to approach, and because she did not want her wheelchair, her array of elaborate cosmetics, prescriptions, ointments and creams to be noted, she turned visitors away from her suite. When Princess Margaret arrived to greet her, however, Dietrich was forced to emerge. According to Bernard Hall, "her quick eye spotted the Princess gazing at a row of vitamin bottles on a table, obviously thinking they were some kind of 'stay young' pills. Furious, Marlene then headed for the table, pointed at me and exclaimed, 'They're his! Remove them, Bernard!' The Princess clearly did not believe it."

Remarkably, Dietrich summoned the stamina for several more concerts in early 1975, but that spring in San Francisco she was clearly more frail than ever, and her unsteady gait was not helped by her increasing reliance on large beakers of Johnnie Walker Black Label scotch whiskey, which she sipped throughout the afternoon and evening (and which she made no attempt to conceal even from interviewers). The boredom of which she had so plangently complained was now more painful than her weak leg.

But she insisted on working—most of all, she said, because she needed the money. She maintained the pretense of being poor, according to Bernard Hall, yet a New York safe still held a valuable cache of jewels; additionally, her income after 1960 was never less than a million dollars annually, and even after American taxes her allowable deductions left her with more than $400,000. In 1987, some of her jewelry was put up for auction at Christie's, who eventually sent her a check for $81,500.

Yet she often and loudly cried, "I need the money. Nobody believes me when I tell them I am poor." This was a far cry from the pretense of great wealth that she had insisted on for years, and the reason she gave did not much please her son-in-law, whom she implicitly represented to the press as an inadequate provider. "I have to support my daughter Maria and four grandchildren . . . The money I make will keep them going for years, [but] Maria went to Switzerland to ski with my money and left me alone."

Finally there was a last stage appearance (although not, as it happened, her last professional engagement). After shows in Melbourne and Canberra, Dietrich was concluding her Australian tour in Sydney when, on September 29, 1975, she collapsed just seconds after walking slowly onto the stage of Her Majesty's Theatre. She had drunk too much whiskey and had not eaten all day, and so it was more difficult than ever for her to walk in her tight dress. Dietrich fell awkwardly, and an examination determined that she had broken her left femur. Her shattered leg was encased in plaster and next day she was flown to the Medical Center of the University of California at Los Angeles. From Houston, Michael De Bakey returned her telephone call, recommending a New York orthopedist, and three days later she was in Columbia University–Presbyterian Hospital Medical Center, New York.

There she remained until the spring of 1976, first supine and immobilized by traction and then, after weeks in another plaster cast, subjected to protocols of physical therapy that left her exhausted and angry. For a woman of resonant independence, this was the most frustrating experience of her life, as the medical staff quickly learned. Dietrich dismissed three private nurses in as many weeks, she threw across her room platefuls of what she called "chunks of indigestible, half-frozen food," and she denounced the American (but not the foreign) Medical Center nurses for being "keen on only two things: their 'rights' and their salary." But her anger might really have been self-directed, for when she fell with such disastrous effects it was into the harsh light of day. There could be no more illusion—and hence, for one defined by illusion, no more identity. "You can't live without illusions," she had said during a London tour, "even if you must fight for them."

DIETRICH WAS FURTHER DISPIRITED BY THE NEWS OF several more deaths, among them that of Frederick Hollander, at age seventy-nine in Munich. He had written her songs for many films, from *The Blue Angel* to *A Foreign Affair*—melodies sassy and pungent that he fitted to her personality. From "Falling in Love Again" to "Illusions," Hollander's tunes became identified with Dietrich's voice and presence, and composers for her other films invariably turned to those recordings for inspiration.

This death was followed, on June 24, by that of Rudi, who was also seventy-nine. He had suffered a fatal heart attack and was found by his housekeeper sitting upright in a rocking chair in his San Fernando cottage. For several years, he had lived alone, for Tamara —who had finally endured irreversible mental breakdown—had to spend the last years of her life in an institution, care which Dietrich underwrote. Hectored for years by the press, Rudolf Sieber had resolutely negated every request for interviews and had kept a dignified silence about his marriage to Marlene Dietrich. She had occasionally visited him, and there was no doubt of their loyalty, manifest in his financial advice and her ongoing support. According to their old friend Stefan Lorant, who had known them both for over half a century, the Sieber marriage—always more accurately defined as a friendship—was preserved by its very nonconformity to any standard. Marriage was a legal and social status they saw no reason to forgo. "Poor Rudi," Marlene Dietrich Sieber said a few years after his death. "He was such a sensitive, sensitive man. I don't know how he could have put up with it, living his whole life in the shadow of a famous woman."

Her confinement throughout 1976 reinforced Dietrich's tendency toward seclusion; thenceforth, she declined all requests for visits from friends (much less photographers or interviewers) either in hospitals or at her Paris apartment, to which she finally returned, with Maria's help, late in 1976. She had devoted her entire life to the manufacture and presentation of a carefully calculated artifact, and when it was no longer presentable she seemed to feel there was nothing for anyone to see—that in a way Marlene Dietrich no longer existed.

Apparently at Maria's suggestion, Dietrich decided to make her solitude creative by writing her memoirs. This turned out to be a more intriguing possibility than a satisfying reality, and the publishing history of Marlene Dietrich's autobiographies was finally somewhat byzantine.

A book was indeed contracted in 1976, and it appeared in Germany three years later, published by Bertelsmann as *Nehmt nur mein Leben—Reflexionen (Just Take My Life—Reflections;* the words are taken from Goethe). Condensed, these random, shallow anecdotes formed the basis of Dietrich's own English manuscript, submitted to and summarily rejected by her British publisher, Collins, to whom she was forced to return the advance. In this book, Dietrich offered nothing like a life story, gave not a single date, ignored the basic facts of her background and family and provided little more than a few vague comments on people she had known. Any journalist could have revealed more.

Undaunted, Dietrich's agents then marketed the rejected English manuscript in France, where it was translated and published in 1984 by Grasset as *Marlène D.* Three years later, Ullstein published an abbreviated German rendering of this as *Ich bin, Gott sei Dank, Berlinerin (Thank God I'm from Berlin).* The first publication of any of this in English was a translation of *Ich bin,* issued by Grove Press in 1989 as *Marlene.*

In each version, Dietrich warned her editors and readers that "facts are unimportant," a prudent caution since she provided so few. There was no mention of a sister; she conveniently combined father and stepfather; Rudi was hardly mentioned, and Maria was only a vague parenthesis across a page or two. More alarming were her frank errors: actors, writers and producers are assigned the wrong credits, and some of her most important colleagues (Paramount's designer Travis Banton, for example) are misidentified. The dates of several of her films are given incorrectly (by as much as a decade), and she has a remarkably vague idea of the characters she played and the stories in which they figured. The pages are further diminished by an abrasive, defensive petulance; the book was not even, alas, an engaging novelette.

There were also unintentionally hilarious gaffes. Writing approvingly of the Jewish tradition of grieving at funerals, Dietrich added that "in the Christian world we are taught to hide our feelings"—an assertion doubtless shocking to Italian, Greek and Iberian cultures, among others. She also claims that acting is not, after all, the right profession for men, "but only for those with talent." Regarding her private life there was not a single disclosure.

FROM 1976 TO HER DEATH IN MAY 1992—EXCEPT for her two half-days of work on *Just a Gigolo* and one month when she allowed a colleague to record an interview—Dietrich resided in a twilight of isolation, a woman vaguely connected to the world by newspapers, books and telephone but insistently reclusive, inaccessible to all but an employee or two, receiving no visitors except (on infrequent occasions) her daughter Maria. In a way she became a character in a von Sternberg picture—veiled and remote, victimized by the legacy of the fame for which she always expressed undiluted contempt, but on which she counted for her very existence.

Only once since *Just a Gigolo* did she mitigate that severe disengagement, and then only partially. Dietrich and actor-director Maximilian Schell (who had also appeared in *Judgment at Nuremberg*) came to an agreement about a documentary on her life and career. There was, however, a difficult proviso, for just before filming was to begin in her apartment she refused to be photographed; only her voice would be heard. From this appalling requirement, Schell somehow fashioned a work of considerable virtues, intercutting documentary footage, film clips, still photographs and a series of hallucinatory images reminiscent of a Fellini dreamscape. The result, called simply *Marlene,* was rightly praised. Connecting the visuals of this film are the voices of director and star (speaking now in German, now in English), as he coaxed, cajoled, grew impatient with her scolding—and finally evoked more of the real Marlene Dietrich than any cameraman had ever dared attempt.

There are, of course, the usual snappy Dietrich retorts and outrageous contradictions peppering the occasional honest assessment:

—Of her old films, she says: "I'm not at all interested. Do you think I'd go and sit in some stuffy cinema and watch movies?"
—Of Emil Jannings in *The Blue Angel:* "What a ham!"
—Of Josef von Sternberg: "He was always forcing me to think, to use my brain and learn something when I was working—not merely to do what I was told."
—Of women: "In universities they've weighed women's brains— they weigh half as much as men's, you know."
—Of feeling in poetry, sentiment in films, nostalgia in real life: "Quatsch!"—"Nonsense! Rubbish!"
—Of herself: "I'm no romantic dreamer. I have no time for that. I'm a logical, practical person who has worked all her life."
—Of God and the afterlife: "I don't believe in a superior power. Once you're dead, that's it—it's all over!"

She did, however, agree to watch with Schell some excerpts from a few of her films on videocassette, and to discuss certain interesting moments. Despite her stated insistence that she found herself and her career monumentally boring, it was clear from her sudden animation that she found only these moments really interesting. But seeing her younger self was evidently painful, for as she continued to comment there was a rueful but futile attempt to disconnect herself from her own memories. Her agent had handed Schell a slip of paper with a citation from Dante, a clue to Dietrich's vulnerability during the tapings:

Nessun maggior dolore
Che ricordarsi del tempo felice
Nella miseria.

There is no greater pain
Than the recollection of past happiness
In times of misery.

According to the conventional wisdom, people do not change very much, especially in senior years; like figures in stories, it is believed, men and women usually become fixed in their own characters.

But something indeed shifted in Marlene Dietrich during the last years of her life—something that was perhaps due to the simple transforming effect of time and solitude. A woman who never showed the slightest inclination to share her feelings, who gloried in her Teutonic training to conceal emotions, was at last led to a kind of epiphany.

Surrounded by a tangle of wires and a crew of technicians, she listened while Schell began to read the old lines from Ferdinand Freiligrath. Then her memory recaptured a few words, and, on the soundtrack of the film *Marlene,* the voices of Maximilian Schell and Marlene Dietrich meet, part, blend again:

O love, as long as you can love,
O love, as long as you may love.
The hour comes when you will stand at gravesides weeping.
Whoever opens you their heart, do all you can to please them.
Fill all their lives with joy and never cause them sadness—
And guard your tongue! Harsh words are easily said—
O God, I meant no harm!
The other leaves and complains.
You kneel down at the graveside and say,
"O look down upon me, crying here on your grave,
Forgive me for hurting you—oh God, I meant no harm."
But he neither hears nor sees you,
he shuns the welcome of your arms—

the mouth which often kissed you says no more
"I've long since forgiven you."
In truth, he has forgiven you,
though many a tear was shed for you and your harsh words.
But still, he rests—he's reached his end.

There is a moment of silence, and then Marlene Dietrich begins to weep, softly, uncontrollably. "I'm afraid I can't say that—I just can't," she whispers, unable to hold back after so many years.

The film's final image holds just a few seconds—it is her last screen appearance, as the frail baroness in *Just a Gigolo*—and then this picture, too, slowly fades.

"It makes me cry," Marlene Dietrich says as we see the blurred image gradually vanish. And then there is only her voice, veiled with memory:

"Maybe it's just a kitschy poem. But I don't know. My mother —my mother really loved it. It's something so many people say—'I meant no harm.' Maybe nowadays it's too sentimental. Maybe."

OTHERWISE, VERY LITTLE HAPPENED OUTWARDLY IN Marlene Dietrich's life in the final years. She had in a way become like one of her favorite poets, Heinrich Heine, living in voluntary Parisian self-exile, an inactive recluse claiming the pedestal to which she believed her fame entitled her. Her career had for years kept her away from her daughter and grandchildren and all during her life she had never made the kind of time necessary for establishing authentic friendships. Her distance from others, her pursuit of affirmation, her longing to be a buddy to as many men and women as possible—all these exacted a fearful cost. A lifetime of emotional isolation, long before her final physical seclusion, had in fact necessitated and sustained precisely the illusions she lived by, the fantastic chimeras she constantly denied. "All her life she was wearing a mask," said Maximilian Schell. "The real Marlene has never been visible. Her mind is filled with the creation of a legend as she conceives it."

Agreeing with Coward's assessment that she was confined within her own legend, Bernard Hall (eventually her live-in majordomo as well as secretary) said that she "made herself a prisoner in her own home, striding around like a caged tigress, because she had a fear that someone would photograph her in her twilight years—like they did her old rival Greta Garbo in the streets of Manhattan. So she rarely went out."

In her retreat from society, one day became very like the next, and few were happy. Awake before six in the morning, she cried out to Hall for some food and by eight o'clock she began drinking scotch. According to Hall, "I didn't know what to do. I gave [the whiskey] to her—it was impossible saying no. Anyway, she had two bottles under the bed. She was brilliant until ten A.M., then zonk, she'd collapse. It was sad to watch, heartbreaking." In fact Dietrich was in her last years a restless, pathetic alcoholic. "It's difficult to say when she became so," Hall added. "But even when we were on tour together, I'd think, 'How much can a person drink?'"

At last—about the spring of 1979—weak, weary and angry, Marlene Dietrich simply announced, "I'm going to bed." Hall had attended her for over thirty years, but finally her condition so saddened him that, as he later admitted, he "simply couldn't cope with caring for her full-time any more. She was totally impossible to live with." In 1987, he moved to London, and Dietrich was cared for by a series of secretaries, daytime companions and, occasionally, visiting nurses.

Her cluttered, modest apartment was filled with mementos, glorious photographs of Dietrich in the films she loved the most—primarily *The Devil Is a Woman* ("because I was never more beautiful")—and pictures of her with her great and adoring mentor von Sternberg, with her comrade Ernest Hemingway, with the handsome young Gary Cooper, the confidently charming Maurice Chevalier, the jealous peasant Jean Gabin. "I'm never lonely," she insisted to Maximilian Schell at the start of their interviews in 1983. Bernard Hall, as well as friends like Stefan Lorant and Billy Wilder, disagreed.

Her reclusiveness, said Douglas Fairbanks, Jr., "was very strange and unfortunate. For years she rang up to chat with me and my wife, and then this stopped. Once I visited Paris and telephoned. I recognized her voice and greeted her, but she denied it was she and pretended to be the maid." Jean-Pierre Aumont, among many others, had a similar telephone experience of Dietrich's denial of self.

"We were in Paris in 1987," recalled Billy Wilder, "and after pretending to be her own masseuse or a cook, she admitted it was herself. At first Marlene had agreed to see my wife and me. We offered to take her out to dinner, or to bring food to her apartment —anything that would please her. But then she changed her mind, saying that she had to go to an eye doctor. It was obvious she just didn't want to see anyone. Or anyone to see her."

When Dietrich did wish to communicate, however, her telephone bills must have been among the highest in Europe, for a two-hour conversation with an old acquaintance in London, New York or Los Angeles was quite typical. Among the regular recipient of such calls was Stefan Lorant, a friend for seventy years.

But the name Marlene Dietrich was still worthy of page one of the *New York Times:* on the occasion of Germany's celebration of reunification in 1990, a headline proclaimed, "United Germany's Joy, and Marlene Dietrich Too." The accompanying story announced:

> The day also brought a legendary voice from the past. Marlene Dietrich, the screen star, welcomed the unification of the homeland she has not visited in thirty years in a rare public statement: "Of course I'm happy. Anything that brings people together and encourages peace always makes me happy. Happiness is so rare in this troubled world."

And despite her disclaimer of sentiment, she told German television on January 14, 1991, that the old UFA film studios in Babelsberg, south of Berlin, ought not to be demolished for merely economic reasons. "I'm still nostalgic for Babelsberg," she said, "and I only hope you find the success you rightly expect. Goodbye—I'll cross my fingers for you!"

Occasionally, she wrote to the author of a book that delighted her: "Thanks a million for writing *Hit Me With a Rainbow,*" she typed in a note to the American novelist James Kirkwood, whom she had never met. "If you could send me [the book's character]

Stash, it would make me happy. I really cried laughing—a rare event in this lousy world. Love and kisses, Marlene Dietrich."

Kirkwood replied, sending his other works and threatening to "set the witches to work on you" if an autographed picture were not forthcoming from her. The photo arrived, on which Dietrich had written, "Don't set the witches to work—it is bad enough as it is. Please send books and write again. Am lonely. Love, Marlene."

SHE HAD IN FACT BEEN LONELY FOR YEARS—EVEN when she was on tour, as Bernard Hall confirmed. Thus her final return to work on a film, *Just a Gigolo* in February 1978, had been singularly important for her.

Dietrich had prepared meticulously for this appearance. Not long before, *Vogue Paris* had featured a photoessay in which models were made up to resemble the great stars of earlier decades. She was impressed with the facsimile of herself—especially with the makeup devised by a wizard of the craft named Anthony Clavet. At Dietrich's request, he met her at the studio and opened his makeup kit, attempting the transformation of an exhausted old lady into an elegant, timeless beauty. When he put the final touches to her lips, Dietrich suddenly reached out and clasped Clavet's wrist.

"You have done it," she whispered fiercely. "You must understand—I cannot see well enough any longer—I cannot see to do Marlene." He was then astonished when she added, with utter gravity, "If—if I ever go on tour again—to do my show—will you please do the makeup for me?"

Marlene Dietrich drew closer to the reflection in the mirror, straining to see, as if by sheer effort she could find again the lost lineaments, the classic features adored by von Sternberg, improved by light, rouge, line and shadow—the enigmatic stare, the ambiguous smile idolized by millions but never duplicated ever, by anyone. Clavet saw only a painted old woman he had painstakingly made over for a color film. But then he saw that Dietrich continued to sit quietly at her dressing table, as if she beheld someone else returning her gaze: the serious young violin student she had been years before, perhaps. Or the prancing Thielscher Girl. Or the saucy Lola Lola

. . . Amy Jolly or Shanghai Lily . . . Frenchy the barmaid . . . or Major Marlene Dietrich, mistress of generals in wartime and comforter of soldiers languishing in army hospitals . . . lover to dozens, perhaps scores of those she met and liked. Perhaps she saw her most artful creation, the dauntless performer of her worldwide show, proclaiming that she was not only Eternal Woman but a kind of theatrical phoenix, ever rising from the cinders of one life to triumph in another.

Unheedful of the damp chill in the studio, she remained a long while at her dressing table. Motionless, silent, statuesque, she simply sat gazing into the mirror. And so in perhaps the truest sense she was at home, content at last with the half-glimpsed memories and dreams—with the illusions of Marlene created and recreated for decades by Maria Magdalene. She smiled.

Notes

For brevity, details of interviews conducted for this book are supplied only at the first citation; unless otherwise stated, subsequent quotations from the same source derive from the interview with that source.

Chapter One
1-her jaw set: Hughes Pierce, "Aged 77—and she still looks stunning," *The Sunday Times,* March 7, 1978.
2-I will sing: Quoted in *Newsweek,* Aug. 7, 1978.

Chapter Two
4-He who writes: Suzanne Everett, *Lost Berlin* (New York: Gallery Books, 1979), p. 18.
9-Sie selbst glich: Marlene Dietrich, *Ich bin, Gott sei Dank, Berlinerin* (Berlin: Ullstein, 1987), p. 31. (For an account of Dietrich's publish-

ing history, see my comments on page 294.) (New York: Grove, 1989), a translation by Salvator Attanasio of *Ich bin.*

9-Tu etwas: *Ibid.,* p. 58.

9-My whole upbringing: Leslie Frewin, *Dietrich* (New York: Stein and Day, 1967), pp. 15–16.

13-We lived in: Marlene Dietrich, *Marlene* (New York: Grove, 1989), p. 22.

14-Every face looks: Everett, p. 24.

15-did not seem: *Marlene,* p. 22.

16-No. You can't: MD to Maximilian Schell, in his film *Marlene* (1983).

16-She didn't want: *Marlene,* pp. 14–15.

CHAPTER THREE

20-a wonderful affair: Quoted in Werner Frisch and K. W. Obermeyer, *Brecht in Augsburg* (Frankfurt, 1976), translated in Ronald Hayman, *Brecht* (New York: Oxford University Press, 1983), p. 53.

23-a completely negative: Nora Hodges (trans.), *George Grosz: An Autobiography* (New York: Imago/Macmillan, 1983), p. 149.

26-She was anything: Geza von Cziffra (trans. Jon Zimmermann), in Renate Seydel, *Marlene Dietrich: Eine Chronik ihres Lebens in Bildern und Dokumenten* (Munich: Nymphenburger, 1984), p. 82.

26-a very strange: Lotte Andor to DS, May 25, 1990.

27-And if they: William Dieterle, in Seydel, p. 82.

28-Wie dann dein: Hugo von Hofmannsthal, *Death and the Fool* (Boston: Richard G. Badger, 1914); trans. Elisabeth Walter.

29-One day, Held: Unpublished memoirs of Grete Mosheim, published here with the kind permission of Mosheim's family.

30-She tried: Stefan Lorant to DS, May 16, 1991.

32-This is too: Quoted in Mosheim memoirs.

34-One had the: William Dieterle, in Seydel, p. 82.

CHAPTER FOUR

37-The role should: *Berliner Tageblatt,* Feb. 22, 1926.

38-wearing neither: Elisabeth Lennartz in Seydel, p. 82.

38-It was chic: Bill Davidson, "The Dietrich Legend," *McCall's,* March 1960, p. 170.

38-Only one woman: Käte Haack, *ibid.*

39-Take some pictures: *New York Times,* Sept. 5, 1976.

42-constantly pursued: Mia May, *ibid.*

43-Oh, don't worry: Quoted by Stefan Lorant to DS, May 16, 1991.

44-She showed only: Karl Hartl in Seydel, p. 83 (trans. Jon Zimmermann).

45-I haven't a: Quoted in Sheridan Morley, *Marlene Dietrich* (New York: McGraw-Hill, 1976).

45-Among the girls: *Neve Freie Presse,* Nov. 30, 1927.

47-Marlene Dietrich sings: Herbert Jhering, in the *Berliner Bösen-Courier,* May 16, 1928.

48-When Dietrich mimes: Unsigned review in *Film-Kurier,* Sept. 6, 1928 (trans. Jon Zimmermann).

49-She simply sat: Lili Darvas, in Seydel, p. 85 (trans. Henriette Fremont).

49-Marlene waged intrigues: Mary Kiersch (interviewer), *Curtis Bernhardt* (Metuchen, N.J.: Scarecrow Press, 1986), p. 38.

50-rare Garboesque: *New York Times,* Sept. 9, 1929, p. 30.

51-plump but agile: Erich Urban, in *Börsen-Zeitung,* Sept. 6, 1929.

51–52-with a cold: Josef von Sternberg, *Fun in a Chinese Laundry* (New York: Macmillan, 1965), p. 231.

CHAPTER FIVE

53-I feel as: *Film-Kurier,* Aug. 17, 1929.

54-without my knowledge: Von Sternberg, p. 154.

56-bovine listlessness: *Ibid.,* p. 233.

56-She came to life: *Ibid.,* p. 237.

57-von Sternberg had: *Marlene,* p. 51.

57-Even while rehearsals: Willi Frischauer, "The Marlene Dietrich Story," Reynolds News Service (London), June 13, 1954.

58-Her behavior: Von Sternberg, p. 239.

58-I didn't know: Quoted in Peter Bogdanovich, "Hollywood," *Esquire,* January 1972, p. 56.

59-He pulled out: Quoted in Frank Westmore and Muriel Davidson, *The Westmores of Hollywood* (Philadelphia: Lippincott, 1976), pp. 69–70.

59-I did not: Von Sternberg, p. 227.

60-I am Miss Dietrich: Often quoted by von Sternberg; see, e.g., "Le Montreur d'Ombres," *Cahiers du Cinéma,* no. 168 (July 1965), p. 21: "Marlène, c'est moi, et elle le sait mieux que personne."

63-Regardless: Von Sternberg, p. 242.

63-simply wasn't ambitious: E.g., *Marlene,* p. 58.

64-She had pinned: Ruth Landshoff-Yorck, "Sensual Indolence Only Part of Marlene Dietrich's Allure," *Los Angeles Herald-Examiner,* Dec. 29, 1977.

65-In Europe it: Budd Schulberg, *Moving Pictures: Memories of a Hollywood Prince* (New York: Stein and Day, 1981), p. 278.

CHAPTER SIX

68–69-von Sternberg controlled: John Kobal, *People Will Talk* (New York: Knopf, 1985), p. 529.

71-They didn't like: Bogdanovich, *art. cit.,* p. 56.

71-Jo was jealous: Kobal, pp. 298–99.

74-I planned to: Von Sternberg, p. 247.

74-Woman is no: F. A. Macklin, "Interview with Josef von Sternberg," *Film Heritage,* vol. 1, no. 2 (Winter 1965–66), pp. 5–6.

75-I would much: E.g., Paramount press release dated May 18, 1937, and, much later, the (London) *Evening News,* May 31, 1949.

77-The light source: *Marlène D.,* pp. 68–69 (trans. DS); the published English version is not quite accurate in this case.

78-Turn your shoulders: Von Sternberg, p. 253.

79-I made seven: Herman Weinberg, *Josef von Sternberg* (New York: Dutton, 1967), pp. 126, 83; see also "Le Montreur d'Ombres, déclarations de Josef von Sternberg," *Cahiers du Cinéma,* no. 168 (July 1965), p. 19.

CHAPTER SEVEN

85-to be Mr. Dietrich: *New York Times,* May 6, 1931.

85-Mr. von Sternberg: Quoted in the *Los Angeles Herald,* Sept. 28, 1931.

86-Mr. von Sternberg: Bogdanovich, *art. cit.*

86-living in sin: Diane Johnson, *Dashiell Hammett: A Life* (New York: Random House, 1983), p. 100.

87-to photograph me: *Marlene,* p. 97.

87-Cooper was very: Bogdanovich, *art. cit.*

88-Marlene worshipped: Nicholas von Sternberg to DS, May 16, 1989.

88-I had nothing: From a Paramount Studios press release dated Oct. 27, 1933, issued under MD's name.

88-I never think: *Motion Picture Classic,* January 1932.

88-She attached no: Von Sternberg, p. 225.

89–90-People have said: Ruth Biery, "Is Dietrich Through?" *Photoplay,* Jan. 1933, p. 110.

90-I felt: *New York Mirror,* June 18, 1961, p. 2; see also Selma Robinson, "I couldn't compete with my Mother," *Ladies Home Journal,* October 1951, p. 56.

90-I remember: John Calendo, "Dietrich and the Devil," *Interview,* November 1972.

91-I am here: "Charges Bared in Mrs. von Sternberg's Suits on Film Star," *Los Angeles Herald,* Aug. 8, 1931.

93-Clive Brook wanted: Lee Garmes to DS, Aug. 20, 1977.

94-genuine and tremendous: *Vanity Fair,* December 1931, p. 41.

94-careful elimination: Quoted in Homer Dickens, *The Films of Marlene Dietrich* (Secaucus, N.J.: Citadel, 1968), p. 103.

95-I have enjoyed: Whitney Williams, "Marlene Dietrich Hints at Quitting Hollywood," *Los Angeles Herald,* Feb. 7, 1932.

99-a joy to: Sam Coslow, *Cocktails for Two* (New Rochelle: Arlington House, 1977), p. 127.

99-obviously on close: Dick Moore, *Twinkle, Twinkle, Little Star* (New York: Harper and Row, 1984), p. 138.

99–100-I do not: Eileen Creelman, "Picture Plays and Players," *New York Sun,* Sept. 28, 1933. See also Biery, *art. cit.,* p. 29.

100-It is behind: Creelman, *art. cit.*

101-All right, George: Whitney Stine, *The Hurrell Style: 50 Years of Photographing Hollywood* (New York: John Day, 1976), p. 109.

CHAPTER EIGHT

104-Like every German: *Los Angeles Times,* Jan. 26, 1933.

105-a little blackbird: Jean Howard to DS, July 15, 1990.

105-seemed such: Mercedes de Acosta, *Here Lies the Heart* (New York: Reynal, 1960), pp. 72, 74, 103.

106-put records on: *Ibid.,* p. 215.

106-I was moving: *Ibid.,* p. 271.

106-sometimes twice: *Ibid.,* p. 243.

106-You are the: *Ibid.,* pp. 242ff.

108-This created: Davidson, *art. cit.,* pp. 166–67.

108-I had the: Bogdanovich, *art. cit.,* p. 57.

110-I am very: *New York World-Telegram,* July 29, 1933.

111-everything bad: Anthony Heilbut, *Exiled in Paradise* (New York: Viking, 1983), p. 34.

111-We poor Germans: *Ibid.,* p. 321.

114-They say von Sternberg: Jack Grant, "Marlene Dietrich Answers Her Critics," a 1934 interview: reprinted in Martin Levin, ed., *Hollywood and the Great Fan Magazines* (New York: Arbor House, 1970), p. 178.

114-If you want: Quoted by Joel McCrea in Kobal, p. 301.

115-He was killing: Leatrice Gilbert Fountain, *Dark Star* (New York: St. Martin's Press, 1985), p. 247.

115-loveliest dreams: Scott Donaldson, *By Force of Will* (New York: Viking, 1977), p. 189.

116-I never ask: A. E. Hotchner, *Papa Hemingway* (New York: William Morrow, 1983), p. 25.

116-run by the stars: Donaldson, p. 232.

116-She is a complete: *Los Angeles Examiner,* Oct. 12, 1934.

119-Von Sternberg made: Cesar Romero to DS, Oct. 2, 1988.

120-an insult to: *Daily Telegraph* (London), Oct. 30, 1935.

120-I am no longer: Edwin Schallert, "Dietrich Discloses Why She Left von Sternberg," *Los Angeles Times,* March 3, 1935.

120-He dreaded the day: *Marlène D.,* pp. 85, 93–94.

121-My salary is: *Evening Standard* (London), Jan. 4, 1936.

CHAPTER NINE

124-fragrant and cool: Basil Rathbone, *In and Out of Character* (New York: Doubleday, 1962), p. 147.

125-Permitted to walk: Frank S. Nugent, *New York Times,* April 13, 1936, p. 15.

125-She was a: Edith Head and Paddy Calistro, *Edith Head's Hollywood* (New York: Dutton, 1983), p. 29.

126-Falling into: Engstead, p. 76.

127-I adored: Fountain, p. 257.

129-I told her: Rudy Behlmer, ed., *Memo from David O. Selznick* (New York: Viking, 1972), pp. 100–101.

130-It's twash: Joshua Logan, *Josh: My Up and Down, In and Out Life* (New York: Delacorte, 1976), pp. 87–104.

131-It isn't that: *Brooklyn Daily Eagle,* Feb. 23, 1936.

132-she only makes: Jacques Feyder and Françoise Rosay, *Le Cinéma—notre métier* (Geneva: Pierre Cailler, 1946), pp. 56–58. For Harry Stradling's recollections, see Richard Whitehall, "The Blue Angel," *Films and Filming,* Oct. 1962, p. 20.

133-slipped and sprawled: *Time,* vol. 28, no. 22 (Nov. 30, 1936), p. 41.

133-You can have: Willi Frischauer, *European Commuter* (New York: Macmillan, 1964), p. 113.

135-really like brother: Douglas Fairbanks, Jr., to DS, March 29, 1990.

135-only her passing: Douglas Fairbanks, Jr., *The Salad Days* (New York: Doubleday, 1988), p. 260.

136-rarely seemed: *Ibid.,* pp. 30–31.

at the root: Frank Nugent, *New York Times,* Nov. 4, 1937, p. 29.

140-Marlene Dietrich: *Der Stürmer,* Oct. 6, 1937 (trans. in *New York Times,* Oct. 7, 1937, from Reuters).

141-really a rather: Douglas Fairbanks, Jr., to DS, March 29, 1990.

CHAPTER TEN

145-motions of secrecy: Fairbanks, pp. 273, 275.

146-I am glad: *Los Angeles Examiner,* June 10, 1939.

148-His melancholy: Dietrich, p. 152.

149-Nobody knows: Davidson, *art. cit.,* p. 168.

156-sailor's daughter: *Ibid.,* p. 175. Remarque wrote as he felt.

156–57-an exciting and forlorn: Erich Maria Remarque (trans. Walter Sorell and Denver Lindley), *Arch of Triumph* (London: Hutchinson Library Services, 1946), pp. 92, 101, 103, 120.

157-Joan, he said: *Ibid.,* pp. 145, 203.

one of the first: Dietrich, p. 153.

158-The greatest compliment: In Ed Sullivan's syndicated column

"Hollywood" (e.g., *Los Angeles Herald, New York Daily News*), Jan. 17, 1940.

159-I had no friends: Selma Robinson, "I couldn't compete with my Mother," *Ladies Home Journal*, October 1951, p. 56.

159-I was always: *Ibid.*

160-Maria is as: Duncan Underhill, "Marlene Dietrich in Pants for *Seven Sinners* Role," *New York World-Telegram*, July 6, 1940.

161-With that wonderful: Tay Garnett with Fredda Dudley Balling, *Light Your Torches and Pull Up Your Tights* (New Rochelle: Arlington House, 1973), p. 245.

161-It's very early: Pilar Wayne, with Alex Thorleifson, *John Wayne—My Life with the Duke* (New York: McGraw-Hill, 1987), p. 39.

161-one that wouldn't: *Ibid.*, p. 40.

162-Unpleasant people: Dietrich, pp. 183–84.

163-giving one of the: *Hollywood Reporter*, Oct. 24, 1940.

CHAPTER ELEVEN

165-One American critic: Charles Thomas Samuels, *Encountering Directors* (New York: Putnam, 1972), pp. 79–80.

166-a flop: *Marlene*, p. 184.

166-he wasn't exactly: *Ibid.*, p. 132.

166-an awfully stupid: *Ibid.*, p. 184.

167-like an orphan: *Ibid.*, p. 135.

168-He called her: Jean Renoir, *My Life and My Films* (New York: Atheneum, 1974), p. 226.

169-Oh, hello: Fred Lawrence Guiles, *Tyrone Power: The Last Idol* (New York: Doubleday, 1979), p. 144.

169-Gabin glanced: *Ibid.*, pp. 144–45.

169-The mothering: Quoted to Dean Goodman by Maria Sieber in 1943; Dean Goodman to DS, May 27, 1989.

169-She is mother: Edward G. Robinson, with Leonard Spiegelgass, *All My Yesterdays* (New York: Hawthorn, 1973), p. 219.

169–70-almost overnight: *New York Journal-American*, June 21, 1941.

170-so subtly: Robinson, *ibid.*

171-Oh, Georgie: *New York Post*, May 27, 1941.

171-Watch Mama: *Life*, Aug. 18, 1952, p. 90.

172-She couldn't understand: David Chierichetti, *Hollywood Director* (New York: Curtis, 1973), p. 177.

176-I'm not thinking: Associated Press wire release, March 9, 1942.

176-not only contributed: Bette Davis, *The Lonely Life* (New York: Putnam, 1962), p. 261.

177-but she also: Cheryl Crawford to DS, Aug. 18, 1983; see also her book *One Naked Individual* (Indianapolis: Bobbs-Merrill, 1977), pp. 117–24.

180-I cannot play: Crawford, p. 124.

181-Maria was the: Dean Goodman to DS, May 27, 1989.

183-Do you have: Juliet Benita Colman, *Ronald Colman* (New York: Morrow, 1975), p. 214.

184-I don't want: Selma Robinson, *art. cit.*

CHAPTER TWELVE

187-He taught me: John Fisher, *Call Them Irreplaceable* (New York: Stein and Day, 1974), p. 143.

190-Wherever I went: Arthur Pollock, "Theater Time," syndicated column (e.g., *New York Journal-American),* June 1, 1944.

190-attached themselves: Danny Thomas, with Bill Davidson, *Make Room for Danny* (New York: Putnam, 1991), p. 138.

190-I was more afraid: *Marlene,* p. 206.

190-It was my first: "Marlene Sees Night Air Fight," United Press International wire dispatch dated Algiers, April 12, 1944.

191-I went in: Thomas, p. 139.

193-Being made prisoner: Jean-Pierre Aumont, *Le Soleil et les Ombres* (Paris: Laffont, 1976), p. 125; trans. DS. See also Aumont's *Souvenirs Provisoires* (Paris: René Julliard, 1957), p. 229.

194-If they don't: Louis Berg, "Dietrich Rides Again," *This Week,* Aug. 13, 1944, p. 10.

194-Anyone who has: *New York Post,* July 2, 1944.

194-It gave me: Willi Frischauer, "The Marlene Dietrich Story," *Reynolds News* (London), June 13, 1954; see also "Dietrich, the body and the soul," *Collier's,* May 14, 1954, p. 27.

194-The Germany I knew: Mel Heimer, "Dietrich 'Home' Again," *New York Journal-American,* Aug. 26, 1944, p. 2.

195-Only the door: Col. Barney Oldfield, USAF (Ret.) to DS, May 29, 1989.

196-Dietrich was a: *Ibid.*

197–98-the Paris command: Baker, p. 444.

198-But Marlene: Renoir, p. 226.

199-but I would: *Marlene,* p. 201.

199-But, darling: Billy Wilder to DS, Nov. 19, 1991.

201-I am through: Frank Conniff, "Marlene Dietrich Quits as Film Actress," syndicated for International News Service (e.g., New York *Journal-American),* Feb. 2, 1945.

203-Patton seemed to: James M. Gavin, *On to Berlin* (New York: Viking, 1978), p. 244.

CHAPTER THIRTEEN

206-Her feet: Barbara Leaming, *Orson Welles* (New York: Viking, 1985), p. 309.

206-She is the: Sidney Skolsky, "Tintypes," *Hollywood Citizen-News,* Aug. 30, 1945.

207-Marlene had stipulated: Marcel Carné, *La Vie à belles dents* (Paris: Jean-Vuarnet, 1979), p. 257 (trans. DS).

208-looked lovely but: Graham Payn and Sheridan Morley, eds., *The Noël Coward Diaries* (Boston: Little, Brown, 1982), p. 54.

208-Are you alone: Max Colpet, *Sag mir, wo die Jahre sind* (Munich: Georg Müller, 1981), p. 196.

209-Because he wanted: Arthur M. Schlesinger, Jr., *Robert Kennedy and His Times* (Boston: Houghton Mifflin, 1978), p. 590.

209-When I devote: Biery, *art. cit.*

210-I could compete: Davidson, *art. cit.*

212-living quietly at: Quoted in Elizabeth Wilson, "You Won't Know Marlene," *Liberty,* January 1948, p. 29.

216-a strange combination: Billy Wilder to DS, Nov. 19, 1991.

217-I'm doing the chores: Hildegarde Knef, *The Gift Horse* (New York: McGraw-Hill, 1971), p. 222.

217-When she heard: Richard Todd, *Caught in the Act* (London: Hutchinson, 1986), p. 240.

218-I am not: *Daily Mail* (London), June 28, 1949.

219-Marlene was a: Alfred Hitchcock to DS, Sept. 13, 1976.

224-I am too old: Michael Wilding, *The Wilding Way* (New York: St. Martin's Press, 1982), pp. 60–76.

225-What's Liz Taylor: *Ibid.,* p. 76.

CHAPTER FOURTEEN

227-I had my: Bob Thomas, "Grandma Dietrich's Riding Piggy-Back," Associated Press syndicated article dated April 1, 1951.

228-I'm the baby-sitter: Lillian Ross, "How Do You Like It Now, Gentlemen?" *The New Yorker,* vol. 26, no. 12 (May 13, 1950), p. 45.

228-Papa, you look: *Ibid.,* pp. 44–46.

229-She looked at me: Ginette Spanier, *It Isn't All Mink* (New York: Random House, 1960), p. 181.

230-Darling: MD to Ginette Spanier, July [21?] 1974.

232-Married?: Quoted in *Los Angeles Herald-Examiner,* July 15, 1951.

232-Women talk when: *Ibid.*

233-I had the foolish: Charles Higham and Joel Greenberg, *The Celluloid Muse: Hollywood Directors Speak* (Sydney: Angus and Robertson, 1969), p. 119; see also Peter Bogdanovich, *Fritz Lang in America* (London: Studio Vista, 1967), p. 77.

237-I admire men's: Winthrop Sargeant, "Dietrich and Her Magic Myth," *Life,* Aug. 18, 1952, p. 101.

237-they could almost: Rock Brynner, *Yul: The Man Who Would Be King* (New York: Berkley, 1991), p. 57.

238-Her movement: Leonard Blair to DS, July 23, 1991.

239-soup [and]: Kirk Douglas, *The Ragman's Son* (New York: Simon and Schuster, 1988), p. 192.

240-I know you're: Ronald Schiller, "Miraculous Marlene Dietrich," *Woman's Home Companion,* vol. 80, no. 8 (Aug. 1953), p. 51.

241-Wouldn't it: *Paris Match,* May 28, 1992, p. 82.

241-I invented the: *Marlene,* p. 227.

CHAPTER FIFTEEN

243-A wayfarer: Gladwin Hill, "Klondike in the Desert," *New York Times,* June 7, 1953, sec. 6, p. 14.

243-the audience is: Lena Horne and Richard Schickel, *Lena* (New York: Doubleday, 1965), p. 234.

244-Eddie, I was: Eddie Fisher, *Eddie—My Life, My Loves* (New York: Harper and Row, 1981), p. 92.

245-Her voice deficiencies: Howard McClay, "Dietrich's a real gown gal in Las Vegas debut," *Las Vegas Daily News,* Dec. 17, 1953.

246-My outward appearance: *Marlene,* p. 229.

246-almost a mania: Jean Louis to DS, July 15, 1991.

246-Jean Louis's creations: *Marlene,* p. 179.

247-Well, this is: Joe Hyams, "Miss Dietrich in Night-Club Debut, $90,000 for 3 Weeks," *New York Herald Tribune,* Dec. 16, 1953.

247-Technique and control: John Fisher, *Call Them Irreplaceable* (New York: Stein and Day, 1974), p. 138.

247-You don't take: Stine, p. 109.

252-Van Johnson: Jean Howard to DS, July 15, 1990.

254-taken advantage of: MD to Charles Feldman, Feb. 7, 1955.

254-fairly tiresome: Cole Lesley, *Remembered Laughter* (New York: Knopf, 1976), p. 346.

255-a twosome: *New York Daily News,* Dec. 5, 1955, p. 34.

255-Mike knew: Fisher, p. 123.

256-with her intense: Payn and Morley, p. 322.

256-in a tremendously: *Ibid.,* p. 333.

259-You call these: Bernard Hall, "The strange, lonely world of Dietrich," *Daily Mail* (London), April 19, 1985.

CHAPTER SIXTEEN

262-There was no talk: Leaming, p. 423.

262–63-the best thing: "No Star Nonsense About Marlene Dietrich," *The Times* (London), Nov. 23, 1964; see also Frank Brady, *Citizen Welles* (New York: Scribner, 1989), p. 500.

264-It is not: Payn and Morley, p. 361.

264-too well: Radie Harris, "Broadway Ballyhoo," *Hollywood Reporter,* Dec. 23, 1985, p. 28.

265-she always admitted: Bernard Hall, in *The* (Belfast) *Sunday News,* May 17, 1992.

265-I understand you're: Robert Anderson to DS, Oct. 4, 1989.

265-She looks ravishing: Payn and Morley, p. 422.

266-She plugged in: "The Day I Called On 'Dr.' Dietrich," *Sunday Express* (London), Dec. 12, 1959.

267-Let's not fool: Lloyd Shearer, "Marlene Dietrich: How to be glamorous and happy at 55," *Parade,* Aug. 2, 1959, p. 6.

267-But enuff: "The Queen Is Not Amused," *Show,* June 1963.

268-I don't ask: Ed McCarthy, "Marlene, You're Incredible!" *This Week,* Nov. 29, 1959, p. 5.

268-I didn't really: Davidson, *art. cit.,* p. 164.

268-boring and: Payn and Morley, p. 419.

268-You could say: Art Buchwald, "La Dietrich Great Anywhere She Goes," *International Herald Tribune,* Dec. 13, 1959.

269-a man who took: *Marlene,* pp. 230ff.

270-She was in: Payn and Morley, p. 433.

270-If they had: Sargeant, *art. cit.,* p. 94.

271-Who showed: Cited in "How Will Berlin Treat Marlene on Return?", *New York Post,* March 21, 1960.

271-An impudent wench: "Marlene Go Home! Briefe und Flügblätter zur Deutschlandtournee im Mai 1960," Werner Sudendorf, ed., *Marlene Dietrich: Dokumente, Essays, Filme* (Munich: Carl Hanser, 1977), vol. 1, pp. 20–21.

271-Aren't you: *Ibid.,* p. 21.

272-The major error: Jean Améry, "Die Künstlerin Dietrich und die Öffentliche Sache," in Sudendorf, *op. cit.,* pp. 15, 19.

272-I am singing: Joseph Barry, "Marlene in Berlin: 'Love and Hate,' " *New York Post,* May 2, 1960, p. 4.

273-I am not: Joseph Barry, "Marlene Faces Her Toughest Audience," *New York Post,* May 3, 1960, p. 8.

274-Dear Marlene: *Life,* May 23, 1960.

274-a woman who: Gaston Coblentz, "Marlene Dietrich on Stage in Berlin After 30 Years," *New York Herald Tribune,* May 4, 1960.

275-That's the old: "Music: Suitcase in Berlin," *Newsweek,* May 16, 1960, p. 80.

CHAPTER SEVENTEEN

276-never again: "Has Marlene 'Had It' in Germany?" *Variety,* June 15, 1960.

277-As an actress: Roland Cosandey, ed., *Chronique et filmographie, 40 ans du Festival internazionale del film Locarno* (Locarno, 1988), pp. 113, 115. Speaking in French, Dietrich said, "Comme actrice j'appartiens à l'album de souvenirs, et cet album reste muet."

278-He doesn't look: Neil Rau, " 'Judgment' Headache," *Los Angeles Herald-Examiner,* May 7, 1961.

278-She came on: Quoted by Stanley Kramer to DS, May 8, 1991.

278–79-a typical: Quoted in Seydel, p. 29.

279-She really believed: Quoted in the *Evening Standard* (London), May 7, 1992, p. 5.

280-The showmanship: *Variety,* April 17, 1974.

280-Well, I would have: Rosalie MacRae, "Turning every head in Paris today," *Daily Express* (London), April 23, 1962.

282-a remarkable piece: Richard Buckle, ed., *Self-Portrait with Friends: The Selected Diaries of Cecil Beaton, 1926–1974* (New York: Times Books, 1979), pp. 417–18 (diary entry for June 16, 1973).

282-I give the audience: E.g., *Newsweek,* Dec. 7, 1964.

283-How have you: *New York Times* (Associated Press wire report), May 20, 1964.

283-I have a: *New York Journal-American* (United Press International wire report), May 22, 1964.

283-You must be: *New York Herald Tribune,* May 20, 1964.

283–84-That horrible woman: Rex Reed, "Dietrich: She Just Wants to Be Alone," *Los Angeles Times,* Jan. 8, 1973.

284-You with the: Jim Sirmans, "Marlene Spectacular," *Vogue,* February 1973, p. 201.

285-You are all: "It's Dietrich vs. Newsmen," *Los Angeles Times* (Reuters), Feb. 1, 1975.

285-It is not: Vivien Byerley to DS, June 12, 1990.

285-the least enjoyable: Alexander H. Cohen to DS, March 31, 1990.

286-She said repeatedly: Peter White to DS, Nov. 8, 1991.

286-I told her: Frederick Combs to DS, June 12, 1991.

287-at times intolerable: Sirmans, *art. cit.*

287-How sweet: Radie Harris, "Broadway Ballyhoo," *Hollywood Reporter,* July 28, 1972.

288-All I demand: Payn and Morley, p. 653.

288-Oh, he could: Reed, *art. cit.;* see also Lesley, p. 471.

289-There was someone: Reed, *art. cit.*

289-When he became: *Marlene,* pp. 241–42.

CHAPTER EIGHTEEN

291-a perfectionist: Stan Freeman, *New York Daily News,* May 7, 1992, p. 30.

291-her quick eye: Hall, *art. cit.*

292-I need the money: Reed, *art. cit.*

292–93-chunks of indigestible: *Marlene,* p. 247.

293-Poor Rudi: To Maximilian Schell, 1983.

298-All her life: Dick Lemon, "Marlene Dietrich," *People,* Sept. 3, 1984, p. 93.

299-made herself: Hall, *art. cit.*

299-I didn't know: Hall, *Evening Standard* (London), May 7, 1992, p. 5.

300-United Germany's Joy: *New York Times,* Oct. 4, 1990, pp. 1, A8.

300-I'm still nostalgic: Quoted in *New York Times,* Jan. 14, 1991, p. B4.

300-Thanks a million: "Notes on People," *New York Times,* Sept. 26, 1980.

301-You have done it: Anthony Clavet, quoted by Robert Colbaugh to DS, Jan. 23, 1992.

Bibliography

IN ADDITION TO THE ARTICLES, ESSAYS AND INTER-
views cited in the Notes, the following books were especially helpful.

Adressbuch für Berlin und seine Vororte: 1901, 1904, 1907, 1908, 1909.
　Berlin: Druck und Verlag.
Aherne, Brian. *A Proper Job*. Boston: Houghton Mifflin, 1969.
Arce, Hector. *Gary Cooper: An Intimate Biography*. New York: Mor-
　row, 1979.
Aumont, Jean-Pierre. *Le Soleil et les Ombres*. Paris: Laffont, 1976.
―――. *Souvenirs Provisoires*. Paris: René Julliard, 1957.
Baker, Carlos. *Ernest Hemingway: A Life Story*. New York: Scribner,
　1969.
Baxter, Peter, ed. *Sternberg*. London: British Film Institute, 1980.
Beaton, Cecil, and Kenneth Tynan. *Persona Grata*. London: Allan
　Wingate, 1953.

Beausoleil, Claude. *Promenade Modern Style*. Montreal: Editions Cul-Q, 1975.

Behlmer, Rudy. *America's Favorite Movies: Behind the Scenes*. New York: Frederick Ungar, 1982.

———, ed. *Memo from David O. Selznick*. New York: Viking, 1972; repr. Los Angeles: Samuel French, 1989.

Best, Katherine, and Katharine Hillyer. *Las Vegas: Playtown U.S.A.* New York: David McKay, 1955.

Bogdanovich, Peter. *Fritz Lang in America*. London: Studio Vista, 1967.

Bosworth, Patricia. *Montgomery Clift: A Biography*. New York: Harcourt Brace Jovanovich, 1978.

Brady, Frank. *Citizen Welles*. New York: Scribner, 1989.

Brownlow, Kevin. *The Parade's Gone By*. New York: Knopf, 1968.

Bruno, Michael. *Venus in Hollywood*. New York: Lyle Stuart, 1970.

Brynner, Rock. *Yul: The Man Who Would Be King*. New York: Berkley, 1991.

Buckle, Richard, ed. *Self Portrait with Friends: The Selected Diaries of Cecil Beaton, 1926–1974*. New York: Times Books, 1979.

Buxton, Frank, and Bill Owen. *The Big Broadcast, 1920–1950*. New York: Viking, 1972.

Carné, Marcel. *La Vie à Belles Dents*. Paris: Jean-Vuarnet, 1979.

Castle, Charles. *Oliver Messel*. New York: Thames and Hudson, 1986.

Chevalier, Maurice. *With Love*. New York: Bantam, 1960.

Chierichetti, David. *Hollywood Director*. New York: Curtis Books, 1973.

Colman, Juliet Benita. *Ronald Colman*. New York: Morrow, 1975.

Colpet, Max. *Sag mir, wo die Jahre sind*. Munich: Georg Müller, 1981.

Cosandey, Roland, ed. *Chronique et filmographie, 40 ans du Festival internazionale del film Locarno*. Locarno: The Film Festival Printery, 1988.

Coslow, Sam. *Cocktails for Two*. New Rochelle: Arlington House, 1977.

Crawford, Cheryl. *One Naked Individual*. Indianapolis: Bobbs-Merrill, 1977.

Davis, Bette. *The Lonely Life*. New York: Putnam, 1962.

de Navacelle, Thierry. *Sublime Marlene*. London: Sidgwick and Jackson, 1984.

Dickens, Homer. *The Films of Marlene Dietrich*. Secaucus, N.J.: Citadel, 1968.

Dietrich, Marlene. *Ich bin, Gott sei Dank, Berlinerin*. Frankfurt: Ullstein, 1987.

————. *Marlene* (trans. Salvatore Attanasio). New York: Grove Press, 1989.

————. *Marlène D.* (trans. Boris Mattews and Françoise Ducout). Paris: Bernard Grasset, 1984.

————. *Marlene Dietrich's ABC* (rev. ed.). New York: Frederick Ungar, 1984.

————. *Nehmt nur mein Leben . . . Reflexionen*. Munich: Bertelsmann, 1979.

Donaldson, Scott. *By Force of Will*. New York: Viking, 1977.

Douglas, Kirk. *The Ragman's Son*. New York: Simon and Schuster, 1988.

Dunning, John. *Tune In Yesterday: The Ultimate Encyclopedia of Old-Time Radio, 1925–1976*. Englewood Cliffs: Prentice-Hall, 1976.

Engstead, John. *Star Shots*. New York: Dutton, 1978.

Everett, Susanne. *Lost Berlin*. New York: Gallery Books, 1979.

Eyles, Allen. *John Wayne and the Movies*. New York: A. S. Barnes, 1976.

Fairbanks, Douglas, Jr., *The Salad Days*. New York: Doubleday, 1988.

Feyder, Jacques, and Françoise Rosay. *Le Cinéma—Notre Métier*. Geneva: Pierre Cailler, 1946.

Fisher, Eddie. *Eddie—My Life, My Loves*. New York: Harper and Row, 1981.

Fischer, John. *Call Them Irreplaceable*. New York: Stein and Day, 1974.

Fountain, Leatrice Gilbert. *Dark Star*. New York: St. Martin's Press, 1985.

Frewin, Leslie. *Blonde Venus*. London: MacGibbon and Kee, 1955 (and New York: Roy Publishers, 1956). Updated and revised as *Dietrich*, New York: Stein and Day, 1967.

Friedrich, Otto. *Before the Deluge*. New York: Fromm, 1986.

Frischauer, Willi. *European Commuter*. New York: Macmillan, 1964.

Fryer, Jonathan. *Isherwood*. New York: Doubleday, 1978.

Garnett, Tay, with Fredda Dudley Balling. *Light Your Torches and Pull Up Your Tights*. New Rochelle: Arlington House, 1973.

Gavin, James M. *On to Berlin*. New York: Viking, 1978.

Geist, Kenneth L. *Pictures Will Talk: The Life and Films of Joseph L. Mankiewicz*. New York: Scribner, 1978.

Godfrey, Lionel. *Cary Grant: The Light Touch*. New York: St. Martin's Press, 1981.

Griffith, Richard. *Marlene Dietrich: Image and Legend*. New York: Museum of Modern Art/Doubleday, 1959.

Guiles, Fred Lawrence. *Tyrone Power: The Last Idol*. New York: Doubleday, 1979.

Harding, James. *Maurice Chevalier: His Life*. London: Secker and Warburg, 1982.

Head, Edith, and Paddy Calistro. *Edith Head's Hollywood*. New York: Dutton, 1983.

Higham, Charles, and Joel Greenberg. *The Celluloid Muse: Hollywood Directors Speak*. Sydney: Angus and Robertson, 1969.

Higham, Charles. *Marlene: The Life of Marlene Dietrich*. New York: Norton, 1977.

Hodges, Nora (trans.). *George Grosz: An Autobiography*. New York: Imago/Macmillan, 1983.

Horne, Lena, and Richard Schickel. *Lena*. New York: Doubleday, 1965.

Hotchner, A. E. *Papa Hemingway*. New York: Morrow, 1983.

Jannings, Emil. *Theater-Film—Das Leben und Ich*. Berchtesgaden: Verlag Zimmer und Herzog, 1951.

Johnson, Diane. *Dashiell Hammett: A Life*. New York: Random House, 1983.

Knef, Hildegarde. *The Gift Horse*. New York: McGraw-Hill, 1971.

Kobal, John. *Marlene Dietrich*. London: Studio Vista, 1968.

Korda, Michael. *Charmed Lives*. New York: Random House, 1979.

Kulik, Karol. *Alexander Korda: The Man Who Could Work Miracles*. New Rochelle: Arlington House, 1975.

Liang, Hsi–Huey. *The Berlin Police Force in the Weimar Republic.* Berkeley: University of California Press, 1970.

Kiersch, Mary. *Curtis Bernhardt.* Metuchen, N.J.: Scarecrow Press, 1986.

Kobal, John. *People Will Talk.* New York: Knopf, 1985.

Lasky, Jesse L., with Don Weldon. *I Blow My Own Horn.* New York: Doubleday, 1957.

Lasky, Jesse L., Jr. *Whatever Happened to Hollywood?* New York: Funk and Wagnalls, 1975.

Leaming, Barbara. *Orson Welles.* New York: Viking, 1985.

Lerner, Alan Jay. *The Street Where I Live.* New York: Norton, 1978.

LeRoy, Mervin, and Dick Kleiner. *Mervyn LeRoy: Take One.* New York: Hawthorn, 1974.

Lesley, Cole. *Remembered Laughter.* New York: Knopf, 1976.

Levin, Martin, ed. *Hollywood and the Great Fan Magazines.* New York: Arbor House, 1970.

Logan, Joshua. *Josh: My Up and Down, In and Out Life.* New York: Delacorte, 1976.

McGerr, Celia. *René Clair.* Boston: Twayne, 1980.

Marion, Frances. *Off With Their Heads.* New York: Macmillan, 1972.

Milne, Tom. *Rouben Mamoulian.* Bloomington: Indiana University Press, 1969.

Moore, Dick. *Twinkle, Twinkle, Little Star.* New York: Harper and Row, 1984.

Noa, Wolfgang, *Marlene Dietrich.* Berlin: Henschelverlag, 1966.

Oldfield, Col. Barney, USAF (Ret). *Never a Shot in Anger (Battle of Normandy Museum Edition).* New York: Da Capo, 1989.

Parris, Thomas, ed. *The Simon and Schuster Encyclopedia of World War II.* New York: Simon and Schuster, 1978.

Pasternak, Joe. *Easy the Hard Way.* New York: Putnam, 1956.

Payn, Graham, and Sheridan Morley, eds. *The Noël Coward Diaries.* Boston: Little, Brown, 1982.

Piaf, Edith, trans. Peter Trewartha and Andrée Masoin de Vireton. *The Wheel of Fortune.* Philadelphia: Chilton, 1965.

Rathbone, Basil. *In and Out of Character.* New York: Doubleday, 1962.

Reed, Rex. *Do You Sleep in the Nude?* New York: New American Library, 1968.

Reissner, Alexander. *Berlin 1675–1945*. London: Oswald Wolff, 1984.

Remarque, Erich Maria. *Arch of Triumph* (trans. Walter Sorell and Denver Lindley). London: Hutchinson Library Services, 1946.

Renoir, Jean. *My Life and My Films*. New York: Atheneum, 1974.

Robinson, Edward G., with Leonard Spiegelgass. *All My Yesterdays*. New York: Hawthorn, 1973.

Roters, Eberhard. *Berlin 1910–1933*. New York: Rizzoli, 1982.

Samuels, Charles Thomas. *Encountering Directors*. New York: Putnam, 1972.

Sarris, Andrew. *The Films of Josef von Sternberg*. New York: Museum of Modern Art/Doubleday, 1966.

Schulberg, Budd. *Moving Pictures: Memories of a Hollywood Prince*. New York: Stein and Day, 1981.

Seydel, Renate (arranged by Bernd Meier). *Marlene Dietrich, eine Chronik ihres Lebens in Bildern und Dokumenten*. Munich: Nymphenburger, 1984.

Silver, Charles. *Marlene Dietrich*. New York: Pyramid, 1974.

Spanier, Ginette. *It Isn't All Mink*. New York: Random House, 1960.

Spoto, Donald. *The Dark Side of Genius: The Life of Alfred Hitchcock*. Boston: Little, Brown, 1983.

———. *Falling in Love Again: Marlene Dietrich* (A Photoessay). Boston: Little, Brown, 1985.

———. *Lenya: A Life*. Boston: Little, Brown, 1989.

Stine, Whitney. *The Hurrell Style: 50 Years of Photographing Hollywood*. New York: John Day, 1976.

Sudendorf, Werner, ed. *Marlene Dietrich: Dokumente, Essays, Filme* (2 vols.). Munich: Carl Haner, 1977.

Swindell, Larry. *The Last Hero: A Biography of Gary Cooper*. New York: Doubleday, 1980.

Thomas, Danny, with Bill Davidson. *Make Room for Danny*. New York: Putnam, 1991.

Todd, Richard. *Caught in the Act*. London: Hutchinson, 1986.

Trewin, J. C. *Robert Donat: A Biography*. London: Heinemann, 1968.

von Sternberg, Josef. *The Blue Angel*. London: Lorrimer, 1968.

———. *Fun in a Chinese Laundry*. New York: Macmillan, 1965.

———. *Morocco/Shanghai Express*. London: Lorrimer, 1973.

Walker, Alexander. *Dietrich*. New York: Harper and Row, 1984.

Wayne, Jane Ellen. *Cooper's Women*. Englewood Cliffs: Prentice-Hall, 1988.

Wayne, Pilar, with Alex Thorleifson. *John Wayne—My Life with the Duke*. New York: McGraw-Hill, 1987.

Weinberg, Herman G. *Josef von Sternberg*. New York: Dutton, 1967.

Westmore, Frank, and Muriel Davidson. *The Westmores of Hollywood*. Philadelphia: Lippincott, 1976.

Wilding, Michael. *The Wilding Way*. New York: St. Martin's Press, 1982.

Willett, John. *The Weimar Years: A Culture Cut Short*. London: Thames and Hudson, 1984.

Yablonsky, Lewis. *George Raft*. New York: McGraw-Hill, 1974.

Zuckmayer, Carl. *A Part of Myself*. New York: Harcourt Brace Jovanovich, 1966.

Index

About the Author

DONALD SPOTO is the author of ten books, among them internationally best-selling biographies of Alfred Hitchcock, Tennessee Williams, Lotte Lenya and Laurence Olivier. He earned the Ph.D. degree from Fordham University and has taught and lectured worldwide. Raised in Westchester and Fairfield Counties, he lives in Los Angeles, New York and London.